BID SHEET

Heritage Auctions • HA.com
Direct Client Service Line—Toll Free:
866-835-3243
3500 Maple Avenue
Dallas, Texas 75219-3941

MW01177978

Animation Art...

Submit Your Bids By Fax | FAX HOTLINE: 214-409-1425

ALL INFORMATION MUST BE COMPLETED AND FORM SIGNED

NAME _____

ADDRESS _____

CITY/STATE/ZIP _____

DAYTIME PHONE (_____) _____

CLIENT # (if known)_____ BIDDER #_____

E-MAIL ADDRESS _____

CELL PHONE _____

EVENING PHONE (_____) _____

Would you like a FAX or e-mail confirming receipt of your bids? If so, please

print your FAX # _____

or e-mail address here: _____

I would like to limit my bidding to a total of $ _____

at the hammer amount for all lots listed on this bid sheet. I am aware
that by utilizing the Budget Bidding feature all bids on this sheet will be
affected. If I intend to have regular bidding on other lots I will need to
use a separate bid sheet.

Payment by check may result in your property not being released until
purchase funds clear our bank. Checks must be drawn on a U.S. bank.
(Bid in whole dollar amounts only.)

All bids are subject to the applicable Buyer's Premium. See HA.com for details.

Non-Internet bids (including but not limited to, podium, fax, phone and mail
bids) may be submitted at any time and are treated similar to floor bids. These
types of bids must be on-increment or at a half increment (called a cut bid). Any
podium, fax, phone or mail bids that do not conform to a full or half increment
will be rounded up or down to the nearest full or half increment and will be
considered your high bid.

Current Bid	Bid Increment
< - $10	$1
$10 - $29	$2
$30 - $49	$3
$50 - $99	$5
$100 - $199	$10
$200 - $299	$20
$300 - $499	$25
$500 - $999	$50
$1,000 - $1,999	$100
$2,000 - $2,999	$200
$3,000 - $4,999	$250
$5,000 - $9,999	$500

$10,000 - $19,999	$1,000
$20,000 - $29,999	$2,000
$30,000 - $49,999	$2,500
$50,000 - $99,999	$5,000
$100,000 - $199,999	$10,000
$200,000 - $299,999	$20,000
$300,000 - $499,999	$25,000
$500,000 - $999,999	$50,000
$1,000,000 - $1,999,999	$100,000
$2,000,000- $2,999,999	$200,000
$3,000,000- $4,999,999	$250,000
$5,000,000 - $9,999,999	$500,000
>$10,000,000	$1,000,000

These bids are for Auction: # _____ Auction Description _____ *(ex. See catalog spine for auction # and description)*

LOT NO.	AMOUNT	LOT NO.	AMOUNT	LOT NO.	AMOUNT	LOT NO.	AMOUNT

PLEASE COMPLETE THIS INFORMATION:

1. IF NECESSARY, PLEASE INCREASE MY BIDS BY:
   ☐ 10%   ☐ 20%   ☐ 30%
   Lots will be purchased as much below top bids as possible.

2. ☐ I HAVE PREVIOUSLY BOUGHT FROM HERITAGE

3. ☐ I HAVE A RESALE PERMIT
   (please contact 1-800-872-6467)

I have read and agree to all of the Terms and Conditions of Auction: inclusive of paying
interest at the lesser of 1.5% per month (18% per annum) or the maximum contract
interest rate under applicable state law from the date of auction.

REFERENCES: New bidders who are unknown to us must furnish
satisfactory industry references or a valid credit card in advance of the
auction date.

REV. 11-3-11

SUBTOTAL	
TOTAL from other side	
TOTAL BID	

_____
(Signature required) *Please make a copy of your bid sheet for your records.*

FAX HOTLINE: 214-409-1425

LOT NO.	AMOUNT	LOT NO.	AMOUNT	LOT NO.	AMOUNT	LOT NO.	AMOUNT

Please make a copy of your bid sheet for your records.

TOTAL this side

7 *easy ways to bid*

1 Bid By Internet
Simply go to www.HA.com, find the auction you are looking for and click "View Lots" or type your desired Lot # into the "Search" field. Every lot is listed with full descriptions and images. Enter your bid and click "Place Bid." Internet bids will be accepted until 10:00 PM CT the day before the live auction session takes place.

2 Bid By e-Mail
You can also e-mail your bids to us at Bid@HA.com. List lot numbers and bids, and include your name, address, phone, and customer # (if known) as well as a statement of your acceptance of the Terms and Conditions of Sale. Email bids will be accepted up to 24 hours before the live auction.

3 Bid By Postal Mail
Simply complete the Bid Sheet on the reverse side of this page with your bids on the lots you want, sign it and mail it in. If yours is the high bid on any lot, we act as your representative at the auction and buy the lot as cheaply as competition permits.

4 Bid In Person
Come to the auction and view the lots in person and bid live on the floor.

5 Bid By FAX
Follow the instructions for completing your mail bid, but this time FAX it to (214) 409-1425. FAX bids will be accepted until 3:00 p.m. CT the day prior to the auction date.

6 Bid Live By Phone
Call 1-800-872-6467 Ext. 1150 and ask for phone bidding assistance at least 24 hours prior to the auction.

7 Bid Live using Heritage Live!™
Auctions designated as "Heritage Live Enabled" have continuous bidding from the time the auction is posted on our site through the live event. When normal Internet bidding ends, visit HA.com/Live and continue to place Live Proxy bids. When the item hits the auction block, you can continue to bid live against the floor and other live bidders.

Because of the many avenues by which bids may be submitted, there is the real possibility of a tie for the high bid. In the event of a tie, Internet bidders, within their credit limit, will win by default

Heritage Signature® Auction #7052

Animation Art

February 21 & 23, 2013 | New York

LIVE AUCTION Signature® Floor Session 1
(Floor, Telephone, HERITAGE Live!® Internet, Fax, and Mail)

2 E. 79th Street • New York, NY 10075
(Ukrainian Institute of America at the Fletcher-Sinclair Mansion)

Session 1
Thursday, February 21 • 3:00 PM ET • Lots 30001–30425
Walt Disney Studios, Disneyland/Disneyana, The Chuck Jones Collection, The McKimson Collection, Warner Brothers Studios, Charlie Brown and Peanuts, The Jackson 5ive, TerryToons, Hanna-Barbera Studios, The Simpsons, Nickelodeon, and Other Studios

HERITAGE Live!® Internet, Fax, & Mail only Session 2

Session 2
Saturday, February 23 • 3:00 PM CT • Lots 31001-31278
Walt Disney Studios, Disneyland/Disneyana, The McKimson Collection and other Warner Brothers Studios, TerryToons, Hanna-Barbera Studios, Jay Ward Studios, Nickelodeon, Walter Lantz Productions, Fleischer Studios, and Other Studios

LOT SETTLEMENT AND PICK-UP
Available immediately following each Floor session at the auction. After Friday, February 22, 2013, all lots will be taken back to Dallas and will be available to be shipped starting Wednesday, February 27. (Session 2 lots not available for pickup in New York).

Extended Payment Terms available. Email: Credit@HA.com

Lots are sold at an approximate rate of 100 lots per hour, but it is not uncommon to sell 75 lots or 125 lots in any given hour.

This auction is subject to a 19.5% Buyer's Premium.

Heritage Auctioneers & Galleries, Inc.: NYC #41513036 and NYC Second Hand Dealers License #1364739. NYC Auctioneer licenses: Samuel Foose 0952360; Robert Korver 1096338; Kathleen Guzman 0762165; Michael J. Sadler 1304630; Scott Peterson 1306933; Andrea Voss 1320558; Nicholas Dawes 1304724; Ed Beardsley 1183220.

LOT VIEWING
2 E. 79th Street • New York, NY 10075
(Ukrainian Institute of America at the Fletcher-Sinclair Mansion)

Wednesday, February 20 – 10:00 AM-6:00PM ET
Thursday, February 21 – 10:00 AM-6:00PM ET
Friday, February 22 – 10:00 AM-2:00 PM ET

View lots & auction results online at HA.com/7052

BIDDING METHODS:
HERITAGE Live!® Bidding
Bid live on your computer or mobile, anywhere in the world, during the Auction using our HERITAGE Live!® program at HA.com/Live

Live Floor Bidding
Bid in person during the floor sessions.

Live Telephone Bidding (floor sessions only)
Phone bidding must be arranged on or before Wednesday, February 20, by 12:00 PM CT.
Client Service: 866-835-3243.

Internet Bidding
Internet absentee bidding ends at 10:00 PM CT the evening before each session. HA.com/7052

Fax Bidding
Fax bids must be received on or before Wednesday, February 20, by 12:00 PM CT. Fax: 214-409-1425

Mail Bidding
Mail bids must be received on or before Wednesday, February 20.

Phone: 214.528.3500 • 800.872.6467
Fax: 214.409.1425
Direct Client Service Line: 866.835.3243
Email: Bid@HA.com

This Auction is presented and cataloged by Heritage Auctions

© 2013 Heritage Auctioneers & Galleries, Inc.

HERITAGE is a registered trademark and service mark of Heritage Capital Corporation. Registered in U.S. Patent and Trademark Office.

26012

Hello Animation Fans and Collectors!

Let me tell you why Heritage is so bullish on Animation Art. We feel it has been undervalued in recent years, and by putting together a strong selection with lots of fresh material, and by educating collectors on the art form, we can realize the untapped potential of this market.

As a collector and former dealer with decades of experience, I am the biggest fan of the medium you will find, and I'm very proud of this selection, in particular the many collections direct from the creators or their estates that have never been offered to the public before. This will be your only chance at this material, so bid aggressively!

This catalog has something for everyone! The entire era of hand-drawn and hand-painted animation art is well represented. From "Steamboat Willie" to Sponge Bob, it can all be found inside this amazing catalog.

If you're a collector who is branching out into this field for the first time, and would like tips on what to look for, what makes a given lot special, or estimates of what a given lot might be expected to sell for, by all means drop me an email or give me a call.

In closing, I hope you can join us in New York for this groundbreaking event, watch and bid live on HA.com, or sign up to bid by telephone. I tell people all the time, *my grandparents* always wanted a Renoir, *my parents* always wanted a Rockwell, I always wanted a Mickey Mouse, and a Bugs Bunny, and a Snoopy...

Best wishes,

Jim Lentz
Director of Animation Art
Heritage Auctions
JimL@HA.com
214-409-1991

HERITAGE CHARITY AUCTIONS PRESENTS

DOODLE FOR HUNGER

ART AUCTION, BENEFITING ST. FRANCIS FOOD PANTRIES AND SHELTERS
ONLINE BIDDING: MARCH 24, 2013 AT 10:00 PM CT — APRIL 14, 2013 10:00 PM CT
HA.COM/532

Tom Wilson
Cartoonist's Doodle for Hunger
Ink on paper
9 x 12 in.

Matthew Van Fleet
Illustrator's Doodle for Hunger
Conte crayon on paper
9 x 12 in.

Bil Keane
Cartoonist's Doodle for Hunger
Ink on paper
9 x 12 in.

Dan Andreasen
Illustrator's Doodle for Hunger
Colored pencil on paper
9 x 12 in.

Rick Stromoski
Cartoonist's Doodle for Hunger
Ink on paper
9 x 12 in.

Mort Walker
Cartoonist's Doodle for Hunger
Ink on paper
9 x 12 in.

Carla Ventresca
Cartoonist's Doodle for Hunger
Conte crayon on paper
9 x 12 in.

Heritage Auctions would like to help worthy charities save time and resources while raising more money, goodwill and awareness for your cause. We are offering our services to approved charities and their donors as a way for Heritage to give back and to meet new friends. Any and all of Heritage's profits after direct expenses will be donated to charities selected by our employees.

Glossary of Terms

ANIMATION DRAWINGS A drawing produced to be traced onto cel and photographed for animating motion. Animation drawings are almost invariably rendered in pencil, graphite and/or colored, on animation paper.

Clean-Up Drawing: cleaned-up animation drawing traced from or directly over a rough drawing.

Extreme Drawing: drawing indicating extreme points of a character's motion.

Rough Drawing:: a very quick drawing used to primarily indicate motion.

BACKGROUNDS Usually a watercolor or tempera on paper, of a scenic location for the character to interact with, or on. Any one of numerous types of drawing, painting or print on which a cel is placed.

CEL A sheet of cellulose acetate or cellulose nitrate on which an animation drawing is traced and colored to be placed over a background and photographed.

CEL SETUP A setup consists of one or more cels overlaid on a background, which may also include overlay cels depicting foreground scenery.

COLOR MODEL CEL A model cel or color model cel is created in the studio as guide for the inkers and painters. Colors may be different from those used in the film, and poses tend to be ideal. They usually say "color model" on bottom of the cel.

CONCEPT (or Inspirational Drawing/Painting) Drawings, sketches and paintings which depict the overall look or mood of a scene, including colors and background. Frequently rendered in watercolor, pastel, crayon and other colorful media.

COURVOISIER BACKGROUND A setup released by Courvoisier Galleries of San Francisco between 1937 and 1946. Early pieces had backgrounds produced by Disney, later ones being produced by Courvoisier. The background medium was frequently airbrushed. Other painted media might be used, and an airbrushed wooden veneer was very common, as well as patterned paper. The cels were usually trimmed to outlines, sometimes laminated, and distinctive mats and labels were used.

FULL CEL Believed to be full size as created.

HAND-PREPARED BACKGROUND A custom-made background created to enhance the presentation of cels.

INKERS TEST An inkers test cel or test cel is inked but not painted, being used as practice or as a test by the inkers.

KEY SETUP A production background and cel combined from the same scene, which appeared on it in the final release of the film.

LAMINATED CEL Cels have at various times been laminated in an attempt at preservation.

LAYOUT Drawings, usually in pencil, depicting the details of a background, the characters as they appear on the background in key positions, and frame lines indicating camera movements. Sometimes difficult to tell from storyboards.

LIMITED EDITION CEL A limited edition cel is generally inked from original animation drawings, painted, and sold in numbered editions. Poses are generally ideal.

LITHO/PRINT BACKGROUND A reproduction of a background produced by any one of numerous printing processes. Those produced by Disney and sold through the Disney parks are usually called "litho backgrounds" or "Disneyland backgrounds."

MODEL SHEET (or Model Drawings) A model sheet consists of a set of drawings depicting various poses and expressions of a character, as a guide for animators. An original model sheet is composed of original drawings (generally pencil, possibly colored), usually cut out and pasted together on a new sheet. Most model sheets on the market are prints produced in-studio from original drawings by photostatic or other processes.

MODEL STATUE OR MAQUETTE A three dimension statue or figurine, produced in the studio in very limited numbers as a reference to what the character will look like from 360 degrees. Usually constructed of plaster with wire armature, painted in colors.

MULTI-CEL A multi-cel consists of two or more cels stacked together to present a single image; the cels need not be matching. A multi-cel is considered as a single piece of artwork.

PRELIMINARY BACKGROUND A background created during production but not actually used.

PRODUCTION CEL A normal production cel will have peg holes at the bottom and also will have a number or a series of numbers in the lower right hand side of the cel.

PRODUCTION/MASTER BACKGROUND A background created during production of an animated film and actually photographed. Usually painted in watercolors, sometimes in airbrush or tempera. If sold as a setup, the cels and background may not be from the same production or even from the same studio.

PUBLICATION BACKGROUND A background which taken from a book or other publication and used like a hand background to enhance a cel.

PUBLICITY CEL A publicity or promotional cel may be inked from original drawings, or may depict an idealized scene, and was produced for illustration or giveaway purposes.

SETUP The combination of a background and one or more cels generally being known as a setup.

SERICEL A sericel is a limited edition cel produced by a silkscreen process.

STORYBOARD DRAWING A drawing that depicts a key moment in a scene designed to show visually the plot of the story. It is usually a guide for animators. Also, several drawings posted together on a board are used to illustrate an entire scene or sequence. Generally done in pencils.

STUDIO BACKGROUND (Art Props Background for Disney) A background produced in the studio for promotional or publicity purposes rather than production. (May duplicate a production background).

TITLE CARD A special cel and background setup used for titles or credits.

TRIMMED CEL Known to be cut down from full size. The cel is then attached directly to a background or to a new cel.

XEROXED CEL A cel from the late fifties that used the Xerox process to transfer the ink lines on a cel.

From *Animation Art The Early Years 1911-1953*
©1995 by Jeff Lotman

Ten Most Notable Lots

TABLE OF CONTENTS

The Art of Walt Disney's
Snow White and the Seven Dwarfs

Walt Disney once said "Of all the fairy tales, I loved Snow White the best, and when I planned my first full-length cartoon, she inevitably was the heroine."

2012 celebrated the 75th anniversary of the Walt Disney Studio's masterpiece and first animated feature film, "Snow White and the Seven Dwarfs." In 2012, J.B. Kaufman, working with the Walt Disney Family Museum, released a magnificent coffee table book that pictured over 200 pieces of art, including original concept sketches, background paintings and production cels. Heritage is proud to offer more than 50 pieces from the ground-breaking film, many of which have never before been seen by the collecting public.

Animation drawings, rare original model sheets, layout drawings, production cels, Courvoisier cel set-ups and even the animators' gag drawings done for each other during the making of this film are included in this offering. The sheer amount of never-before-seen hand-drawn and hand-painted elements of this classic film in this catalog is staggering.

The Walt Disney Family Museum in November of 2012 launched its first special exhibit *"Snow White and the Seven Dwarfs*: The Creation of a Classic." It is scheduled to run November 15, 2012 – April 14, 2013, at the Walt Disney Family Museum in San Francisco, California. This timeless treasure continues to touch generation after generation. We're proud to present one of the largest auction offerings of original art from this film ever put together.

SESSION ONE

Floor, Telephone, Heritage Live!®, Internet, Fax, and Mail Signature® Auction # 7052
Thursday, February 21, 2013 | 3:00PM ET | New York, NY | Lots 30001-30425

A 19.5% Buyer's Premium ($14 minimum) Will Be Added To All Lots
To view full descriptions, enlargeable images and bid online, visit HA.com/7052

WALT DISNEY STUDIOS

30001 *Snow White and the Seven Dwarfs* "Some Day My Prince Will Come" Production Cel With Hand-Painted Background (Walt Disney, 1937).
Snow White and six of the seven dwarfs from the "Some Day My Prince Will Come" musical number. The set-up is in its original Courvoisier wood veneer set-up with beautiful hand-painted background effects. Framed to 28" x 25.5" with an image area of 14.25" x 11.25". The paint is in Fine condition. A wonderful, museum-worthy piece.

The Joe Magro Collection

Joe Magro was an animator at Walt Disney Studios in the 1930's. He worked as in in-between and clean-up animator, sometimes working in Woolie Reitherman's unit. Some of the films he worked on included "Peculiar Penguins" (1934), "Don Donald "(1937)," Hawaiian Holiday" (1937) and "Clock Cleaners" (1937). He left the company right after "Snow White" came out and a virtual who's who of Disney Animation sent him off with a gag sketch, with many incorporating Snow White into their artwork. The list includes Woolie Reitherman, Mark Davis, Fred Moore, and Ward Kimball to name a few. What a keen insight into the studio in that early year of 1937! Mr. Magro went back East for a job, but soon found himself drafted. After the war he worked in advertising for Coca-Cola for a number of years in Italy. His binder of in-studio gag drawings and his going away artwork from his fellow employees has been in the same binder he put them in back in 1937 until now, and we're excited to offer it to our bidders.

30002   Marc Davis and Charles "Nick" Nichols Going Away Drawing for Joe Magro (Walt Disney, 1937). Unique "going away" drawing for animator Joe Magro by Disney legend, Marc Davis and Charles "Nick" Nichols. Mixed media on 12-field 5-peghole (10" x 12"). Some paper aging and light soiling; otherwise the art is in Very Good condition. Signed and inscribed by the artist at the lower right. *From the Joe Magro Collection.*

30003   Marc Davis Going Away Drawing for Joe Magro (Walt Disney, 1937). This "going away" drawing for animator Joe Magro is by Disney legend and Nine Old Man, Marc Davis. Mixed media on 12-field 5-peghole (10" x 12"). Some paper aging and light soiling; otherwise the art is in Very Good condition. Signed and inscribed by the artist at the lower right. *From the Joe Magro Collection.*

30004 Charles "Nick" Nichols Going Away Drawing for Joe Magro (Walt Disney, 1937). Joe Magro received this "going away" drawing by fellow animator, Charles "Nick" Nichols. Graphite and colored pencil on 12-field 5-peghole (10" x 12"). Some paper aging and light soiling; otherwise the art is in Very Good condition. Signed and inscribed by the artist at the lower right. Includes a "half cell" gag award written in grease crayon on a small piece of acetate (9.5" x 4"), in Good condition. *From the Joe Magro Collection.*

30007 *Snow White and the Seven Dwarfs* Poison Apple Antidote Layout Drawing (Walt Disney, 1937). Here is the original layout drawing of the poison apple antidote, which has been collaged with another piece of art and used as a going away gag cartoon for animator Joe Magro. Graphite and colored pencil on 12-field 5-peghole animation paper, measuring 12" x 10". There is paper aging, and soiling; otherwise the art is in Good condition. Signed and inscribed by animator Dave Rose along the top edge. *From the Joe Magro Collection.*

30005 Grim Natwick *Snow White* Going Away Drawing for Joe Magro (Walt Disney, 1937). The fairest on the beach meets animator Joe Magro, courtesy of one of her most illustrious original animators, the legendary Grim Natwick. This frolicsome drawing was rendered in colored pencil on 12-field, 5-peghole sheet of animation paper. Some paper aging, and light wear; otherwise the work is in Very Good condition. Signed by the artist at the lower right. *From the Joe Magro Collection.*

30008 Bill Tytla Going Away Drawing for Joe Magro (Walt Disney, 1937). Special "going away" drawing for animator Joe Magro by legendary Disney animator, Vladimir "Bill" Tytla. Note Mickey Mouse on the blackboard and Dopey as one of the students. Graphite and colored pencil on 12-field 5-peghole (10" x 12"). Some paper aging and light soiling; otherwise the art is in Very Good condition. Signed and inscribed by the artist at the lower right. *From the Joe Magro Collection.*

30006 Hugh Hennesy Going Away Drawing for Joe Magro (Walt Disney, 1937). Animator Joe Magro goes nose to nose with *Snow White's* Old Hag, in this original "going away" drawing by Disney art director, Hugh Hennesy. Mixed media on 12-field 5-peghole (12" x 10"). Some paper aging and light soiling; otherwise the art is in Very Good condition. Signed and inscribed by the artist at the lower right. *From the Joe Magro Collection.*

30009 Bob Leffingwell Going Away Drawing for Joe Magro (Walt Disney, 1937). Original "going away" drawing for Joe Magro by Disney/Fleischer Studios animator, Bob Leffingwell. Mixed media on 12-field 5-peghole (10" x 12"). Some paper aging and light edge wear; otherwise the art is in Very Good condition. Signed by the artist at the lower right. *From the Joe Magro Collection.*

30010 *Snow White and the Seven Dwarfs* **Gag Drawing (Walt Disney, 1937).** Animator Joe Magro is in the lap of luxury, in this hilarious drawing by fellow Disney animator, Jack Larsen. Created during the production of Disney's first animated feature, this piece was rendered in colored pencil on a 12-field, 5-peghole sheet of animation paper. Some paper aging, and light soiling; otherwise the work is in Very Good condition. Signed by Jack Larsen at the lower right. *From the Joe Magro Collection.*

30011   Joe Magro Going Away Drawing (Walt Disney, 1937). Caption: "But Mr. Drake told me the same thing!" Unique "going away" drawing for animator Joe Magro. Appears to be Fred Moore style, but is signed "Chuck" at the lower right. Mixed media on 12-field 5-peghole (10" x 12"). Some paper aging and light soiling; otherwise the art is in Very Good condition. *From the Joe Magro Collection.*

30012   Joshua Meador Going Away Drawing for Joe Magro (Walt Disney, 1937). Special effects animator, Joshua Meador renders a caricature of animator Joe Magro in waves, in this "going away" drawing. Graphite and colored pencil on 12-field 5-peghole (10" x 12"). Some paper aging and light soiling; otherwise the art is in Very Good condition. Signed by the artist at the lower right. *From the Joe Magro Collection.*

30013   Fred Moore Going Away Drawing for Joe Magro (Walt Disney, 1937). Caption reads: "But — what could you possibly do with me in New York?" This tongue-in-touch "going away" drawing for animator Joe Magro is by veteran Disney animator, Fred Moore. Mixed media on 12-field 5-peghole (10" x 12"). Some paper aging and light soiling; otherwise the art is in Very Good condition. Signed and inscribed by the artist at the lower right. *From the Joe Magro Collection.*

30014   Ward Kimball Going Away Drawing for Joe Magro (Walt Disney, 1937). Caption reads: "Well, Mr. Disney - here I am. My 20 years leave of absence is up." Original "going away" drawing for Joe Magro by Disney animator, Ward Kimball. Mixed media on 12-field 5-peghole (10" x 12"). Some paper aging and light soiling; otherwise the art is in Very Good condition. Signed by the artist "Ward K. Age 12" at the lower right. *From the Joe Magro Collection.*

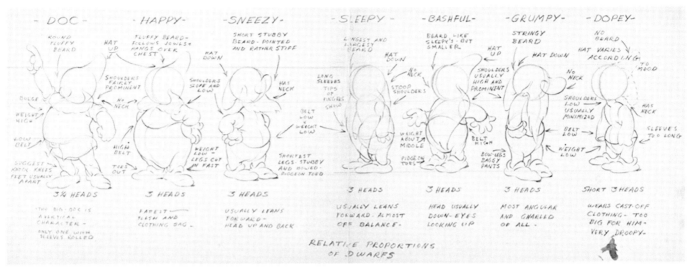

30015 *Snow White and the Seven Dwarfs* **Character Model Sheet (Walt Disney, 1937).** One of the most important pieces related to this movie to surface! This is an original hand-drawn Walt Disney Studios model sheet featuring concept drawings for each of the seven dwarfs plus detailed notations. Pencil on drawing paper, it measures 24" x 10". In Good condition with some tanning, some wear and small tears to the corners and edges, a vertical fold crease in the center and a small red stain at the extreme right. A true piece of animation history. *From the Joe Magro Collection.*

30016 *Snow White and the Seven Dwarfs* **Printed Model Sheet Group (Walt Disney, 1937).** These six model sheets belonged to animator Joe Magro, who stapled three sets of two back-to-back and put them behind nitrate clear cels. Included are a hand-drawn title (this one is not printed, there is a stain on the left side), one of Snow White and three Dwarfs for size comparison, one of all seven Dwarfs' faces (the red highlights are hand-drawn, not printed), two showing the physiques and posture of the Dwarfs, and one of Doc. All printed on photographic paper. All measure approximately 12.5" x 10". *From the Joe Magro Collection.*

30017 *Snow White and the Seven Dwarfs* **Snow White Model Sheet Drawing (Walt Disney, 1937).** This original drawing features ten facial expressions of Snow White rendered in graphite and red pencil on a 12" x 10" sheet of animation paper. Some paper aging, and pin holes on two edges; otherwise the art is in Very Good condition. A piece of animation history! *From the Joe Magro Collection.*

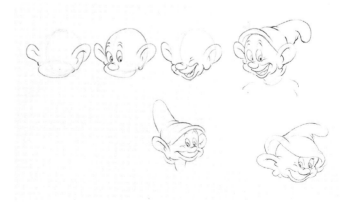

30018 *Snow White and the Seven Dwarfs* **Dopey Model Sheet (Walt Disney, 1936).** Rare animator's practice model sheet of Dopey. Graphite on paper, measuring 12" x 10". There is paper aging, and light edge wear; otherwise the art is in Very Good condition. *From the Joe Magro Collection.*

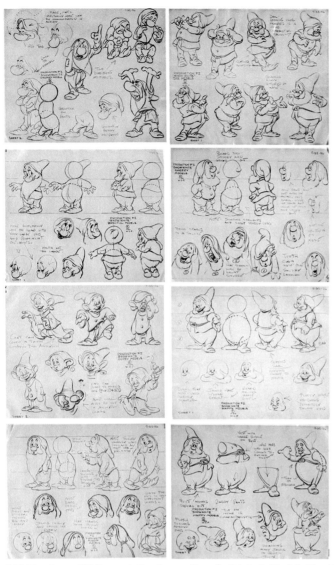

30020 *Snow White and the Seven Dwarfs* **Concept Drawing (Walt Disney, 1937).** Beautiful concept drawing of Snow White's face on Disney Studio 12-field 5-peghole animation paper. Red, Brown, and blue color highlights. Possibly Grim Natwick's work. A great piece of concept artwork that went into the making of the feature film. Image area measures approximately 3.5" x 4". Very Good condition.

30019 *Snow White and the Seven Dwarfs* **Printed Model Sheet Group (Walt Disney, 1937).** Get all seven Dwarfs with one bid, in this lot of eight model sheets, made for distribution to the animators. These belonged to animator Joe Magro, who stapled four sets of two back-to-back and put them behind nitrate clear cels. The two-sided sets here are Doc/Happy, Grumpy/Dopey, Sleepy/Bashful, and Sneezy/Happy.

All printed on photographic paper. All measure approximately 12.5" x 10". *From the Joe Magro Collection.*

30021 *Snow White and the Seven Dwarfs* **Snow White With Little Bird Production Drawing (Walt Disney, 1937).** On 12-field 5-peghole animation paper. Graphite pencil with slight red highlights. "#78" written in the right hand corner. Image area measures approximately 5" x 5.75". Excellent condition.

LOOK FOR A GLOSSARY OF ANIMATION ART TERMS ELSEWHERE IN THIS CATALOG.

30022 *Snow White and the Seven Dwarfs* **Snow White Production Drawing (Walt Disney, 1937).** Original animation drawing of Snow White, in graphite with green and yellow highlights on 12-field, 5-peghole animation paper. The image of Snow White measures 3". "Walt Disney Productions" is embossed on the paper, which indicates this drawing was originally sold through Courvoisier Gallery. Matted to 18.5" x 15.5" and in Fine condition.

30024 *Snow White and the Seven Dwarfs* **Snow White Production Drawing (Walt Disney, 1937).** This original production drawing features two lovely images of Snow White. Rendered in graphite and red pencil on a 12" x 10" sheet of animation paper. There is paper aging, soiling, and edge wear especially noticeable along the top; otherwise the art is in Very Good condition. *From the Joe Magro Collection.*

30023 *Snow White and the Seven Dwarfs* **Production Drawing (Walt Disney, 1937).** Original 12-field, 5-peghole animation drawing of Snow White in graphite with red highlights ("367") in bottom right corner. The image measures 5.5". Framed to 19.75" x 17.5" with an image area of 11" x 9". In Excellent condition.

30025 *Snow White and the Seven Dwarfs* **Dopey Production Drawing (Walt Disney, 1937).** Rough production drawing of Dopey from Disney's beloved *Snow White and the Seven Dwarfs*. Graphite on a 12" x 10" sheet of animation paper. There is some paper aging and light edge wear; otherwise the art is in Very Good condition. *From the Joe Magro Collection.*

12-FIELD: AN INDUSTRY STANDARD CEL (AND DRAWING PAPER) SIZE APPROXIMATELY 10" X 12", DEPENDING ON THE STUDIO AND YEAR.

16-FIELD: AN INDUSTRY STANDARD CEL (AND DRAWING PAPER) SIZE APPROXIMATELY 12" X 16", DEPENDING ON THE STUDIO AND YEAR.

30026 *Snow White and the Seven Dwarfs* **Dopey Production Drawing (Walt Disney, 1937).** Dopey lifts his candle high in this production drawing from Disney's *Snow White and the Seven Dwarfs*. Graphite on a 12" x 10" sheet of animation paper. There is some paper aging and light edge wear; otherwise the art is in Very Good condition. *From the Joe Magro Collection.*

30027 *Snow White and the Seven Dwarfs* **Dopey Production Drawing (Walt Disney, 1937).** A rough drawing of Dopey the Dwarf, in pencil on 16-field animation paper. The large image measures approximately 6.5". The drawing is in Very Good condition with some wear and tanning to the edges and a vertical fold crease, none of which affects the drawing. *From the Joe Magro Collection.*

30028 *Snow White and the Seven Dwarfs* **Grumpy Production Drawing (Walt Disney, 1937).** Expressive production drawing of Grumpy from Disney's premiere animated feature. Rendered in graphite on a 12" x 10" sheet of animation paper. There is some paper aging, surface wear, soiling and a horizontal crease in the upper portion; otherwise the art is in Very Good condition. *From the Joe Magro Collection.*

30029 *Snow White and the Seven Dwarfs* **Doc Production Drawing (Walt Disney, 1937).** Dramatic production drawing of Doc from Disney's masterpiece, *Snow White and the Seven Dwarfs*. Graphite and red pencil on a 12" x 10" sheet of animation paper. There is some paper aging, edge wear and two torn corners; otherwise the art is in Very Good condition. *From the Joe Magro Collection.*

30030 *Snow White and the Seven Dwarfs* **Bashful Production Drawing (Walt Disney, 1937).** Huge image of Bashful from Disney's first feature cartoon. Rendered in graphite and red pencil on a 12" x 10" sheet of animation paper. There is some paper aging, and edge wear; otherwise the art is in Very Good condition. *From the Joe Magro Collection.*

30031 **Marc Davis** *Snow White and the Seven Dwarfs* **Production Drawing Group (Walt Disney, 1937).** All seven dwarfs at the end of Snow White's bed are featured in this original production drawing from Disney's first feature film. The art is rendered in graphite and red pencil on a sheet of 12" x 9.5" sheet of animation bond paper. There is paper aging and edge wear; otherwise the work is in Very Good condition. *From the Joe Magro Collection.*

30032 *Snow White and the Seven Dwarfs* **Grumpy Production Drawing (Walt Disney, 1937.** An outstanding full figure pose! 12-field 5-peghole animation paper. Graphite with red highlights. "#111" written in the bottom right corner. Image area approximately 6" x 4". Very Good condition.

30033 *Snow White and the Seven Dwarfs* **Doc Production Drawing (Walt Disney, 1937).** Graphite pencil with distinct red and green highlights. "#65" written in right hand corner. Excellent condition.

30034 *Snow White and the Seven Dwarfs* **Snow White with Apple Production Drawing (Walt Disney, 1937).** An outstanding animation drawing of Snow White holding the fateful apple from Disney's first feature-length animated film. In red pencil on animation paper with "39" written in the lower right corner; the image measures approximately 6". Matted to an overall size of 18" x 15.5". In Excellent condition.

30035 *Snow White and the Seven Dwarfs* **Old Hag Production Drawing (Walt Disney, 1937).** A key scene is represented here! A 16-field drawing of the Old Hag/Witch with the poison apple. Graphite pencil with slight red and green highlights. Matted to an overall size of 17.5 x 15.25. Very Good condition.

A SNOW WHITE
SUNDAY STRIP
BY HANK PORTER
IS FEATURED IN
OUR COMIC ART
AUCTION!

SEE IT AT
HA.COM/7073

30036 *Snow White and the Seven Dwarfs* **The Evil Queen and the Old Hag Production Cel with Courvoisier Background (Walt Disney, 1937).** Two of the most epic evil characters in the Disney oeuvre, the Evil Queen and her alter-ego the Old Hag, share space in this splendid Courvoisier set-up. This set of two hand-inked and hand-painted cels from Disney's first feature film includes a hand-painted Courvoisier background. Framed and matted to an image area of 11" x 10.5". There is light buckling to the acetate, light paint stress on the Queen's dress with one small chip lost from the upper portion of her cape, and a 1" vertical tear in the lower portion of her podium; otherwise the work is in Very Good condition.

30037 *Snow White and the Seven Dwarfs* **The Old Hag Production Cel with Courvoisier Background (Walt Disney, 1937).** The Old Hag guides her raft towards the dwarf's cottage, in this wondrous Courvoisier set-up. This hand-inked and hand-painted cel from Disney's premiere animated feature includes a hand-painted Courvoisier background. Framed and matted to an image area of 12" x 9.25". There is light buckling to the acetate and background, one small area of ink line loss on the Hags cheek, and some loose paint in the area of her raised hand; otherwise the work is in Very Good condition.

30038 ***Snow White and the Seven Dwarfs* Crow and Skull Courvoisier Production Cel (Walt Disney, 1937).** This scene of the Queen's pet crow, reacting in horror to the Old Hag with her poisoned apple, is one of the most memorable moments of this classic animated film. This Courvoisier trimmed cel set-up includes the crow on its human skull perch, alongside the burning candle that dimly lights the scene. The art has been reframed with glass and a triple mat; the image area measures approximately 10.25" x 9", with an overall size of 18" x 17.25". In Excellent condition.

30039 *Snow White and the Seven Dwarfs* **The Old Hag Courvoisier Production Cel (Walt Disney, 1937).** The evil queen, in her magical disguise as an old hag, prepares the poison potion for Snow White's apple in this wonderful image from Disney's first full-length animated film. This Courvoisier set-up incorporates a trimmed image of the Hag with her pet crow against a custom painted background, for an image area of approximately 6" x 6.25". The set-up has been reframed with Plexiglas and a special mat, for an overall size of 17.25" x 17.75". In Very Good condition.

30040 *Snow White and the Seven Dwarfs* **The Evil Queen Production Cel with Courvoisier Background (Walt Disney, 1937).** One of the most wicked characters in the Disney pantheon lifts the box she hopes one day will hold Snow White's heart, in this unforgettable treasure from the beloved film. This stunning cel and Courvoisier painted background are framed and matted to an image area of 7.75" x 9.5". Some buckling on the cel; otherwise the art is in Excellent condition.

30041 *Snow White and the Seven Dwarfs* **Evil Queen Courvoisier Production Cel (Walt Disney, 1937).** The Evil Queen holds the box meant to keep the heart of Snow White in this chillingly beautiful Courvoisier set-up with a "full moon" background. The art has been reframed with a double mat; the image area is approximately 8.25" x 8.25", with an overall framed (with glass) size of 17.5" x 17.5". In Excellent condition.

30042 *Snow White and the Seven Dwarfs* **Dopey and Sneezy Production Cel with Courvoisier Background (Walt Disney, 1937).** Dopey, perched on Sneezy's shoulders, dances with Snow White in this hand-inked and hand-painted cel from Disney's first animated feature. This stunning work includes a hand-painted Courvoisier background, and is framed and matted to an image area of 6.5" x 9.25". There is light buckling to the acetate and background; otherwise the work is in Very Good condition.

30043 *Snow White and the Seven Dwarfs* **Production Cel with Courvoisier Background (Walt Disney, 1937).** Original hand-inked and painted cel of four dwarfs from Disney's Classic feature film in original Courvoisier Set-Up and airbrushed background. Two small original labels are on back. Nice large image of Dopey, Doc, Happy, and Bashful, with an approximate image area of 8" x 5"; matted and Plexiglas framed to an overall 17" x 14". Some slight warping of the cels, but the paint is in Fine condition.

30045 *Snow White and the Seven Dwarfs* **Doc Production Cel and Courvoisier Background (Walt Disney, 1937).** An original Courvoisier set-up. The cel is trimmed and has been placed over a hand-prepared hand-painted Courvoisier background. Framed. Frame opening is approximately 8" x 8". Image is a large 6" x 4". Paint is in good condition with slight cracking in bottom body part. No paint loss.

30044 *Snow White and the Seven Dwarfs* **Doc Production Cel with Courvoisier Background (Walt Disney, 1937).** Doc picks a pretty tune on his duck-shaped lute in this attractive hand-inked and painted cel, in an original Courvoisier set-up. The cel is trimmed and placed over a hand prepared, hand-painted Courvoisier background. Doc is a large 6" x 4" and the combined image area measures 8" x 8"; matted and framed to an overall 17.25" x 17.75". There are a few dings on the wooden frame. The paint is in Good condition with slight cracking in bottom body part, but no paint loss.

30046 *Snow White and the Seven Dwarfs* **Grumpy Production Cel Set-Up (Walt Disney, 1937).** Original hand-inked and hand-painted production cel of Grumpy in its original mat, trimmed and installed in an original Courvoisier set-up with a wood veneer background. The image of the irritable dwarf measures approximately 4" x 2". Small "©WDP" embossed in lower right corner and a small "Original work from Snow White" is printed on the reverse. Paint is in Fine condition.

30047 *Snow White and the Seven Dwarfs* **Sleepy Production Cel and Courvoisier Background (Walt Disney, 1938).** Original, one-of-a-kind hand-inked and painted production cel of Sleepy about to grab a pesky fly. The Fly is on a separate cel level. In the original Courvoisier set-up on a wood veneer background. Image area is a large 4" x 6"; matted and framed with glass to an overall 17.5" x 14.5". Paint is in Fine Condition.

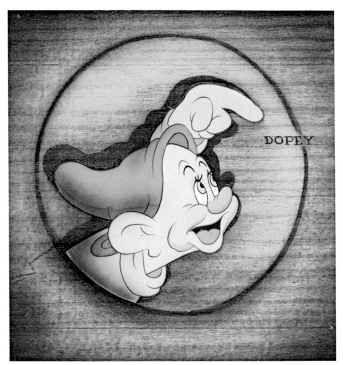

30049 *Snow White and the Seven Dwarfs* **Dopey Production Cel with Courvoisier Background (Walt Disney, 1937).** In an original wood grain Courvoisier Gallery set-up. Two small original stickers remain on the reverse. Matted with an image area of 5.25" x 5.5". Some overall aging; otherwise the condition is Very Good. The only Dwarf with *blue eyes*!

30048 *Snow White and the Seven Dwarfs* **Dopey Production Cel Set-Up (Walt Disney, 1937).** Original hand-inked and hand-painted production cel of Dopey in an original Courvoisier wood veneer background. Image area is 7" x 8"; image size is 5.5" x 5.75". Paint is in Fine condition.

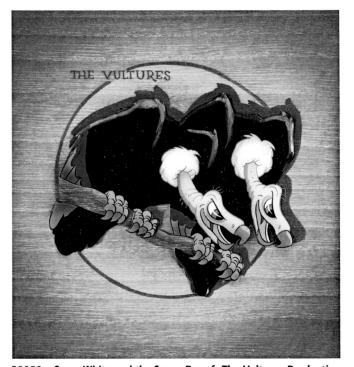

30050 *Snow White and the Seven Dwarfs* **The Vultures Production Cel and Courvoisier Background (Walt Disney, 1938).** A grinning pair of hungry vultures is ready to snack on something (or someone) in this original production cel from *Snow White*. Cel art pieces featuring the vultures are among the toughest to find from this classic film, as they appear only briefly, as the Old Hag makes her way to the Dwarf's cabin. Trimmed and set-up on an original Courvoisier woodgrain background. The birds are approximately 3" x 4" within an image area of 6" x 6"; matted and framed with non-reflective glass for an overall 13.25" x 13.25".

30051 *Snow White and the Seven Dwarfs* **Evil Queen Production Cel with Signed Card (Walt Disney, 1937).** As good a Snow White cel as we've seen. In an original Courvoisier set-up, complete with a Courvoisier hand-painted background. "Now I look for a formula to transform my beauty to ugliness." Large 8" x 8" image. Paint in fine condition with only slight separation in her cheek, no paint loss. Framed with a Walt Disney signature that reads "To G With best Wishes Walt Disney".

30052 *Snow White and the Seven Dwarfs* **The Old Hag Production Cel with Presentation Background (Walt Disney, 1937).** With a basketful of apples and a devious smile, the Old Hag sets out on her deadly mission to destroy Snow White. Includes a hand-painted presentation art background. Framed and matted to an image area of 14" x 9.5". Some buckling on the cel; otherwise the art is in Excellent condition.

30053 *Snow White and the Seven Dwarfs* **The Old Hag Production Cel with Presentation Background (Walt Disney, 1937).** Resolved to do away with her stepdaughter, the Queen, in the guise of an Old Hag, takes matters into her own nefarious hands here. Includes a hand-painted presentation art background. Framed and matted to an image area of 12" x 8.5". In Excellent condition. Includes a Certificate of Authenticity.

30054 *Snow White and the Seven Dwarfs* **Production Cel with Presentation Background (Walt Disney, 1937).** Here's a real treat for lovers of the first full-length animation feature from the Walt Disney Studios, *Snow White and the Seven Dwarfs*. All seven dwarfs are present in this delightful scene, with Dopey barely noticeable, shown doing a flip with his head obscured. The wonderful hand-painted background has two separate layers, giving the piece a three-dimensional feel. The combined image area measures approximately 21.5" x 12.5", and the scene has been matted and framed with glass for an overall size of 29.5" x 21". In Excellent condition.

YOU'LL FIND A GLOSSARY OF ANIMATION ART TERMS ELSEWHERE IN THIS CATALOG!

30055 *Snow White and the Seven Dwarfs* **Snow White and the Old Hag Production Cel Set-Up (Walt Disney Studios, 1937).** We chose this as our cover lot with good reason: it's one of the most remarkable examples of our Snow White selection. Exquisite original production cels in an original Courvoisier set-up of Snow White with the Old Hag, from a key scene in the Disney classic. The image of Snow White measures 4", while the Old Hag measures 4.25". Originally sold in Sotheby's animation art Sale #6520 (Lot #719) on December 16, 1993. Two original 1937 labels are still on the back. The set-up features a Courvoisier-prepared hand-painted background, and is framed to 16.5" x 15.5" with a frame opening of 9" x 7.5". The paint is in Fine Condition.

30056   *Snow White and the Seven Dwarfs* **The Old Hag Production Cel with Presentation Background (Walt Disney, 1937).** The Old Hag attempts to dislodge a huge rock upon the pursuing dwarfs, in this hand-inked and hand-painted production cel from the climactic scene just before the death of one of Disney's most memorable villains. Includes a hand-painted presentation art background. Framed and matted to an image area of 12" x 8.5". Some very light buckling; otherwise in Excellent condition.

30057 *Snow White and the Seven Dwarfs* **Prince with Snow White Production Cel and Courvoisier Background (Walt Disney, 1937).** Snow White stares into her Prince's eyes as three of the seven dwarfs look on. This is a lovely Courvoisier set-up, and the cel is registered to a hand-painted and air-brushed gradated background, with foreground foliage. There is some rippling to the cel, causing some visual separation from the background, but the paint has held up very well and is in Fine condition. This is one of the nicest *Snow White* cels we have ever offered. Expertly framed to an overall size of 24.25" x 34", with an image area of approximately 8.75" x 8.45".

30058 Gene Ware Snow White with Grumpy, Dopey, and Bashful Book Illustration Art (Walt Disney, c. 1980s). Outstanding one-of-a-kind Gene Ware original watercolor painting done for a Disney children's book. Framed with an image area of 18″ x 12″. Signed by the late Mr. Ware. In Excellent condition. *From the Gene Ware Collection.*

30059 Gene Ware *Snow White and Seven Dwarfs* Book Illustration Art (Walt Disney, 1987). Original acrylic painting of Snow White and the Seven Dwarfs by Gene Ware for a children's book, published for the 50th anniversary of the movie. Framed image size is 12″ x 12″. In Excellent condition. *From the Gene Ware Collection.*

ALL ORIGINAL ARTWORK IN THIS CATALOG IS SHOWN TIGHTLY CROPPED TO THE PUBLISHED IMAGE AREA. YOU CAN SEE THE COMPLETE ART, INCLUDING EXTRA BORDER AREAS, BY VIEWING THE LOTS ONLINE AT HA.COM

The Art of the Walt Disney Studio
Animation Drawing

In the 2012 book "A Disney Sketchbook," Ken Shue, Vice President of Disney Global Art Development, wrote, "Hand-drawn Disney animation holds a unique place in the history of modern art and culture. Disney artists and animators bring great performances to the screen by drawing with emotion, sincerity, and intensity. Knowing full-well that many of their drawings would only be seen in pencil tests and preliminary screenings, or never at all, the artists drew from within themselves onto a sheet of paper. In the process, they created incredible works of art in their own right."

Animation historian Charles Solomon noted, "Walt Disney advanced the art of animation by giving his animators the time they needed to explore and experiment. Disney had only one rule, says Snow White animator Grim Natwick: whatever we did had to be better than anyone else could do it, even if you had to animate it nine times, as I once did!"

John Lasseter of Pixar provided another perspective: "To be an animator, you have master two skills. First, you have to have an eye for movement and understand the specifics of how movement conveys meaning. How do you show personality of a character in the way he or she moves? How do you adjust the timing of a gesture or glance to convey the right emotion? Every animator is really an actor performing in slow motion, living the character a drawing at a time. Second you have to be able to translate your understanding and movement to paper; your draftsmanship must be able to capture and convey your intent. Anyone who has watched a Disney film has seen its animators acting talent on display. But it's only when you see the individual drawings that you are able to fully appreciate the rock-solid artistry that provides the foundation for the moving image."

In today's age of digital computer-drawn artwork , these simple Walt Disney Studio animation drawings, drawn by hand by the team of Disney artists and animators, present a unique opportunity to own a piece of what they call "Disney Magic."

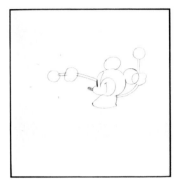  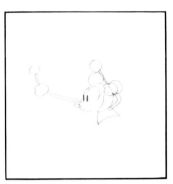

30060   Ub Iwerks Steamboat Willie Mickey Mouse Production Drawings Group (Walt Disney, 1928). From the very first Mickey Mouse cartoon – drawings attributed to Ub Iwerks. The framed trio includes one of just a few full figure Mickey drawings we've ever seen from this scene from the legendary cartoon. The art is rendered in graphite on 2-peghole animation sheets, measuring 12" x 9.5". There is some paper aging, and very light creasing present; otherwise, the art is in Very Good condition. Framed to an overall size of 18/75" x 40.5", with image areas of approximately 7" x 7". It doesn't get more historic than this!

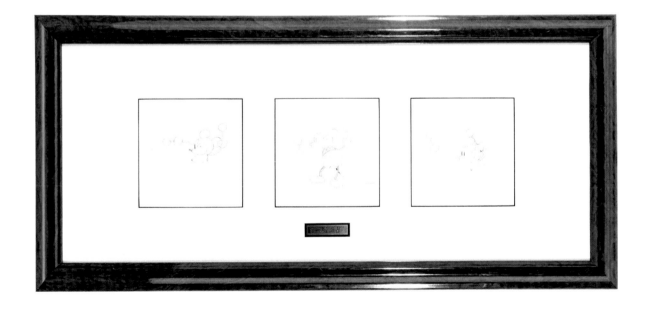

30061 *Steamboat Willie* **Mickey Mouse Production Drawing Group (Walt Disney, 1928).** A pair of 12-field, 2-peghole animation drawings of Mickey Mouse drawn by Ube Iwerks, from the first Mickey Mouse short released by Walt Disney Studios. (Mickey was voiced by Walt Disney himself in this landmark theatrical short.) The images are from the scene where Mickey is playing the hippo's teeth. The two drawings form a complete figure of Mickey. Mickey's top half is 4" long, while is bottom half is 2.5". Framed to 21.5" x 15.5". A Sotheby's sticker is on the reverse.

30062   Ub Iwerks and Walt Disney In-Studio Gag Drawing (circa late 1920s). Quite the role reversal here with Ub Iwerks pushing Walt Disney to produce art on deadline! Rendered in pencil, 11" x 8.5". There's a stain at lower right, otherwise Very Good condition.

30063 *Pluto* **Production Drawing Group (Walt Disney, 1930s).** Sequence of nine lively production drawings of Pluto from a theatrical short. Each drawing measures 12" x 10". There is paper tanning, and edge wear; otherwise the work averages Very Good condition. *From the Joe Magro Collection.*

30064 *Traffic Troubles* **Mickey Mouse Black and White Nitrate Production Cel with Presentation Background (Walt Disney, 1931).** Taxi driver Mickey takes his cab out on a very dilapidated city street in this exceedingly rare hand-inked and hand-painted production cel from the early B&W Mickey short, *Traffic Troubles*. The cel has been trimmed to the line and remounted onto a recent hand-painted presentation background. Framed and matted to an image area of 12" x 9.5", the trimmed cel measures 5" x 3.25". As to be expected for a Nitrate item, there is cel discoloration, ink and paint loss, and slight buckling; otherwise the art is in Good condition and still presents well. As most animation collectors know, finding choice black and white Nitrates featuring Mickey Mouse is a difficult task, with only 50 currently known to exist; don't let this one zip by without bidding!

30065 *The Mail Pilot* Mickey Mouse Production Drawing (Walt Disney, 1933). A dangerous situation for Mickey, and an outstanding piece of art! This amazing graphite pencil drawing takes up almost the entire 12-field 2-peghole animation paper with the plane stretching out to 10.5". The Disney theatrical short "The Mail Pilot" (comic collectors will know it from the key Big Little Book) was directed by Dave Hand. "#161" is written in the bottom corner of the piece. Very Good condition.

30066 *Puppy Love* Mickey Mouse and Pluto Production Drawing (Walt Disney, 1933). You won't find a more heartfelt drawing of Mickey on his way to court Minnie! From the theatrical short directed by Wilfred Jackson. 12-field 2-peghole animation paper, graphite with red and green highlights. Number 200 in bottom right corner. Image area approximately 8" x 4". Very Good condition.

30068 *Grasshopper and the Ant* Color Model Cel and Background (Walt Disney, c. 1933). This attractive set-up had us puzzled, but we now believe this to be a Color Model cel and background, done during the early stages of production for Disney's 1934 adaptation of the classic Aesop Fable's story. The final version of this character changed, but both the cel and background illustration have all the hallmarks of being from the Disney studios. The Grasshopper has an approximate image area of 4" x 4", and the background (which is composed of two separate items — the blue sky being on a separate piece glued to the tree and mushroom houses) measures 11" x 8.5". The cel is in Excellent condition; the background a solid Fine with some fading apparent in places. Overall, this is a rare and unusual item, sure to appeal to advanced Disney collectors.

30067 *Ye Olden Days* Mickey Mouse Production Drawing (Walt Disney, 1933). Everyone's all smiles in the finale of the 1933 theatrical short directed by the Bert Gillett. Graphite with red, green and blue highlights. 12-field 2-peghole animation paper. An outstanding piece. Very Good condition.

30069 *Hawaiian Holiday* **Mickey Mouse and Donald Duck Promotional Original Art Painting (Walt Disney, 1937).** This wonderful gouache on board painting, done by the Hank Porter Group, of Mickey Mouse and Donald Duck "hangin' eight," was inspired by the Disney short *Hawaiian Holiday*. It was given as a gift, by Walt Disney, to an employee of Disney's art supply company, A. C. Friedrichs Co., for the birth of the employee's daughter, in 1936. It has been in their family collection until now! The piece has been matted to an overall size of 13.75" x 18", with an image area of approximately 11.25" x 15.5" and is in Excellent condition.

30071 *Funny Little Bunnies* **Disney Painting Original Art (Walt Disney, mid-1930s).** This painting was a gift from Disney to a friend who worked at A. C. Friedrichs art supply company to celebrate the birth of the friend's daughter in the mid-1930s. The art was probably done by Hank Porter's group. The image was inspired by the 1934 theatrical short "Funny Little Bunnies." This gouache on board piece is good-sized, with an image area of 10" x 13", and it's in Excellent condition.

30070 **Mickey Mouse, Minnie Mouse, and Donald Duck Painting Original Art (Walt Disney, mid-1930s).** This painting was a gift from Walt Disney to a friend who worked at A. C. Friedrichs art supply company to celebrate the birth of the friend's daughter in the mid-1930s. The art was probably done by Hank Porter's group. A remarkable, good-sized piece! The image was inspired by the 1933 theatrical short "Ye Olden Days." This gouache on board piece has an image area of 10" by 13" and is in Excellent condition.

30072 *Funny Little Bunnies* **Disney Painting Original Art (Walt Disney, 1934).** This painting was a gift from Walt Disney to a friend who worked at A. C. Friedrichs art supply company to celebrate the birth of the friend's daughter in the mid-1930s. The art was probably done by Hank Porter's group. A large piece, with an adorable image! The image was inspired by the 1934 theatrical short "Funny Bunnies." This gouache on board piece has an image area of 10" x 13" and is in Excellent condition.

30075 *On Ice* **Goofy Production Drawing (Walt Disney, 1935).** Goofy tries a new form of ice fishing in the 1935 short, *On Ice*. This original production drawing of Goofy is rendered in graphite and red pencil on a 12-field sheet of paper (12" x 10"). There is paper aging and light soiling; otherwise the art is in Very Good condition. *From the Joe Magro Collection.*

30073 *Two Gun Mickey* **Pete and Mickey Mouse Production Drawing (Walt Disney, 1934).** A life-and-death struggle makes for a great two-character drawing! From the theatrical short directed by Ben Sharpsteen. Graphite pencil on 12-field 2-peghole animation paper. "#30" written in the bottom right corner. Image area measures approximately 5" x 4.75". Excellent condition.

30076 *Moving Day* **Production Drawing Group (Walt Disney, 1936).** Seven sequential drawings of Goofy created for the 1936 short, *Moving Day*. Rendered in graphite and red pencil on 12-field 5-peghole animation paper, each measuring 12" x 10". Some paper aging, and light edge wear; otherwise the art averages Very Good condition. *From the Joe Magro Collection.*

30074 *The Big Bad Wolf* **Production Drawing (Walt Disney, 1934).** "All the better to EAT you with, my dear!" Fantastic original production drawing from one of the best-loved Disney cartoons of all time, featuring the Big Bad Wolf dressed in Granny's bonnet and laying in bed. It's a full image including background, drawn in graphite with red pencil borders, and an approximate image area of 10.5" x 7.5". Drawn on 2-peghole animation paper, and numbered 45. Excellent condition.

30077 **Joe Magro** *Goofy* **Model Sheet Drawing (Walt Disney, 1936).** Four original working model sheets of Goofy created for the 1936 short, *Moving Day*. Four 12-field 5-peghole animation paper sheets, each measuring 12" x 10". Some paper aging, edge wear, and light soiling; otherwise the art averages Very Good condition. Two of the sheets have been signed by animator Joe Magro at the lower right corner. *From the Joe Magro Collection.*

30078 *Mother Pluto* **Production Cel on Key Master Background (Walt Disney, 1936).** One of the highlights of our Disney selection is this cel from the 1936 theatrical short. Not only is Pluto's expression adorable, be sure to zoom in on our online image to see the chicks on the other side of the fence. Cute! Matted to an image area of approximately 11" x 8".

MOTHER PLUTO
- 1936 -

30079 *Mother Pluto* **Production Cel and Key Master Background (Walt Disney, 1936).** A forlorn Pluto dreams of his adopted "babies" in this tender scene from *Mother Pluto*. It's a wonderful hand-painted production cel set-up, from one of Pluto's best short features. It's been paired with a key master background, with a combined image area of 10.25" x 8.25", very nicely matted to an overall 18.25" x 16.5". It's in Excellent condition and ready to frame and find a new home!

30080 *Mickey's Circus* **Production Drawing Group (Walt Disney, 1936).** Two production drawings, including a rare title drawing and one with a great Mickey Mouse expression. Both from the theatrical short, *Mickey's Circus*, on 5-peghole 12-filed animation paper. Graphite pencil with red and green highlights. Image areas are approximately 8.25 x 4" (Mickey) and 6.75 x 7.5" (title). Very Good condition.

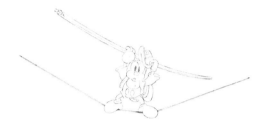

30081 *Mickey's Circus* **Tightrope Production Drawing (Walt Disney, 1936).** On 12-field 5-peghole animation paper from the 1936 Ben Sharpsteen-directed theatrical short. Graphite pencil with red highlights. "#30" written in bottom right corner. Excellent condition.

30082 *Three Little Wolves* **Production Cel and Drawing Group (Walt Disney, 1936).** An original hand-inked and hand-painted production cel of two of the Three Little Wolves, along with a layout sketch of the scene. The figures in the cel have been trimmed and mounted to another sheet of acetate, and the background is a color photocopy. The drawing is rendered in graphite and red pencil. Framed together, the cel and drawing are each matted to an image area of 11.25" x 7.5". Some slight foxing in the paint and paper aging and light soiling in the drawing; otherwise the art averages Very Good condition.

30083 *Lonesome Ghosts* **Production Cel (Walt Disney, 1937).** Ajax Ghost Exterminator Mickey Mouse takes aim in this original hand-inked and hand-painted production cel from the 1937 short, *Lonesome Ghosts*. Mounted against a color photocopy, the art is framed and matted to an image area of 11" x 8". There is some slight aging and buckling on the cel; otherwise this work is in Very Good condition. Includes a COA.

30084 *Don Donald* **Production Drawing (Walt Disney, 1937).** Original layout model drawing of Donald Duck from his first starring role in the short, *Don Donald*. Graphite and multi-color pencil on 12" x 10" 5-peghole animation paper. Some paper aging, and light edge wear; otherwise the art is in Very Good condition. *From the Joe Magro Collection.*

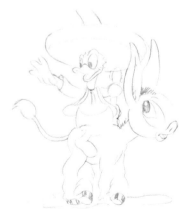

30085 *Don Donald* **Production Drawing Group (Walt Disney, 1937).** Five animation drawings of Donald Duck from his first starring-role short, *Don Donald*. Graphite on 12" x 10" 5-peghole animation paper. Some paper aging, edge wear, and light soiling; otherwise the art averages Very Good condition. *From the Joe Magro Collection.*

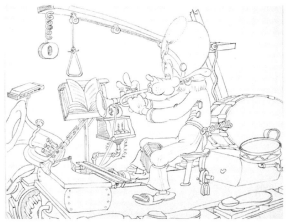

30086 *Mickey's Amateurs* **Goofy Production Drawing (Walt Disney, 1937).** An outstanding and dramatic original layout drawing of Goofy from the 1937 Walt Disney Studio theatrical short "Mickey's Amateurs". 12-field 5-peghole animation paper, with an approximate image area of 10.5" x 8". Nicely detailed graphite pencil with slight blue and green highlights. Some minor edge wear, but the image area remains in Excellent condition. *From the Joe Magro Collection.*

30087 *Moose Hunters* **Production Drawing Group (Walt Disney, 1937).** Series of three drawings of Mickey and Donald, and Goofy as a moose from the 1937 Disney short, *Moose Hunters*. Graphite and colored pencil on 12" x 10" 5-peghole animation paper. Some paper aging, edge wear, pinholes and corner tears; otherwise the art averages Good condition. *From the Joe Magro Collection.*

30088 *Little Hiawatha* **Production Cel (Walt Disney, 1937).** Outstanding hand-inked and hand-painted production cel of Little Hiawatha meeting the baby bear cub, from the theatrical short directed by Dave Hand, on a hand-painted Courvoisier background. Originally sold at Arthur Ackermann and Sons; the original paperwork is mounted on the reverse along with the original Courvoisier paperwork. Framed to 15.5" x 13.5", with an image area of 8" x 6". The paint is in Fine condition.

30089 *Clock Cleaners* **Goofy Production Drawing Group (Walt Disney, 1937).** From the Ben Sharpsteen Walt Disney Studios directed theatrical short that also starred Mickey Mouse and Donald Duck. "Clock Cleaners" ranks #27 in Jerry Beck's 1994 book **50 Greatest Cartoons**. There are 33 in all here on 12-field 5-peghole animation drawing paper, graphite with red highlights, ranging from Very Good to Excellent. Goofy's 4" to 6" in these amazing sequences.

30090 *Clock Cleaners* **Donald Duck Production Cel (Walt Disney, 1937).** A busy Donald puts on a happy face in this original hand-inked hand-painted nitrate production cel from the 1937 Walt Disney Studio theatrical short "Clock Cleaners," with "#63" noted in the lower right corner. The paint in good condition, other than a slight loss in top of Donald's hat and within the mop head. The image area is approximately 4" x 3". *From the Joe Magro Collection.*

30091 *Clock Cleaners* **Donald Goofy and Mickey Production Cel (Walt Disney, 1937).** The wheels go 'round for our boys in this original hand-inked hand-painted nitrate cel of Mickey Mouse, Goofy, and Donald Duck, from the 1937 Walt Disney theatrical cartoon "Clock Cleaners". This is a rare example of three major characters on one cel, with the number "111" written in the lower right corner. There is slight paint loss on the characters, but the overall image condition is Fine. *From the Joe Magro Collection.*

30093 *Clock Cleaners* **Mickey, Donald, and Goofy Production Cel (Walt Disney, 1937).** Mickey Mouse, Goofy, and Donald Duck can hear no evil in this original hand-inked hand-painted nitrate cel of in the 1937 Walt Disney theatrical cartoon "Clock Cleaners". Cartoon historian Jerry Beck's 1994 book **The 50 Greatest Cartoons** had "Clock Cleaners" listed as the 27th best cartoon of all time, and finding all three main characters on one cel like this is quite unusual. This exact cel was also used as the book illustration for **Key Pose**. The number "368" is written in the lower right corner. The image area measures 7.5" x 5". There are a few pinholes in the top corners and some light smudging, with a few areas of paint loss; overall condition is Good. *From the Joe Magro Collection.*

30092 *Clock Cleaners* **Donald Duck Production Cel (Walt Disney, 1937).** Donald gets down to business in this original hand-inked hand-painted nitrate production cel from the Walt Disney Studio theatrical short "Clock Cleaners". A perfect, full-figure Donald pose, with paint in Fine condition. The image area is approximately 3" x 4". *From the Joe Magro Collection.*

30094 *Clock Cleaners* **Goofy Production Cel and Matching Drawings Group (Walt Disney, 1937).** An original hand-inked hand-painted 12-field nitrate cel of Goofy from the 1937 Walt Disney theatrical short "Clock Cleaners". The addition of the rough animation drawing and clean up animation drawing makes this three-piece lot something special. Cel, rough, and clean-up pieces are all numbered 145, with the drawings on 12-field 5-peghole animation paper. There are slight pinholes in the corners of the drawings, and a couple of tiny areas of paint loss on the cel; overall condition for all three is Very Good. *From the Joe Magro Collection.*

30095 *Hawaiian Holiday* **Goofy Production Drawing Group (Walt Disney, 1937).** Set of three brilliant Goofy drawings from this 1937 theatrical short. Each drawing is rendered in graphite and multi-colored pencil on 12-field paper. There is paper aging, pinholes, and edge wear; otherwise the art averages Very Good condition. *From the Joe Magro Collection.*

30097 *Ferdinand the Bull* **Matador and Fans Production Cel (Walt Disney, 1938).** Original hand-inked and hand-painted production cel of the matador and his fans from the Academy Award-winning theatrical short directed by Dick Richard, trimmed and placed on a Courvoisier wood veneer background with painting effects. Matted, with an image area of 10" x 8". The matador is 5.5" inches tall. The paint is in Fine condition, and the colors are amazing.

30096 *Hawaiian Holiday* **Pluto Production Drawing Group (Walt Disney, 1937).** Pluto is startled in this set of five drawings from the 1937 theatrical short, *Hawaiian Holiday*. Each drawing is rendered in graphite and red pencil on 12-field paper. There is paper aging, and edge wear; otherwise the art averages Very Good condition. *From the Joe Magro Collection.*

30098 *The Brave Little Tailor* **Mickey Mouse Production Drawing (Walt Disney, 1938).** A key pose! This 12-field 5-peghole animation drawing of graphite pencil with red and green highlights is from the Academy Award-nominated theatrical short directed by Bill Roberts. "65 ED" in bottom right corner. Image area measures approximately 5.5" x 3.75". Excellent condition.

LOOK FOR MORE ANIMATION ART
IN THE SUNDAY INTERNET COMICS AUCTIONS
AT HA.COM!

30099 *The Brave Little Tailor* **Mickey Mouse Production Cel and Courvoisier Background (Walt Disney, 1938).** One of Mickey Mouse's greatest roles! Original hand-inked, hand-painted, trimmed production cel placed on a hand-painted Courvoisier background. Directed by Bill Roberts, this Walt Disney theatrical short was nominated for an Academy Award. Mickey is approximately 3" x 4", and the combined image area is 10" x 8". Matted and framed with non-reflective glass for an overall size of 17.75" x 15.25". Paint is in Fine condition. BEAUTIFUL!

30101 *The Boat Builders* **Goofy Production Background with Presentation Cel (Walt Disney, 1938).** An original hand-painted production background, gouache on illustration board, from the theatrical short directed by Ben Sharpsteen. Placed over this background is a newly created hand-inked and hand-painted cel of Goofy, created by the Walt Disney Studio's Ink and Paint Department from the original 1938 archived animation drawings. This is a 1/1 cel placed over a vintage background for presentation purposes, with the image of Goofy measuring 6.5". Framed to 28" x 21", with an image area of 15" x 9". The original 1938 background paperwork and cel paperwork are mounted on the reverse. The cel bears the Disney studio seal. The paint is perfect.

30100 *The Boat Builders* **Mickey Mouse Production Drawing Group (Walt Disney, 1938).** A series of five animation drawings, in sequence, featuring Mickey the 1938 animated short (the first to depict him without a tail!). In Excellent condition.

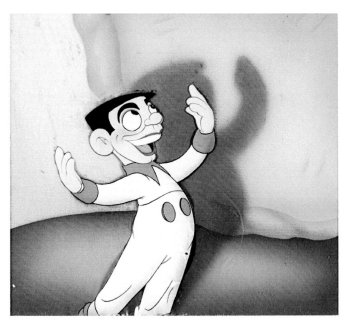

30102 *Mother Goose Goes Hollywood* **Eddie Cantor Production Cel and Courvoisier Background (Walt Disney, 1938).** From the Academy Award-nominated theatrical short directed by Wilfred Jackson, this short was nominated for an Academy Award. Eddie is 4" tall and is applied to hand prepared Courvoisier background. Paint is fine.

30103 *Mother Goose Goes Hollywood* **Laurel and Hardy Storyboard (Walt Disney, 1938).** Original Storyboard artwork (5" x 7") of Laurel and Hardy from the Academy Award-nominated theatrical cartoon short directed by Wilfred Jackson. Red graphite pencil. "#90" in right corner. Excellent condition.

30104 *Sea Scouts* **Donald Duck Production Cel and Background (Walt Disney, 1939).** Original hand-inked, hand-painted production cel of Donald Duck in uniform, on a Walt Disney studio production background, from the Walt Disney theatrical short, directed by Dick Lundy that also starred Huey Dewey and Louie. Nice 5" tall Donald cel, paired with a simply breathtaking background from the same film! Image area of the background is 9" x 7"; matted and framed with Plexiglas for an overall size of 15.5" x 13.5". Very minor missing chip of paint from Don's beak and two pinholes in his right foot, with a few small areas of minor discoloration; a tiny, thin stain on the background. Overall Very Good.

30105 *Autograph Hound* **Donald Duck and Policeman Matched Color Model Drawing Group (Walt Disney, 1939).** Donald's pose here reminds us of a lot of collectors we know, and the expressions on Donald and the cop are guaranteed to make you chuckle. This pair of matched drawings is from the theatrical short directed by Jack King. On 12-field 5-peghole animation paper with red highlights. The entire ink and paint codes are called out in this set of drawings each with "c-23" and "d-23" at bottom right on the respective pieces. Very Good condition.

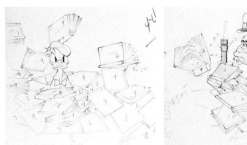

30106 *Society Dog Show* **Pluto and Dog Show Judge Production Drawing (Walt Disney, 1939).** In the theatrical short directed by Bill Roberts, Mickey, and Pluto crashed a posh dog show, presided over by a judge just as snooty as the other handlers. 12-field 5-peghole animation paper, graphite pencil with red and green highlights. "#96" on bottom right corner. Excellent condition.

30107 Joe Grant Jiminy Cricket Concept Artwork (Walt Disney, 1940). Original concept drawing of Jiminy Cricket by Grant, with a "Return to Character Model Dept." studio stamp on the lower right corner. In Very Good condition.

YOU'LL FIND MORE DISNEY ANIMATION ART IN SESSION TWO!

30108 *Mr. Mouse Takes A Trip* **Mickey Mouse Production Cels on Key Master Background (Walt Disney, 1940).** This is as good a Mickey Mouse set-up as we have ever seen. Outstanding cels of Mickey, Pete, and Pluto on a key master hand-painted background from the Clyde Geronimi-directed theatrical short. Matted and framed, with a frame opening of 14" x 8". Mickey Mouse is 4", Pete is 6" and Pluto is 5" long. Paint is in Fine condition.

30109 *Bill Posters* **Donald Duck Pan Production Background Set-Up (Walt Disney, 1940).** An outstanding pan production background, gouache on illustration board, from the theatrical short *Bill Posters*, directed by Clyde Geronimi and starring Goofy and Donald Duck. The detail on the background painting is amazing, and it is enhanced by the addition of a hand-inked and hand-painted production cel of Donald from the same time period. Framed to 33.5" x 16.5" with an image area of 26" x 8"; the image of Donald is 4.75" tall. The paint is in Fine condition. One of the best Donald Duck set-ups we've ever seen.

30110 *Fantasia* **Mickey Mouse as the Sorcerer's Apprentice Production Cel (Walt Disney, 1940).** The crowning moment for Mickey Mouse! Original trimmed cel, applied to an airbrushed background with painted overlay of the stars. There is a small cut in the celluloid at Mickey's feet. No paint loss. An original Courvoisier set-up. Provenance has it that Roy Disney presented this as a gift to an associate. The piece was previously sold at Sotheby's on November 18, 1999. Mickey is 4" tall, and the mat opening is approximately 7" x 6".

30111 *Fantasia* **The Sorcerer's Apprentice Storyboard Sketch (Walt Disney, 1940).** Original color storyboard concept artwork of Mickey Mouse in the most famous sequence of Disney's masterpiece, *Fantasia*. Gouache on board measuring 7.25" x 6". Used in the making of the classic Disney feature film, the work has a pin hole in each of its four corners; otherwise its condition is Excellent.

30112 *Fantasia* **Mlle. Upanova Production Cel (Walt Disney, 1940).** Original hand-inked and hand-painted cel set-up of the first dancer from the "Dance of the Hours" segment of *Fantasia*. One cel is an in-studio specially painted cel overlay for an Ink and Paint Department bride-to-be, and it features the inked signatures of her co-workers. "Best Wishes" is inscribed across the dancer in the center on the top cel. Paint is Fine. Dancer is 7" with a specially painted wedding veil! Cels are trimmed to 8" x 7".

30113 *Fantasia* **Cupids Production Cel with Courvoisier Background (Walt Disney, 1940).** A lovely image from one of the most-loved scene, the Pastoral Symphony sequence of *Fantasia*, featuring three little tree-dwelling cupids on a trimmed cel. The hand-painted Courvoisier background mimics the movie art nicely. There is some color flaking in each of the figures, most noticeably in the first cupid's blond hair, but also within the wrist of the middle cupid, and in the last figure's left hand. In overall Very Good condition, with an approximate image area for the cupids of 6.5" x 3.25", and the combined image area is 8.25" x 7.25". Matted to 15" x 13", with the original Courvoisier label on the back.

30114 *Pinocchio* **Production Cel with Courvoisier Background (Walt Disney, 1940).** A donkey-eared Pinocchio is underwater in this delightful hand-inked and painted original production cel, complete with three fish and lots of bubbles. The Pinocchio figure is approximately 5.25" tall, and the combined image area is 8.25" x 8.25". The original Courvoisier mat is included, with the caption, "Gee, What a Big Place!" seen in the lower left. An additional cloth-covered mat is included, and the piece is Plexiglas framed for an overall size of 16" x 16". There is a bit of cracking of paint within one ear, and a couple of tiny flakes out in the two fish above Pinocchio's head, but the cel presents extremely well, and is in overall Fine condition.

30115 *Pinocchio* **Figaro Production Cel Setup With Courvoisier Background (Walt Disney, 1940).** Trimmed cel in original Courvoisier set-up with a hand-prepared Courvoisier background. Paint is fine. Matt opening is 5" x 4", Figaro is approximately 2" x 2" and includes the original Courvoisier mat. The mat has a Walt Disney studio signature, possibly by Hank Porter or another studio artist.

30116 *Pinocchio* **Production Cel and Master Background (Walt Disney, 1940).** Pinocchio and Figaro the cat are featured in this splendid production cel, paired with an original key master background painted by Disney artist Claude Coats. The 4" tall Pinocchio and 2" long Figaro figures are carefully trimmed, Courvoisier-style, and the scene is beautifully matted and Plexiglas framed, with a brass nameplate, for a size of 19.5" x 17". The paint is in Fine condition; overall condition appears Excellent. Disney's adaptation of Carlo Collodi's classic story of a humble puppeteer and his desire to raise a real-life son remains one of the best of the studio's animated features, and for lovers of that film, this piece is sure to thrill.

30117   *Pinocchio* Geppetto and Figaro Storyboard (Walt Disney, 1940). This 5" x 7" storyboard is mounted to a 12-field 5-peghole animation paper and has a Courvoisier WDP Stamp in the bottom right corner on the animation paper. This storyboard was originally sold through the Courvoisier Art Program. Very Good condition.

30118   *Pinocchio* Cleo Production Cel (Walt Disney, 1940). A 1940 original hand-inked hand-painted production cel of Cleo the fish from the Walt Disney feature film "Pinocchio." Placed over a lovely hand-painted underwater Courvoisier background. Matted with a circular cut frame. The paint on Cleo is Fine. Cleo measures approximately 3.75" tall. The overall mat size is 12.5" x 12.5", with a circular image area of approximately 6.5" in diameter. Overall Very Fine condition.

30119   *Pinocchio* Jiminy Cricket and Seahorse Production Cel (Walt Disney, 1940). Outstanding hand-inked and hand-painted production cel of Jiminy Cricket and the Seahorse, with bubble effects, trimmed and placed over a Courvoisier hand-painted background. Jiminy is 3" tall, while the Seahorse is 6". The paint is in Fine condition.

30120   *Pinocchio* Production Cel with Courvoisier Background (Walt Disney, 1940). Original hand-inked and hand-painted production cel of Pinocchio mounted to a Courvoisier wood veneer background with hand-painted effects. Pinocchio measures 4.5". The paint is in Fine condition.

30121   *Pinocchio* Jiminy Cricket Production Cel (Walt Disney, 1940). Original one-of-a-kind hand-inked and hand-painted production cel of Jiminy Cricket, mounted to a hand-painted Courvoisier background. Framed to 12" x 15.5", with the original paperwork on reverse. The mat is signed with a studio artist signature of Walt Disney. Framed with original Courvoisier-script "Jiminy" on the mat. The frame opening is 6" x 6", and Jiminy is 3.5". The paint is in fine condition. In overall Excellent condition.

30122   *Pinocchio* Geppetto Production Cel Set-Up (Walt Disney, 1940). A striking set-up featuring an original hand-inked and hand-painted cel set-up of Geppetto and Figaro in bed, placed over a hand-painted presentation background, painted to enhance the set-up. The Geppetto image measures 4" x 2.5" and Figaro is 1.25". The paint is in Fine condition.

30123 *Pinocchio* **Pinocchio and Figaro Production Cel Set-Up (Walt Disney, 1940).** Original hand-inked and hand-painted production cel of Pinocchio and Figaro, trimmed and placed over a hand-painted keyed production background. The image of Pinocchio measures 3.5″, while Figaro is 2″. Framed to 24.5″ x 22″, with and image area of 10″ x 8″. In Fine condition.

30124 *Dumbo* **Production Drawing (Walt Disney, 1941).** An original clean-up drawing of Dumbo on the high-wire in the classic animated feature. In Excellent condition.

30125 *Dumbo* **Jim Crow Production Cel and Courvoisier Background (Walt Disney, 1941).** The wise-cracking crows are singing "When I See an Elephant Fly" in this funny scene from Disney's cherished animated feature. While the ink and paint have held up well over the years, someone early on decided to laminate the cel art, which has resulted in the plastic buckling somewhat. This has the unusual effect of giving the three crows a somewhat "3-D" appearance. The cel image area is approximately 8.5" x 4.5", and the Courvoisier background measures approximately 12" x 9.5". There is a bit of rust-colored staining on the background, from the cels; it is mostly hidden when the cel art is in place. Overall condition is Good. The original Courvoisier label is included.

30126 *Dumbo* **Two Crows Production Drawing by Ward Kimball (Walt Disney, 1941).** Original drawing of the two crows on 12-field, 5-peghole animation paper, from the 1941 Disney feature film. The drawing is in graphite with two green highlights, and is signed in the lower right corner by Disney legend Ward Kimball. The images of the crows measure 3" and 4". In Fine condition.

30127 *The Little Whirlwind/The Nifty Nineties* **Mickey and Minnie Mouse Production Cels Set-Up (Walt Disney, 1941).** Features an original hand-inked and hand-painted production cel of Minnie Mouse from the theatrical short *The Little Whirlwind* with a hand-inked and hand-painted production cel of Mickey Mouse from *Nifty Nineties*, both directed by Riley Thomson and released in 1941. The cels are on a Walt Disney Studio pan production background from the same time period. Framed to 31" x 17", with an image area of 22" x 8.5". Minnie measures 5.5", while Mickey is 4.5". The paint is in Fine condition. This is one of the best pure Mickey and Minnie set-ups we have ever seen, with a beautiful background.

30128 *Bambi* **Thumper Illustration (Walt Disney, 1941).** An outstanding original pastel painting of Thumper used for a full page in the 1941 *Walt Disney's Bambi* book published by Simon & Schuster. A first edition copy of the book is included. The artwork measures 11" x 9". In Excellent condition.

30129 **Lew Keller** *Bambi* **Preliminary Color Key Test Background Sketch (Walt Disney, 1942).** The fine artistry of Disney designer Lew Keller sparkles in this color key background from the classic animated feature. Rendered in watercolor on heavy paper, this piece has been matted to an image area of 8.25" x 6". In Excellent condition.

30130 **Lew Keller** *Bambi* **Background Color Key Sketch (Walt Disney, 1942).** Lew Keller captures the majesty of Mother Nature in this original small color key background sketch for Disney's fifth animated feature, *Bambi*. Watercolor on textured paper, the art has been matted to an image area of 5" x 4.75". Some paper aging; otherwise the work is in Excellent condition.

30131 **Lew Keller** *Bambi* **Key Background Illustration (Walt Disney, 1942).** A lush color key background painting done for Disney's classic animated feature film. The gouache painting on paper has an approximate image area of 5.75" x 4.5", and is affixed to 5-peghole animation paper. The paper has a few small bends and discoloration, but the artwork remains in Excellent condition.

30132 **Lew Keller** *Bambi* **Key Background Illustration (Walt Disney, 1942).** A beautiful image of bare trees in the forest, painted in gouache on board. The image area measures approximately 6" x 4.5". The art is taped from the back onto an old mat, which measures approximately 13" x 12.5". While the mat has multiple tack holes, edge wear, and minor staining, the art appears to be in Excellent condition.

30133 *Bambi* Flower Production Cel (Walt Disney, 1942). Original hand-inked and hand-painted trimmed cel of Flower for the Disney animated feature, trimmed and placed on a Courvoisier hand-prepared background which has a small "WDP" stamp. Flower is 4" x 3", and the paint is in Fine condition. Mat opening is 4" x 5". "Copyright Walt Disney Productions All Rights reserved" is printed on the reverse of the mat.

30134 *Donald Gets Drafted* Production Cel (Walt Disney, 1942). Hand-inked and hand-painted production cel of Donald in the Army in one of his World War II cartoon shorts. This trimmed and laminated cel was originally sold through Courvoisier. Placed over a Courvoisier hand-painted background used to enhance the set-up, and matted to an image area of 8" x 7.75". In Good condition with no paint loss.

30136 World War II Marine Utility Squadron 352 Insignia Illustration (Walt Disney, 1943). More than 1,200 World War II insignias were made by Disney, and all artwork requests for this project were handled by Hank Porter's group. This is a rare case of the original artwork being preserved as originally presented by Disney. Two letters accompany this lot: one from Disney to the Marine squadron's commanding officer noting changes having been made (apparently a prior version the squadron received had too much of a "Navy" look to it), and a letter from the squadron to Washington D.C. registering the insignia. By the way, while some might wonder if the duck here is "flipping the bird," the marine major clarifies that it's "thumbing his 'nose' at an imaginary enemy." Gouache on board with a "Walt Disney" signature probably done by Hank Porter. Artwork is almost 7" by 7" and in Very Good condition.

30135 Fred Moore "Reason and Emotion" Model Sheet (Walt Disney, 1943). An original character model sheet for the WWII propaganda film, featuring ten images of the Emotion character (which was a caricature of animator Ward Kimball). In blue pencil on 5-peghole animation paper. In Excellent condition.

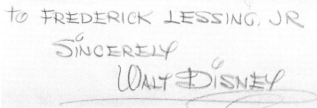

30137 *The Three Caballeros* **José Carioca and Donald Duck Courvoisier Production Cel Set-Up Signed by Walt Disney (Walt Disney, 1945).** Hand-inked and hand-painted cel set-up of Brazilian parrot, José Carioca, and Donald Duck in its original Courvoisier Gallery set-up. Framed and matted art has an image area of 9.25" x 7.5". Some buckling in the cel, and slight cracks in the paint; otherwise the work is in Very Good condition. We believe the matte has been autographed and inscribed by Walt Disney. Includes a photocopy of its original accompanying letter from K. C. Clark, Secretary to Walt Disney.

30139 *Clown of the Jungle* **Donald Duck Production Cel (Walt Disney, 1947).** Shutterbug Donald is featured on this original hand-inked and painted production cel. The image area measures approximately 3.5" x 4.25", and the cel has been double matted for an overall farmable size of 8" x 10". Excellent condition.

30138 *The Three Caballeros* **Pablo the Penguin Production Cel (Walt Disney, 1945).** Original hand-inked and hand-painted production cel of Pablo the Cold-Hearted Penguin from the 1945 Disney feature film, placed on a hand-painted Courvoisier background. Original top mat has slight "WDP" evident. Pablo has been restored and is 5". Snow effects cels are over the image of Pablo. In Fine condition.

30140 *The Adventures of Ichabod and Mr. Toad* **Production Cel Set-Up with Background (Walt Disney, 1949).** Hand-inked and hand-painted cel set-up featuring Angus MacBadger, Rat, and Mole from Disney's adaptation of Kenneth Grahame's **The Wind and the Willows**. Each cel was trimmed to the line of the figure and placed on a hand-painted original production background. Matted to an image area of 9.5" x 7.75". Paint on the cels is fine with some discoloration in the MacBadger and Rat figures. In Very Good condition.

30141 Mary Blair *Cinderella* Concept Painting (Walt Disney, 1950). Concept artwork of Cinderella's coach racing to get home before midnight, painted by Disney designer, Mary Blair. This unusually large piece was rendered in tempera on heavy board, with an image area of 19.75" x 8.5". Aside from pin holes in each of the four corners (outside of the image area), the work is in Excellent condition.

IF YOU'D LIKE ESTIMATED VALUES OF THE LOTS THAT INTEREST YOU, PLEASE EMAIL JIM LENTZ AT JIML@HA.COM.

30142 *Cinderella* **Production Cel (Walt Disney, 1950).** An original hand-inked and hand-painted production cel of Cinderella, placed on a hand-painted production background. The Image of Cinderella measures 6.5". Originally sold by Sotheby's on December 16, 1993 (Sale #6520, Lot 703). Framed to 17.25" x 15.5", with an image area of 7" x 9". The paint is in Fine condition.

30143 *Alice in Wonderland* **Production Cel (Walt Disney, 1951).** An original hand-painted production cel featuring the King of Hearts from Disney's 1951 adaptation of Lewis Carroll's classic novel. Attached to a print background. In Excellent condition.

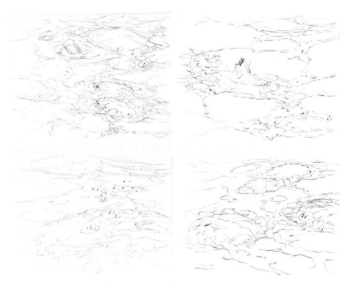

30144 Josh Meador *Alice in Wonderland* **Production Effects Drawings (Walt Disney, 1951).** Four pages of original effects drawings by Meador for the 1951 animated feature, one of which can be found on page 255 of the book **Disney Animation: The Illusion of Life**. In Excellent condition.

30145 Mary Blair *Alice in Wonderland* **Concept Painting Original Art (Walt Disney, 1951).** A stunning and unique Disney Studio concept painting of the Caterpillar. Disney Studio artist Mary Blair brings an unbelievable sense of style to this painting, done in tempera on heavy board, with an image area measuring approximately 8.25" x 7.25". Other than pinholes in the corners and some minor soiling along the borders (outside the image area), the painting is in Excellent condition.

30146 Mary Blair *Alice in Wonderland* **Concept Painting Original Art (Walt Disney, 1951).** A beautiful piece of original, hand-painted artwork by one of Walt Disney's best artists, Mary Blair, showcasing Alice and the March Hare as they attend the Mad Hatter's Tea Party. Painted in tempera colors on heavy board, with an image area of approximately 8.25" x 7". Pin holes in each corner (outside the image area); otherwise Excellent condition.

30147 *Alice in Wonderland* **The Mad Hatter Production Cel (Walt Disney, 1951).** This hand-inked and hand-painted 16-field production cel features the Mad Hatter. The cel measures 15.5" x 12.5", and it is in Excellent condition. The background is a color photocopy.

30148 *Alice In Wonderland* **Alice and Dinah Production Cel (Walt Disney, 1951).** Original hand-inked hand-painted cel set-up of Alice (#59) and Dinah (109) from the Walt Disney feature film. On 16-field cels. The image of Alice is 5" tall, and Dinah is 1.5". The paint is in Fine condition.

30149 *The Cold War* **Title Card Illustration (Walt Disney, 1951).** Hand-painted cartoon title artwork for the Jack Kinney directed Goofy short, *The Cold War*, about the perils of battling a cold. Mixed media on 12-field 3-peghole heavy board, measuring 12" x 10". "2409" and "Title" are written on the bottom border. Includes paperwork that reads "'Cold War' production no. 2412". Some light edge wear; otherwise the art is in Excellent condition.

30150 *Pluto's Party* **Mickey Mouse and Pluto Production Drawing (Walt Disney, 1952).** An adorable drawing from the Milt Schaffer-directed theatrical short. Graphite pencil with blue highlights on 12-field 3-peghole animation paper, with "115" written in the bottom right corner. Very Good condition.

30151 *Two Chips and a Miss* **Chip 'n' Dale Production Cel (Walt Disney, 1952).** An outstanding one-of-a-kind hand-inked production cel over a hand-painted key master background. Gouache on illustration board, from the theatrical short where Chip and Dale court Clarice, directed by Jack Hannah — considered one of Chip and Dale's best shorts. Amazing detail to the stage background. Framed to 25" x 21.25", with an image area of 14" x 10". In Excellent condition.

30152 *Peter Pan* **Production Cel Animation Art (Walt Disney, 1953).** Original hand-inked hand-painted production cel of John Darling. Measures 12" x 10". There is paint loss on John's shoulder and in the upper portion of his hat; otherwise the art is in Very Good condition.

30153   Mary Blair *Peter Pan* Concept Sketch (Walt Disney, 1953).
Outstanding original concept artwork of Peter Pan and Tinker Bell on the roof in London by Disney artist Mary Blair. Tempera on heavy board, measuring 8" x 6". Aside from some pin holes in each of the corners and slight edge wear; the art is in Very Good condition. A beautiful piece of artwork created over 50 years ago in the making of this classic film.

30156   *Peter Pan* Production Cel (Walt Disney, 1953). Original hand-inked hand-painted production cel of John and the Raccoon Twins being taken captive by the Indians. This trimmed 16-field cel has some light paint loss and cracking in Indian's hair and one foot, and John's nightshirt; otherwise it is in Very Good condition. Large image.

30157   *Peter Pan* Production Cel (Walt Disney, 1953). Original hand-inked, hand-painted Walt Disney Studio production cel of Mr. Smee as he gets ready to shave Captain Hook. On 12-field cel with "#109" written in the corner. Nice 6" size and great facial expression. Minor paint separation but no paint loss. In Very Good condition.

30154   *Peter Pan* Production Cel (Walt Disney, 1953). Original hand-inked and hand-painted production cel of Peter Pan on 16-field acetate. A perfect pose! The art measures 16" x 12", and aside from stained tape in the upper three edges, it is in Very Good condition.

30158   *Peter Pan* John and Nibs Production Cel (Walt Disney, 1953). An original hand-inked and hand-painted 12-field cel featuring John Darling and Nibs the Lost Boy, from the 1953 adaptation of the classic story. This the last Disney animated film to feature work from each of the legendary "Nine Old Men". Framed to 16" x 13", with an image area of approximately 10" x 8". There is some craquelure to the grey paint in Johns nightshirt.

30155   *Peter Pan* Production Cel (Walt Disney, 1953). Original hand-inked hand-painted production cel of John in his top hat. Trimmed cel with John at almost 10" high! This beautiful cel is trimmed to 8" x 9.5". In Excellent condition.

30159 *Peter Pan* **Lost Boys Production Cel with Hand-Painted Background (Walt Disney, 1953).** Two of Peter's Lost Boys are featured in this cel, which has been placed over a studio background prepared for another production. The paint shows a couple of tiny cracks on the black outfit, but is in overall Fine condition. The figures measure approximately 7" x 6.75", with a combined image area of 9.75" x 8". Matted and framed with glass to an overall 16" x 13", some scratches on the wooden frame.

30161 *The Lone Chipmunk* **Chip 'n Dale Production Cel Group (Disney, 1954).** Chip is an outstanding 16-field cel marked C141 (image area 3 x 7.75"), and Dale is a 12-field hand-inked cel and the corner is marked #19 (image area 3 x 3"). They're just a couple of crazy rascals out to have some fun! Excellent condition.

30160 *Grin and Bear It* **Donald Duck Production Cel (Walt Disney, 1954).** Donald is on the top cel, and the car is on the bottom one. The car cel is attached to a 3-peghole 12-field animation paper. The cel paint is fine. This Donald Duck and Humphrey the Bear short, directed by Jack Hannah, was the first appearance of Ranger J. Audubon Woodlore. Donald and the car take up the entire cel.

30162 **Chip 'n Dale Production Cel Group (Walt Disney, c. 1950s).** A cut piece of acetate with Dale looking back to the camera, plus a full cel of Chip surrounded by water splashes, which has been taped to an even larger cel, make up this lot. Chip's image area, including the splashes, measures approximately 11" x 7.5", white the image of Dale is approximately 2.75" x 4". Both items are in Excellent condition.

30163 *Lady and the Tramp* **Three-Cel Set-Up With Disney Oil-Painted Art Props Background (Walt Disney, 1955).** One of the most beloved and desirable scenes in the history of Disney Animation, this piece is one of the undisputed highlights of our auction. This "Bella Notte" production cel set-up has Lady on one cel, Tramp with a mouth full of spaghetti on the second cel and the third has the table with tablecloth, spaghetti and the meatballs in the plate along with the bread sticks and the candle.

The background is rendered in oil, which is very rare, and it was created by the Walt Disney Art Props Department using the original background layout drawing as reference.

Disneyland opened in 1955, one month after the release of *Lady and the Tramp*. Inside the park, on Main Street at the Art Corner store where Disney animation cels were sold, this piece was created to hang in that store as a signature piece for the opening of the Art Corner location. The cel is in mint condition and has the original mat and gold sticker on the reverse. Paint is flawless. Tramp is 5", and Lady 4". The single most romantic scene in the history of animation!

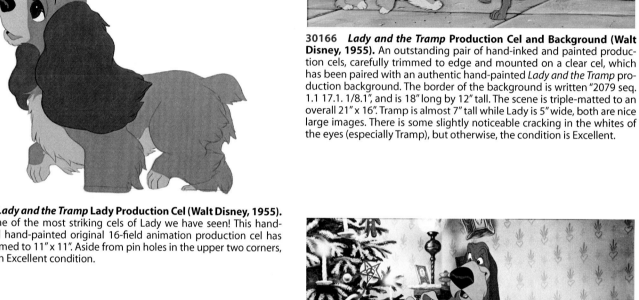

30166   *Lady and the Tramp* Production Cel and Background (Walt Disney, 1955). An outstanding pair of hand-inked and painted production cels, carefully trimmed to edge and mounted on a clear cel, which has been paired with an authentic hand-painted *Lady and the Tramp* production background. The border of the background is written "2079 seq. 1.1 17.1. 1/8.1", and is 18" long by 12" tall. The scene is triple-matted to an overall 21" x 16". Tramp is almost 7" tall while Lady is 5" wide, both are nice large images. There is some slightly noticeable cracking in the whites of the eyes (especially Tramp), but otherwise, the condition is Excellent.

30164   *Lady and the Tramp* Lady Production Cel (Walt Disney, 1955). Here is one of the most striking cels of Lady we have seen! This hand-inked and hand-painted original 16-field animation production cel has been trimmed to 11" x 11". Aside from pin holes in the upper two corners, the art is in Excellent condition.

30165   *Lady and the Tramp* Peg Production Cel (Walt Disney, 1955). Hand-inked hand-painted production cel of Peg from Disney's fifteenth animated feature film. Large 16-field cel with Peg measuring 6" x 5", huge. There is a tiny crack at the top right of her head, but otherwise the cel is in Very Good condition.

30167   *Lady and the Tramp* Studio Dye Transfer Print Signed by Walt Disney (Walt Disney, 1955). Outstanding Walt Disney studio dye transfer high quality print of Lady, Tramp, Jock, Trusty and Scamp the puppies from the finale holiday scene. In the original studio mat with script writing on the mat that says "Walt Disney's Lady and the Tramp." The mat has been boldly signed by Walt Disney. This piece was a contribution by Walt Disney Studios to a fundraising event for Schneck Memorial Hospital in Seymour, Indiana in 1955. Image area is 12" x 9", and the framed size is 23.5" x 20.75". Excellent condition.

30168 *Lady and the Tramp* **Pan Production Background With Four Trimmed and Mounted Production Cels (Walt Disney, 1955).** Jock and Trusty join Lady and Tramp on a superb piece that was originally prepared as a studio gift. The four hand-inked production cels are trimmed to the respective images and mounted to a hand-painted studio production background. The pan background measures approximately 24" x 12". The clue on Lady has come loose on her nose area and there is very minor separation. Good condition.

30169 *The Lady and the Tramp* **Barking Tramp Production Cel (Walt Disney, 1955).** Original hand-inked and hand-painted trimmed production cel of a barking Tramp from the 1955 Walt Disney feature film, placed over a complimentary print background. The cel is trimmed to 10" x 7", and the image of Tramp measures 4" x 4". The paint is in Fine condition.

30170 *Mickey Mouse Club* **Opening Title Sequence Production Cel and Background (Walt Disney, 1955).** "Who's the leader of the Club that's made for you and me? M-I-C-K-E-Y-M-O-U-S-E!" What wonderful memories seeing this iconic item brings to anyone who grew up during the 1950s and '60s! This is the original hand-painted 16-field production cel set-up with a hand-painted production background. In it, Mickey, in his bandleader outfit, is being bounced onto the scene by a group of friendly bears — one of the most famous and important opening title sequences in television history. The background is marked "Prod. 8200 Seq. 02.0 Sc. 57 - Bear." Mickey measures approximately 5" tall, and the combined image area measures about 13.5" x 10", within a 18" x 15" black mat. The cel is in Very Good condition, with only minor cracking within Mickey's left foot. Wow — what an incredible set-up!

30171 *Swamp Fox* **Concept Painting by Charles Ohmann Original Art (Walt Disney, late 1950s).** Swamp Fox was an eight-episode show that ran on the "Wonderful World of Disney" from 1959-1961. It starred none other than a young Leslie Nielsen as a Revolutionary War hero (comic fans will remember the **Four Color** devoted to the feature). The piece is signed in the left bottom corner. A Walt Disney Productions sticker is on the bottom right. Swamp Fox is written in the bottom right border. The dimensions of this pan piece are approximately 24" x 12". Very Good condition.

30172 Eyvind Earle Sleeping Beauty Concept Original Art (Walt Disney, 1959). Original concept artwork painting by legendary artist Mr. Eyvind Earle who shaped the design of this film. An extremely rare black and white tempera painting on heavy board measuring 15" x 6", showcasing Prince Phillip racing to the Castle in the distance. Mr. Earle's signature tree style is evident. Pinholes in each corner. Signed in bottom right corner.

30173   Eyvind Earle *Sleeping Beauty* Concept Painting Original Art (Walt Disney, 1959). Highly stylized concept art painting by Walt Disney Studio Art Director Eyvind Earle. Dramatic painting showing Maleficent with the castle guards. Tempura on heavy board measuring 11" x 6"; other than pinholes in each corner, it's in Excellent condition. Nicely signed in right corner by the artist.

30174   Eyvind Earle *Sleeping Beauty* Concept Painting Original Art (Walt Disney, 1959). Original painting by legendary artist Mr. Eyvind Earle who served as the color stylist and art director for this Disney feature film. This magnificent painting of Prince Phillip battling Maleficent as a dragon in the dramatic finale of this film measures 22" x 9". Rendered in tempera on heavy illustration board, the art is signed in the bottom right corner by the artist. There are pin holes in all four corners, as the artwork was used in the development of this landmark movie; otherwise the condition is Excellent.

30175 *Sleeping Beauty* **Maleficent Hand-Painted Production Cel Set-Up with Presentation Background (Walt Disney, 1959).** The evil queen Maleficent virtually radiates evil in this stunning two-cel set-up. This extra-large pan cel shows the Evil One in all her glory, measuring an impressive 30" x 12.25" overall. Maleficent herself is on one cel, while the purple smoke effect is on another. The art is in Excellent condition.

30177 *Sleeping Beauty* **Dragon Production Drawing (Walt Disney, 1959).** Original 16-field (16" x 12") Walt Disney Studio animation rough drawing of Maleficent as the Dragon. A dramatic drawing in graphite with red highlights. (A5) Image measures 10" x 8". In Excellent condition.

30176 *Sleeping Beauty* **Dragon Production Drawings (Walt Disney, 1959).** A trio of outstanding 16-field Walt Disney Studio animation drawings of Maleficent as the Dragon, as she is slain in the film's dramatic finale — three sequenced drawings that take up almost all of the paper. A dramatic sequence of three, and a fine display of the power of Disney animation at its finest. Drawing #23/45/95. Graphite. Images measure almost a full 12". In Excellent condition.

30178 *Sleeping Beauty* **Production Drawing (Walt Disney, 1959).** Beautiful 16-field animation drawing of Briar Rose in the forest with her basket. "#116" written at the bottom right corner. Aside from some light paper aging and edge wear, it is in Very Good condition.

30179 *Sleeping Beauty* **Production Drawing (Walt Disney, 1959).** Dramatic animation production drawing of Maleficent, rendered in graphite with red highlights on 16-field animation paper (OPD #103). The drawing is a large image of 9" x 10". Aside from some light paper aging, the art is in Very Good condition.

30181 *Sleeping Beauty* **Briar Rose Production Cel (Walt Disney Studios, 1959).** A beautiful original hand-inked, hand-painted production cel of Sleeping Beauty as Briar Rose, from the 1959 Disney feature film. The cel is trimmed to 12" x 11", with Briar Rose measuring almost 8" in height. The inking is striking. Placed over a hand-painted background created to enhance the presentation. In Excellent condition.

30180 *Sleeping Beauty* **Maleficent Production Drawings (Walt Disney, 1959).** Series of four sequenced original one-of-a-kind 16-field rough animation drawings of Maleficent as a dragon. The sequence shows the amazing detail of the close-ups, even though the drawings are in rough animation form. Graphite, with last drawing having some blue under drawing highlights. In Excellent condition.

30182 *101 Dalmatians* **Pongo and Perdita Color Model Cel (Walt Disney, 1961).** Original hand-painted color model cel of Pongo and Perdita from the Walt Disney 1961 feature film, placed on a non-Disney print background. Cels featuring Pongo and Perdita together are very difficult to find. In Excellent condition.

30183 *101 Dalmatians* **Cruella De Vil Production Cel Set-Up (Walt Disney, 1961).** An original, one-of-a-kind, hand-painted production cel set-up featuring vile villainess Cruella De Vil, matted and framed along with a line test cel overlay, applied to a hand-painted key master background. The frame measures 26.5" x 23.25", with an image area of 11" x 14"; the image of Cruella measures 7" tall. the paint is in Fine condition. A classic Disney villain featured in one of the best Cruella set-ups we have seen.

30184   José Carioca Publicity Cel (Walt Disney, undated). Disney's Brazilian-born José Carioca, the cigar-smoking, dapper parrot, starred in two 1940s feature films, *Saludos Amigos,* and *The Three Caballeros.* We can't say for sure, but this handsome hand-inked and painted Publicity cel set-up probably dates from the character's use on a 1960s television special. The image, including smoke trail from José's cigar, measures approximately 5" x 6.5". There is some cracking of the paint in José's right foot and left hand and there are a few tiny areas of paint loss in the hand. Part of the smoke trail is on a separate cel. The cel is taped to an old colored paper background that has been lightstruck from years of being framed. The overall condition is Very Good.

30185   *Winnie-the-Pooh and the Blustery Day* Production Cel and Background Set-Up (Walt Disney, 1968). Original hand-painted production cels of Christopher Robin, Kanga and Roo, and Eeyore, framed on a hand-painted "Blustery Day" production background. The Image of Christopher Robin is 4", Eeyore is 4", and Kanga and Roo are 2". Originally sold at Sotheby's December 16, 1993 animation art sale (#6520, Lot 796). Framed to 23.5" x 18.5" with an image area of 16" x 11". The paint is in Fine condition.

30186   *Aristocats* Scat Cat, Berlioz, and Toulouse Production Cel (Walt Disney, 1970). Original one-of-a-kind hand-painted production cel on a print background of Scat Cat, Berlioz, and Toulouse from the Walt Disney feature film *The Aristocats.* Framed to an overall size of 16" x 18", with an image area of 8" x 10". The paint is in fine condition. Includes a C.O.A. from the Wonderful World of Animation, Inc.

30187   Jack Hannah "Rain Predicted" Donald Duck and Chip 'n Dale Painting Original Art (Walt Disney, undated). After he retired, Disney legend Jack Hannah began to paint original Donald Duck paintings on canvas. This one, titled "Rain Predicted", depicts Chip 'n Dale playing a prank on Donald Duck. The artwork is signed boldly Jack Hannah and framed to 17" x 14", with an image area of 11.75" x 9". In Excellent condition.

30188   *The Rescuers* Medusa Concept Drawing Original Art (Walt Disney, 1977). A graphite, pen, and ink character study with early drawings of the villainous Madame Medusa from the 1977 Disney feature film. Outstanding concept artwork from the hand of the great Milt Kahl, on 16-field animation paper. In Fine condition.

30189   Paul Wenzel *1950s Walt Disney and Friends* Portrait Painting Original Art (undated). Walt Disney shares time with his beloved characters Mickey Mouse, Minnie Mouse, Donald Duck, and Goofy, in this oil on canvas portrait. Disney illustrator, Paul Wenzel is the poster artist for the Academy Award winning feature, *Mary Poppins*, and also painted the portrait of Walt Disney that appeared on a 1968 U.S. commemorative stamp. This stretched canvas painting measures 24" x 18", and it is in Excellent condition. Paul Wenzel signed the piece in the lower left.

30190   *Mickey's Christmas Carol* Mickey Mouse Production Cel (Walt Disney, 1983). Original hand-painted production cel of Mickey Mouse as Bob Cratchit from the Academy Award-nominated theatrical featurette *Mickey's Christmas Carol*. The cel is placed over a hand-painted background created for presentation purposes. Framed to 22.5" x 18.5", with an image area of 15" x 10". The image of Mickey measures 5.5". The paint is in Fine condition.

30191   Gene Ware *Disney's DuckTales Magazine* #1 Cover Original Art (Walt Disney, 1988). Original gouache-on-board painting of Scrooge McDuck, Huey, Dewey, Louie, and Launchpad McQuack used for the cover of the Summer 1988 debut issue of **DuckTales Magazine**. The show, which premiered in 1987, was Disney Studios first daily animated TV series, and at the characters were big stars! Approximate image size is 12" x 17". In Excellent condition. *From the Gene Ware Collection.*

30192   *Who Framed Roger Rabbit* Baby Herman Production Cel (Walt Disney, 1988). Original hand-painted 16-field production cel of Baby Herman from the Maroon Cartoon opening sequence of the 1988 comedy by Robert Zemeckis. A rare signature from animation director Richard Williams is in the lower right corner. Framed to 22" x 17", with and image area of 14.5" x 10". A perfect image! In Excellent condition.

30193   *Who Framed Roger Rabbit* Baby Herman Production Cel (Walt Disney, 1989). Baby Herman stars in this hand-painted original animation cel from the landmark Touchstone Pictures film, presented on a photographic print background. Measures 11.5" x 16.5". Cel has a Disney seal on the acetate. In Excellent condition.

30194 *Who Framed Roger Rabbit* **Jessica Rabbit Production Cel (Walt Disney, 1989).** Superb hand-painted cel of the voluptuous Jessica Rabbit, presented on a photographic print background. Framed and matted to an image area of 12" x 8", and in Excellent condition.

30197 *The Lion King* **Simba Color Model Cel (Walt Disney, 1994).** Original Walt Disney Studios 16-field hand-painted color model cel of Young Simba, with an image measuring almost 6" tall. Painted by the Disney Ink and Paint Department for use in a 1994 Skybox trading card series and other consumer products projects. In Excellent condition.

30195 *The Little Mermaid* **Production Cel with Hand-Painted Background (Walt Disney, 1989).** Ariel and her friends Sebastian, Flounder, and Scuttle share a vibrant seascape sunset, in this production cel with a hand-painted presentation background. The art has an image area of 12.5" x 8". The piece has been matted and framed to an overall size of 15.25" x 16.75" and is in Excellent condition. There is no Disney seal or certificate of authenticity with this cel. In Excellent condition.

30198 *The Lion King* **Scar Color Model Cel (Walt Disney, 1994).** Original Walt Disney Studios 16-field hand-painted color model cel of Scar, with an image measuring more than 9" tall. Painted by the Disney Ink and Paint department for a 1994 Skybox trading cards series and other consumer products projects. In Excellent condition.

30196 **Gene Ware** *The Lion King* **Simba Drawing (undated).** The future King of Pride Rock, Simba by Alvin White Studio artist, Gene Ware. Mixed media on textured paper. Framed and matted to an image area of 13" x 10". Signed by the artist at the lower right.

30199 *The Lion King* **Timon Color Model Cel (Walt Disney, 1994).** An original 16-field Walt Disney Studios hand-painted color model cel of Timon, with the image measuring 6" X 7". An outstanding pose! Painted by the Walt Disney Ink and Paint Department for a 1994 Skybox trading card series and other consumer products projects. In Excellent condition.

30200 *The Lion King* **Pumba Color Model Cel (Walt Disney, 1994).**
An original Walt Disney Studios 16-field hand-painted color model cel of
Pumba, with an image size of 6" x 7". Painted by the Walt Disney Ink and
Paint Department for a 1994 Skybox Trading Card series and other Disney
consumer products projects. In Excellent condition.

30203 *Mickey Mouse Works* **Production Cel with Background (Walt
Disney, 1999).** This hand-inked and hand-painted cel from the episode,
"Pluto vs. The Watchdog," includes its original background art. Framed and
matted to an image area of 12" x 8.5", and in Excellent condition. Includes
a Disney seal and a COA. Signed by Executive Producer, Tony Craig at the
lower left.

30201 *The Lion King* **Rafiki Color Model Cel (Walt Disney, 1994).**
Original Walt Disney Studios 16-field hand-painted color model of Rafiki,
with an image measuring 9" tall. Painted by the Disney Ink and Paint
Department for a 1994 Skybox Trading Card Series, as well as other consumer products. In Excellent condition.

30204 *Mickey Mouse Works* **Production Cel (Walt Disney, 1999).**
Hand-painted cel from the episode, "Pluto vs. The Watchdog," set against
a color photocopy of the original background art. Framed and matted to
an image area of 12" x 9", and in Excellent condition. Includes a Disney
seal and a COA. Signed by Executive Producer, Tony Craig at the lower left.

30202 *Pocahontas* **Production Cel and Background (Walt Disney,
1995).** An original hand-painted cel, by the Disney Ink and Paint
Department from animation drawings used to make the film. The cel has
been placed on a hand-painted production background. Prepared for the
1996 Sotheby's "Art of Pocahontas" auction, this was lot #222. Framed to
an overall size of 18" x 22.25", with an image area of 11" x 15". A Disney
seal is on lower right of the cel. The Pocahontas figure is over 8" tall! This
moody piece from a pivotal scene in the film is in Fine condition.

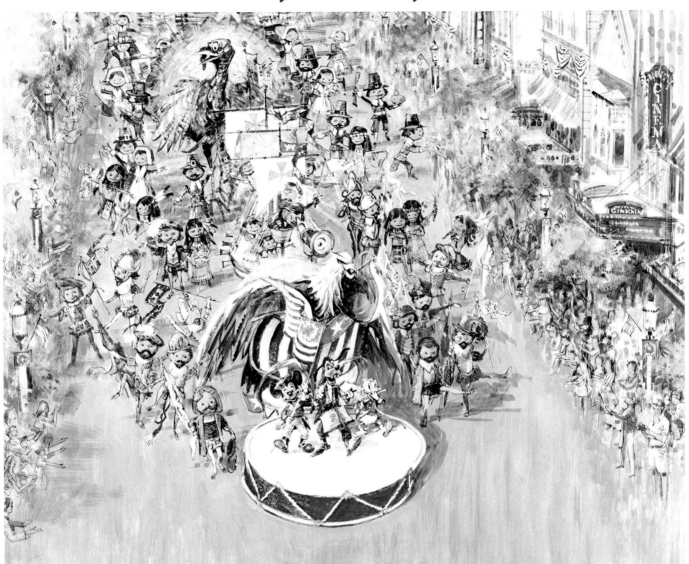

30205 Sam McKin Concept Painting for Bicentennial Disneyland Parade Original Art (Walt Disney, 1976). A huge (30" x 23" image area) painting by Disney Legend Sam McKin, who worked at Walt Disney Studios in WED as an Imagineer for 32 years. He spent almost 12 of those years working closely with Walt Disney. His artwork was used in the development of The Hall of Presidents, Frontierland, Main Street, Great Moments with Mr. Lincoln, The Haunted Mansion, and the 1964 World's Fair to name a few, and people love his artwork for Disney theme park maps. He even came out of retirement in 1992 to do artwork for the first Disneyland Paris souvenir map. In addition to fife-and-drum-playing Mickey Mouse, Goofy, and Donald Duck, there's a huge cast of pilgrims and Indians and even a conquistador or two. Catch the spirit of '76 with this good-sized art!

30206 *Don Quixote* Concept Original Art (Walt Disney, 1967). The Walt Disney Studio has taken stabs at turning *Don Quixote* into a company film project many times in the '40s, '50s, '60s, and early 2000s. This is an important piece of concept artwork for the ill-fated project by Disney legend Walt Peregoy, the noted avant-garde artist who worked at Disney from 1951-1964, and then again from 1974-1983. His work for the House of Mouse includes *Peter Pan*, *Lady and the Tramp*, *Paul Bunyan*, *Mary Poppins*, *The Sword in the Stone*, and *The Jungle Book*, to name a few. He returned to work on design elements of Epcot in Orlando, Florida. This amazing piece of original artwork is signed by Walt Peregoy and dated 1967. "Titles for Don Quixote" is inscribed along the border. This stunning mixed media work in Conte crayon, charcoal, and graphite measures 23" x 5", and is matted to 29.75" x 12". In Excellent condition.

30207 Fred Moore "Foster Girls" Illustration Original Art (1940s). This risqué drawing by Fred Moore features a caricature of Ward Kimball staring at an array of nude women on a beach. The Gae Foster Girls were an all-girl revue popular in the early 1940s-1950s. Mixed media on 12-field, 5-peghole animation paper with an image area of 9" x 7". In Excellent condition.

30208 Fred Moore *Little Boy* Sketch Original Art (Walt Disney, 1940's). Fred Moore sketch in mixed media on 12-field, 5-peghole animation paper (12" x 10"). Some paper aging, pin holes in the corners, light soiling, and edge wear; otherwise the art is in Very Good condition.

30209 Paul Murry (attributed) "The Near-Sighted Photographer" Gag Illustration (Walt Disney, 1940s). In-studio gag drawing, possibly by Paul Murry, in blue pencil on 5-peghole animation paper. In Excellent condition.

30210 Fred Moore Spark Plug Illustration Original Art (Walt Disney, 1940s). Original pen-and-ink and water color painting of a young boy with a spark plug, inscribed "To Milt with love" and signed by Disney animator Fred Moore. The young boy measures 10.5" while the spark plug is 9". "Milt" is possibly animator Milt Kahl, one of the legendary "Nine Old Men". Moore originals such as this one were highlighted on page 121 of the book **The Illusion Of Life** by Frank Thomas and Ollie Johnston, and they are in high demand around the world. Matted to 16" x 20". In Fine condition.

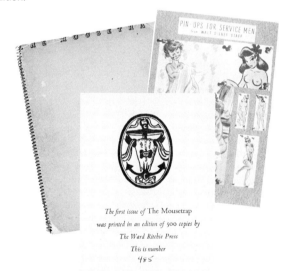

30211 *The Mousetrap* Disney In-House Magazine for Employees In The Service (Walt Disney, 1937). This rarity offers a behind-the-scenes look at 1930s Disney! Only 500 copies were printed by Ward Ritchie Press. This is Joe Magro's personal copy #485. An extra pinup poster with art by Fred Moore and Bill Justice is included. The magazine was done for Disney staffers serving in the military, "to let you know what's going on at the studio." It was definitely meant for insiders and notes, "All references herein to characters, persons, and even places living or dead are purely malicious."

There are two original drawings in this copy: a Goofy by Nick Nichols and a caricature of an aged Snow White signed "Amby" (perhaps Nick Ambro).

Fascinatingly, the list of the pinups has a directory of some of the servicemen this magazine went out to, and in addition to Disney standbys like Frank Thomas, there are a lot of names the comic collector will recognize, some whom we know from the Western Publishing Disney comics like writer Del Connell and artist Tony Strobl, and others who you might be surprised to hear even worked for Disney, like George Baker ("Sad Sack"), Hank Ketcham ("Dennis the Menace"), and the longtime Tarzan artist Jesse Marsh!

About half of the front cover has separated from the ring binding. Measures approximately 9" x 12". *From the Joe Magro Collection.*

30212   Walt Disney-Signed *Bambi* Dye Transfer Print (Walt Disney Studios, 1950s). An original Walt Disney Studios dye transfer print of Bambi, signed boldly on the mat by Walt Disney. These high quality prints were given away by the studio for publicity and as gifts, as well as sold at the Art Corner store in Disneyland. This particular print was given as a gift by Disney publicity employee Joe Reddy.

30213   Walt Disney-Signed Dye Transfer Prints (Walt Disney, 1950s). A pair of dye transfer prints of Pinocchio and Jiminy Cricket, both signed boldly by Walt Disney (Note: The signature on the Jiminy Cricket print is badly faded.) Given as a gift from Walt Disney Studio publicist Joe Reddy. In Excellent condition.

30214   Walt Disney-Signed *Snow White and the Seven Dwarfs* Dye Transfer Print (Walt Disney, 1950s). An original Walt Disney Studio dye transfer print of Snow White and the Seven Dwarfs, signed boldly on the mat by Walt Disney. These high quality prints were given away by the studio for publicity and as gifts, as well as sold at the Art Corner store in Disneyland. This print was given as a gift by Walt Disney Studio publicity employee Mr. Joe Reddy.

30215 Disneyland Pirates of the Caribbean Original Maquette "Prisoners and Pirates" (WED Imagineering, early 1960s). Years before the 1967 debut of the ride that would turn into a billion-dollar franchise, these small sculptures were made to finalize the poses and positioning for Walt Disney to review personally. No molds were ever made of these. Once Disney approved each maquette, it was used as the model for the full-size sculpture.

A 1974 Disney brochure on the ride described the process as follows: "A scale model of the adventure was built as a guide for studying the Pirates of the Caribbean in miniature. The mock-up, as the model is called, enabled the Imagineers to view the entire show as the adventure's guests would later see it. … Clay figures, nine inches high, were placed on the mock-up to portray the pirates as they were to appear in the final version of the show. … These detailed characters…were moved from place to place on the model set, much like a movie director instructs his actors, so that every aspect of the action could be thoroughly envisioned. …The small replicas became the guides for the actual sculpting of… life-size figures." In the meantime this is one of the most popular theme park attraction rides in the world, a major draw not only in Disneyland but at Disney World, Tokyo Disneyland, and Disneyland Paris. Of course, it has also spawned a smash-hit movie franchise. "Pirates of the Caribbean" was the last ride Walt Disney participated in designing. It opened just three months after his death in 1967, and he promoted this ride on the *Wonderful World of Color* TV show before it opened.

Little if any artwork from the creation of this ride has veer been offered in the marketplace. These maquettes were made using an oil-based clay, there was no baking. After sculpting paints were applied directly onto the figures. The major sculptors at the time these were made would have been Ken O'Brien and Blaine Gibson. Disney would review these, set-up at eye level, so he was "moving through the ride" as he walked through the display.

The handmade sculpture offered here has a base measuring 15" x 4" x 8.5". Figure one is 8" x 1.25", figure two is 7.25" x 1.5", and figure three is 8.25" x 2.25" (sizes are approximate). Third-party shipping is required.

30216 Disneyland Pirates of the Caribbean Original Maquette "Two Drunken Pirates" (WED Imagineering, early 1960s). Yo ho, ho, a pirate's life for me! Please see our previous lot for a full description of these original items and how they were used, years before the ride was opened to the public in 1967. One of the highlights of our auction!

Base is 10" x 4" x 8" inches. Pirate one is 7.5" x 2" and pirate two is 10.5" x 3.25". Third-party shipping is required.

30217 Disneyland Haunted Mansion Original Maquette "Three Ghosts" (WED Imagineering, early 1960s). So delicate, yet so scary! Please see our previous lot for the story behind this piece of Disneyland history. The piece measures 15" x 2" x 6". Left to right, ghost one is 10.25" x 3.5", ghost two is 9.75" x 4.75" and ghost three, who is broken off the base, is 8" x 3". Third-party shipping required.

FOR MORE IMAGES OF THESE MAQUETTES, PLEASE SEE THE ONLINE LISTINGS AT HA.COM

30218 Disneyland Haunted Mansion Original Maquette "Two Witches" (WED Imagineering, early 1960s). This small sculpture was made years before the attraction opened for business, to finalize the poses and positioning for Walt Disney's review. No molds were ever made, and once Disney approved each maquette, it was used as the model for the full-size sculpture.

The Haunted Mansion is currently located in Disneyland as well as The Magic Kingdom in Orlando, Tokyo Disneyland and (under the name Phantom Manor) in Disneyland Paris. The world first heard about The Haunted Mansion in a 1965 episode of *Walt Disney's Wonderful World of Color* TV series. Due to Disney's involvement with the New York World's Fair, it did not open in Disneyland until 1969. The attraction featured at various times, the work of many Disney "Legends" including Ken Anderson, Rolly Crump, Yale Gracey, Marc Davis, X Atencio and Claude Coats. A feature film *The Haunted Mansion* starring Eddie Murphy came out in 2003.

Very few pieces for the original design of this monumentally successful theme park ride have been available to the public! The base is 9" x 4" x 6"; witch one is 7" x 7.75"; and witch two is 7.25" x 4". Third-party shipping required.

30219 "Disneyland Hotel" Park Entrance Attraction Poster (Walt Disney, 1956). Starting off this group of impressive, and impressively large posters, is the earliest of the bunch. As Tony Baxter of Walt Disney Imagineering wrote, "Before the advent of high-tech communication, Walt Disney knew the importance of both creating anticipation for, and extending the enjoyment of, a visit to his Magic Kingdom. A great poster sells its story from a distance and needs to be glimpsed just briefly to work its magic."

This poster, like all the first edition posters offered here, was hand-silkscreened and done in the large 36" x 54" size (whereas Disney World was done in more economical 30" x 45" size). The artist is Bjorn Aronson.

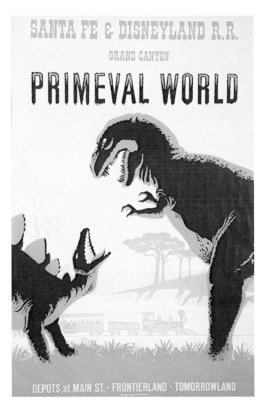

30221 "Primeval World" Disneyland Park Entrance Attraction Poster (Walt Disney, 1966). You can almost feel a child impatiently tugging on your hand as he lays eyes on this one! Hand-silkscreened and done in the large 36" x 54" size. The artist is Claude Coats.

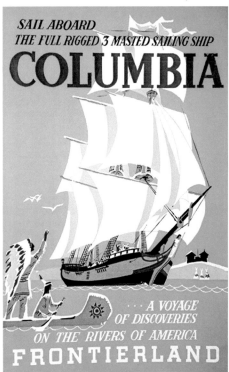

30220 "Columbia" Disneyland Park Entrance Attraction Poster (Walt Disney, 1958). The Sailing Ship Columbia still sets sail from Frontierland in the present day! This poster measures 36" x 54", and features art by Bjorn Aronson.

30222 "Golden Horseshoe Revue" Disneyland Park Entrance Attraction Poster (Walt Disney, 1966). Hand-silkscreened and done in the large 36" x 54" size. The artist is Bjorn Aronson.

30223   "Adventure Thru Inner Space" Disneyland Park Entrance Attraction Poster (Walt Disney, 1967). Hand-silkscreened and done in the large 36" x 54" size. The artist is John Drury.

30224   "America the Beautiful" Disneyland Park Entrance Attraction Poster (Walt Disney, 1967). What pastime could be more all-American than a day at Disneyland in Anaheim? This poster measures an impressive 36" x 54". Art by Ken Chapman.

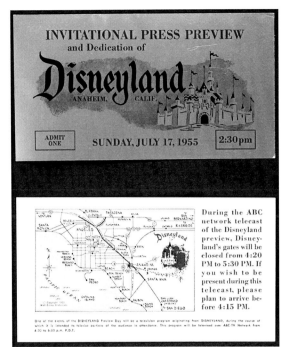

30225   Disneyland Dedication/Press Preview Passes (Walt Disney, 1955). These rare documents of the opening of the world's most famous theme park are framed to showcase the front of the ticket as well as the reverse. The owner of the ticket owned a local citrus cannery company (E. A. Silzle Company) in Anaheim, and in 1953 approached Disney about putting characters in the Anaheim Chamber of Commerce Halloween Parade. The initial meeting with Disney changed the entire float concept to have each float represent a Disney animated film for the parade. This formed a friendship with Mr. Joe Reddy, who worked in publicity at Walt Disney Studios. He would become the family's godfather to their son. This friendship got the family two tickets for the Press Preview, which was held the day before the Park officially opened. A rare piece of Disneyland history.

30226   Mickey Mouse Penny Card Vending Machine Display Sign (Calex Mfg. Inc, c. 1930s). A rare display sign featuring a series of Mickey Mouse Penny Cards, with images taken directly from the newspaper comic strip, and sold through machines at gas stations during the 1930s. Five actual cards are affixed to the yellow paper sign, which has been framed with glass for an overall size of 10.75" x 14.25". In Excellent condition. Includes an extra card from the series, numbered 397, and featuring an Amoco Gas logo.

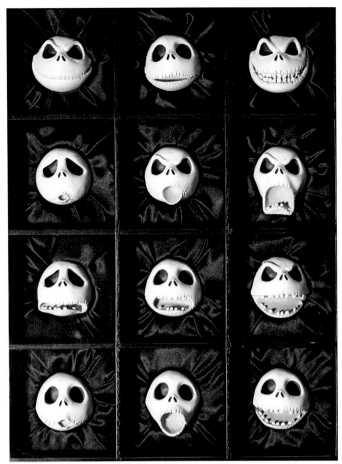

30227 Tim Burton's The Nightmare Before Christmas "Twelve Faces of Jack" Limited Edition Set 32/275 (Disney Art Editions, 1993) An incredible set of twelve hand-painted cast heads of Jack Skellington, from Tim Burton's now-classic stop-motion animation film. The set is housed in an ebonized mahogany glass-framed box measuring 13.25" x 16.5" and 3.5" deep, lined with black satin over a foam insert. The frame opens at the front for closer inspection, and a pair of white cotton gloves is included for handling the pieces. The back of the box has been signed by Tim Burton. A certificate of authenticity is included. This much-in-demand set immediately sold out and has long been unavailable; whenever a set does turn up online, it's is quickly snapped up at prices exceeding $5,000.

YOU CAN BID LIVE
ONLINE DURING
THE AUCTION AT
HA.COM

30228 The Art and Making of Toy Story - Signed, Limited, First Edition, with Sketch (Hyperion Press, 1995). A first edition, lenticular covered, **The Art and Making of Toy Story**, signed by many of the technical and creative artists (more than 15!) who participated in the making of the film. Included is a letter from John Lasseter's assistant Heather Feng (dated March 18, 1996) thanking the collector for being patient, as the book made its way through the studio. Notable signatures include the late Joe Ranft, Randy Newman (page 94) who writes "you Got a Friend in ME!", Don Rickles on the front cover, as well as many other artists throughout the book. The real prize here though is a huge sketch by John Lasseter of Buzz and Woody! Mr. Lasseter writes "To Joe, To infinity and Beyond" and signs his sketch. This would be the equivalent to Walt Disney drawing and signing a sketch in a Snow White book. Don't let this one-of-a-kind treasure pass you by. The book is in Excellent condition.

Original artwork
from the Chuck Jones Archive

 Chuck Jones is a legend in animation. He wore many hats. He was an animator, a cartoon artist, produced fine art, and was a writer, a screen writer, a producer, and a director of some of the greatest cartoons ever made. He directed those classic Looney Tunes characters like Bugs Bunny, Daffy Duck, the Road Runner and Wile E. Coyote, Pepe LePew, and many other classic favorites. Three of the films he directed are in the National Film Registry. In fact, in the 1994 Jerry Beck book "The 50 Greatest Cartoons" (as selected by 1,000 Animation professionals), 9 of the 50 shorts selected were directed by Chuck Jones! Chuck Jones went on to direct Tom and Jerry cartoons and produce many TV specials including the classic specials " Dr. Seuss's How the Grinch Stole Christmas" and " Dr. Seuss's Horton Hears a Who." The list of characters he personally created includes Pussyfoot, Charlie Dog, Michigan J Frog, Marvin Martian, Pepe LePew and The Road Runner and Wile E Coyote.

The legacy of Chuck Jones lives on. 2012 would have been Mr. Jones' 100th birthday. His legacy of artwork continues to make people smile. Chuck Jones galleries are in operation in San Diego, California, Santa Fee, New Mexico and Cost Mesa, California as well.

This unprecedented collection being offered in this catalog on behalf of the Chuck Jones Estate includes many historic pieces. It also includes a rare glimpse in the genius of Chuck Jones through his actual character studies, anatomy and human figure drawings. Other highlights include his original hand drawn animation layout drawing for "What's Opera Doc" as well as an extremely rare "Crawford" pen and ink published daily comic strip, not to mention one of the early sketches Mr. Jones drew of Wile E Coyote as he was figuring out who Wile E Coyote would become. This is simply a piece of animation history.

Heritage is proud to offer one of the largest selections of Chuck Jones artwork ever auctioned as well as over 20 pieces directly from the hand of the man himself.

30229   Chuck Jones Early Wile E. Coyote Concept Sketch (Warner Brothers, 1950s). After the release of the first Wile E. Coyote film, "Fast and Furry-ous" (1949), Chuck Jones decided he wanted to figure out who this character was. One of the most important pieces of Chuck Jones artwork ever offered, this drawing of Wile E. Coyote on 12-field animation paper is one of the first drawings Mr. Jones did when he was working on the early development of this famous character that was paired with the Road Runner. It was done as he was figuring out who this character was and what he looked like. This vintage character development drawing is signed by the late Mr. Jones and is framed to 21" x 20" with a letter of authenticity. A museum worthy piece, in Excellent condition. *From the Chuck Jones Collection.*

30230 Chuck Jones "Very Early Bird" Model Sheet (Warner Brothers., c. 1938-41). Original hand-drawn model sheet featuring drawings of a bluebird in blue, red, brown graphite pencil, cut out and mounted to 2-peghole 12-field animation paper. Signed and annotated "Very early bird" by the late Mr. Jones. Accompanied by a letter of authenticity. *From the Chuck Jones Collection.*

30232 *Duck Dodgers in the 24 1/2 Century* **Conceptual Production Drawing (Warner Brothers, 1953).** A conceptual piece for the 1953 *Duck Dodgers in the 24 ½ Century* Warner Brothers short. An outstanding background layout/concept sketch for the first appearance of Daffy Duck as Duck Dodgers, and consequently the first named appearance of Marvin Martian. The artwork could possibly be from the hand of Mr. Maurice Noble who did the layouts for the film. Graphite on paper. The piece has been framed to an overall size of 13" x 14.5", with an image area of 4" X 5.5". A special piece of Looney Tunes history from the Chuck Jones Archives. In Very Fine condition. *From the Chuck Jones Collection.*

30231 Chuck Jones "Inki" Model Sheet (Warner Brothers, 1940s/50s). Original hand-drawn animator's model sheet featuring drawings of Inki, in conte crayon and graphite. The character was animated by Chuck Jones and appeared in five Warner Bros.. Studio theatrical cartoons from 1939-1950. On 2-peghole 12-field animation paper. Accompanied by a letter of authenticity. *From the Chuck Jones Collection.*

30233 Chuck Jones *What's Opera, Doc?* **Production Drawing (Warner Brothers, 1957).** Rare original production layout drawing of Elmer Fudd in the classic short *What's Opera Doc*, drawn by Chuck Jones! In graphite pencil on 12-field animation paper. "#110" written at the center of the drawing and "#3" in the bottom right corner. The short was voted #1 in the 1994 in book **The 50 Greatest Cartoons** by Jerry Beck. A color copy of the exact scene and a letter of authenticity are included. A wonderful piece of animation history, in Excellent condition. *From the Chuck Jones Collection.*

30234 *Ready, Woolen, and Able* **Wile E. Coyote Production Drawing Group (Warner Brothers, 1960).** Five original layout drawings of a classic Wile E. Coyote gag sequence, drawn by none other than Chuck Jones himself in graphite pencil on 12-field animation paper. Accompanied by a letter of authenticity. *From the Chuck Jones Collection.*

30235 Chuck Jones *Lickety Splat* **Wile E. Coyote Production Drawing (Warner Brothers, 1961).** Original layout drawing of Wile E. Coyote drawn by none other than Chuck Jones. Graphite on 12-field animation paper with "4" written in the lower right corner and "27" in the center of the page. Accompanied by a letter of authenticity. In Excellent condition. *From the Chuck Jones Collection.*

30236   Chuck Jones Bugs Bunny and Daffy Duck Illustration Original Art (Warner Brothers, 2012). This year a book is being released entitled **Chuck Jones: Drawing on Character — 100 Classic Drawings by an American Icon.** This drawing of Bugs Bunny and Daffy Duck (with Daffy pulling the proverbial "rabbit out of a hat!"), by Chuck Jones is in the upcoming book. This outstanding drawing was a sketch/gag concept drawn during the creative process of designing one of his many limited edition hand-painted cels. A rare Bugs and Daffy drawing by the man that made them famous! Framed to an overall size of 16.75" x 20.5", with an image area of approximately 9.5" x 11.5". In Excellent condition. *From the Chuck Jones Collection.*

30237   Chuck Jones Pepe Le Pew Original Signed Watercolor Painting Original art (Warner Brothers, undated). Chuck Jones animated, directed, sketched, produced, lectured, taught, and ran a studio... he basically did it all. This magnificent piece of artwork showcases his true artistic talent. A rare Jones original watercolor painting of Pepe Le Pew, done on acid-free art rag paper, the piece measures 15" x 11", with an image area of 13" x 8". Mr. Jones has signed it at the bottom right. Very few of his watercolors have ever been brought to market, so we expect active bidding on this one! In Excellent condition. A Letter of Authenticity from the Chuck Jones Archives accompanies the painting. *From the Chuck Jones Collection.*

30238 Chuck Jones Signed Road Runner and Wile E. Coyote Publicity Cel Set-Up (Warner Brothers, undated). An outstanding hand-painted studio publicity cel set-up on a studio hand-painted background, featuring two of Chuck Jones' most famous characters and hand-signed by him. One of the nicest Road Runner and Coyote set-ups we have ever seen, it features 12-field animation cels over a hand-painted gouache board background. Accompanied by a letter of authenticity. In Excellent condition. *From the Chuck Jones Collection.*

30239 Chuck Jones Michigan J. Frog Publicity Cel (Warner Brothers, 2004). In 1995, Chuck Jones directed *Another Froggy Evening*, a follow-up to his legendary short *One Froggy Evening*. A major traveling exhibit showcased artwork from this show; this specially prepared cel and background were among the featured works. This one-of-a-kind hand-painted "Exhibit Only" cel on 12-field acetate is placed on a hand-painted background, and bears a silkscreened rendition of Jones' signature in the lower right corner. Possibly one of the best Michigan J. Frog set-ups ever! It's worth noting that when a Chuck Jones Estate signature is applied, the date and time is recorded in the Linda Jones Enterprises Register! Accompanied by a letter of authenticity. In Excellent condition. *From the Chuck Jones Collection.*

30240 Chuck Jones *Captain Hareblower/From Hare to Eternity* Yosemite Sam Production Cel Set-Up (Warner Brothers, 1954/96). Here's something special: A Freleng/Jones set-up! An original hand-painted 12-field production cel of Yosemite Sam from the 1996 cartoon *From Hare to Eternity* signed by director Chuck Jones. The cel has been placed on a rare Warner Bros.. Studios hand-painted production background from the theatrical short *Captain Hareblower*, directed by Friz Freleng. Accompanied by a letter of authenticity. In Excellent condition. *From the Chuck Jones Collection.*

30241   Chuck Jones Bugs Bunny Trading Card Illustration Original Art (Warner Bros./Upper Deck, 1990). In 1990 Upper Deck trading cards partnered with Warner Bros.. and Chuck Jones for a series of baseball cards featuring Warner Bros.. characters in artwork and stories developed by Jones. This rare 12-field hand-painted animation cel of Bugs Bunny hitting the ball with his "bat" (a giant carrot) was created from an original drawing by Jones, and was photographed to make the actual trading card. Accompanied by a letter of authenticity. In Excellent condition. *From the Chuck Jones Collection.*

30242   Chuck Jones Wile E. Coyote and Yosemite Sam Trading Card Illustration Original Art (Warner Bros./Upper Deck, 1990). This matched piece is a great image of Yosemite Sam and Wile E. Coyote (playing for the San Francisco Giants!) going for a ball hit by Bugs Bunny's carrot bat. Original 12-field hand-painted cel created from original artwork by Chuck Jones, this cel was photographed to create one of the Upper Deck Comic Ball series trading cards. Accompanied by a letter of authenticity. In Excellent condition. *From the Chuck Jones Collection.*

30243   Chuck Jones *Crawford* Comic Strip Original Art (Chicago Tribune-New York Times Syndicate Inc., 1978). On Monday, January 9, 1978 the New York Times introduced a new daily comic strip titled *Crawford*, written and drawn by Chuck Jones, and distributed by the Chicago Tribune-New York Times Syndicate. This lot is the art for the May 2, 1978 strip by Jones. Few of his hand-drawn *Crawford*'s have ever come to market. Included with this lot is a letter of authenticity and a copy of the coffee table book **Chuck Jones — The Dream That Never Was** that tells the entire history of the character, with this particular strip featured on page 173. In Excellent condition. *From the Chuck Jones Collection.*

30244   Chuck Jones "Man at Typewriter" Drawing (1960s). An original sketch of a man at a typewriter, drawn by Jones in graphite on MGM animation paper. Accompanied by a letter of authenticity. In Excellent condition. *From the Chuck Jones Collection.*

30247   Chuck Jones "Two Women" Drawing. Outstanding mixed-media artwork by Jones, stunning combination of watercolor and conte crayon on 12-field animation paper, hand-signed by him. A letter of authenticity accompanies this signed piece of original Chuck Jones artwork. In Excellent condition. *From the Chuck Jones Collection.*

30245   Chuck Jones "Leaping Dog" Drawing. A dramatic drawing of a leaping dog by Jones on 12-field animation paper. Chuck frequently used dogs (Charlie, Frisky Puppy, Smidgen, etc.) in many of his cartoons. The dog is over 11" long and 6" tall. This great drawing is accompanied by a letter of Authenticity. In Excellent condition. *From the Chuck Jones Collection.*

30248   Chuck Jones "Two Dogs" Illustration (MGM, c. 1960s). Beautiful drawing of two dogs by Jones in graphite on MGM Studio animation paper which indicates that it was drawn in the early 1960s. Accompanied by a letter of authenticity. In Excellent condition. *From the Chuck Jones Collection.*

30246   Chuck Jones "Horse" Drawing. A beautiful portrait of a horse drawn by the hand of Chuck Jones in graphite on 12-field animation paper. The image measures more than 10". Accompanied by a letter of authenticity. In Excellent condition. *From the Chuck Jones Collection.*

30249   Chuck Jones "Woman" Drawing. A rare charcoal sketch of a woman by Jones on 12-field animation paper. A large image, measuring almost 8". Accompanied by a letter of authenticity. In Excellent conditions. *From the Chuck Jones Collection.*

with an image size of approximately 17" x 12". This breathtaking original artwork is signed by Jones and accompanied by a letter of authenticity. In Excellent condition. *From the Chuck Jones Collection.*

30250   Chuck Jones "Dog and Bone" Drawing. Outstanding original drawing of a dog being given a bone by a friend, by Jones in graphite on 12-field animation paper. Signed by Jones in the lower right corner. Accompanied by a letter of authenticity. In Excellent conditions. *From the Chuck Jones Collection.*

30251   Chuck Jones "Young Woman" Drawing. Stunning portrait of a young woman from the hand of Chuck Jones, drawn in graphite on 12-field animation paper. So simple, yet so much more. Accompanied by a letter of authenticity. In Very Good condition. *From the Chuck Jones Collection.*

30252   Chuck Jones "Female Nude" Drawing. Magnificent charcoal drawing of a nude woman by Jones. Framed, the paper measures 18" x 24"

30253   Chuck Jones "Two Women in Shawls" Drawing. Outstanding pastel/charcoal mixed media drawing from the hand of Chuck Jones, featuring two women in shawls. The work measures 12" x 18" with an approximate image size of 11" x 9"; it is framed to a size of 22" x 28.5". The artwork is signed by Jones and accompanied by a letter of authenticity. In Excellent condition. *From the Chuck Jones Collection.*

30254   *How the Grinch Stole Christmas* Chuck Jones Signed Grinch Production Cel (Chuck Jones, 1966). Outstanding hand-painted production cel from the holiday classic directed by Chuck Jones. The 12-field cel is hand-signed by Jones and comes with a letter of authenticity. In Excellent condition. *From the Chuck Jones Collection.*

30255 *Surf-Bored Cat* **Tom and Jerry Production Cel Signed by Chuck Jones (MGM, 1966).** Original hand-inked and hand-painted production cel of Tom Cat from the MGM theatrical short, directed by Abe Levitow and produced by Chuck Jones. It was said Mr. Jones felt that the character design didn't belong to him and he consequently hasn't signed many Tom and Jerry cels. A great image to boot! This 12-field cel is accompanied by a letter of authenticity and a Linda Jones Enterprises seal. *From the Chuck Jones Collection.*

30256 *Now Hear This* **Production Cel (Warner Brothers, 1963).** Original hand-inked and hand-painted production cel from the Chuck Jones and Maurice Noble theatrical short, which was nominated for an Academy Award. The character is holding the devil's horn, the key prop to the short. A 12-field animation cel with # B26 in the lower right corner. Extremely rare, and accompanied by a letter of authenticity. In Excellent condition. *From the Chuck Jones Collection.*

30257 Chuck Jones "Male Character Model" Drawing Group. Original pair of model type drawings of a male character from the hand of Chuck Jones. Drawn in graphite on 12-field animation paper. Very distinctive Jones style. Accompanied by a letter of authenticity. In Excellent condition. *From the Chuck Jones Collection.*

30258 *A Very Merry Cricket* **Harry the Cat Production Drawing (Chuck Jones, 1973).** Original concept artwork of Harry the Cat on 12-field animation paper by Chuck Jones. This was an ABC television special that premiered on December 14, 1973, and a sequel of sorts of *A Cricket in Times Square*. Accompanied by a letter of authenticity. In Excellent condition. *From the Chuck Jones Collection.*

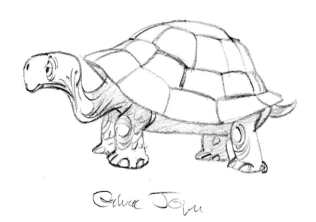

30259 *The White Seal* **Chuck Jones Signed Turtle Production Drawing (Chuck Jones, 1973).** Original layout drawing by the hand of Chuck Jones, from the making of the March 24, 1973 CBS television special *The White Seal*, hand-signed by Mr. Jones. Graphite on 12-field animation paper. "I-2" written in the upper right corner. Accompanied with a letter of authenticity. In Excellent condition. *From the Chuck Jones Collection.*

30260 *Horton Hears A Who* **Production Cel With Hand-Painted Background (Chuck Jones, 1970**). A dramatic cel hand signed by Chuck Jones. This TV special was produced by Chuck Jones Enterprises and premiered on CBS on March 19, 1970. A letter of authenticity accompanies the artwork. *From the Chuck Jones Collection.*

30261 *The Dot and the Line* **Presentation Cel (MGM Studios, 1965).** Released on December 31, 1965, *The Dot and the Line* was directed by Chuck Jones and Maurice Noble, and produced by Jones for MGM. The ten-minute short was the winner of the Academy Award for Animated Short Film for 1965. This is an actual production background used in this film, in a 23" x 24" framed set-up with a recreated hand-painted cel of the line placed on the background for presentation purposes. A special Academy Award presentation matting showcases an image of Jones receiving his Oscar, as well as an image of the nomination certificate for the short. A unique and one of a kind set-up, accompanied by a letter of authenticity. in Excellent condition. *From the Chuck Jones Collection.*

30262 *Doctor Seuss' Horton Hears A Who* **Horton Production Cel (Chuck Jones, 1970).** An outstanding one of a kind hand-painted cel of Horton, at the exact moment that he first hears the Whos! From the CBS March, 1970 TV Special. Signed by Chuck Jones, with a Linda Jones Enterprises seal on the cel. Horton is in fine condition and measures approximately 4″ x 5″. Framed to an overall size of 19.75″ x 20.75″.

30263 *The Night Watchman* **Pretzel Eater Production Cel and Background with Chuck Jones Autograph (Warner Brothers, 1938).** The Merrie Melodies cartoon that launched the career of Chuck Jones! The story involves a kitten "night watchman" who lets the kitchen be overrun with hungry mice, including this pretzel-eater who winds up tied in a knot. The cel is placed over a Warner Brothers studio hand-painted production background. The mouse figure measures approximately 7″ x 3″, with an overall image area of 11″ x 8″. Matted and framed with glass for an overall size of 20″ x 17.75″. The mat has been boldly inscribed, "This is from my first cartoon "The Night-Watchman" — 1938, Chuck Jones, 1979." Considering Mr. Jones' place in the history of animation, we consider this a very important piece. The paint is in Fine condition.

Mel Blanc and
Robert McKimson

The Art of Robert McKimson

Robert McKimson was a major force in the development and style of many of the classic Warner Brothers/Looney Tunes characters. Mr. McKimson was the man behind the design of such classic characters as Foghorn Leghorn, The Tasmanian Devil, Sylvester's son Junior, Henry Hawk, Hippity Hopper , and Speedy Gonzalez to name a few. Robert McKimson along with Friz Freleng, Chuck Jones, Tex Avery, and Bob Clampett helped produce the best of the best of Bugs Bunny and Looney Tunes Cartoons for an entire generation of cartoon fans. Mr. McKimson's work includes such Bugs Bunny classics films as "What's Up Doc," "What's Cookin' Doc" and "A–Lad-in-His-Lamp" to name a few. It is important to note that in a 1944 copyright registration for Bugs Bunny, the artist named is Robert McKimson! Taking the original 1940 model sheet labeled "Tex's Rabbit" for the short "A Wild Hare," Mr. McKimson refined that model sheet in 1943, where it became the gold standard for all Bugs cartoons.

Heritage is proud to exclusively offer original artwork from both Robert McKimson and his brothers Chuck and Tom, legendary animators in their own right.

30264 Robert McKimson *Mouse Tales* Illustration Original Art (1920s). Earliest known artwork by Golden Age Warner Bros. cartoon director, Robert McKimson. Created for a proposed children's book *Mouse Tales*, which was illustrated by Robert and his brother, Tom, and written by their mother, Mildred Porter McKimson. Published on page 21 of **I Say, I Say... Son!** Pen and ink on heavy board, measuring 9" x 10.75". Some paper aging, soiling, and slight edge wear; otherwise the work is in Very Good condition. Signed by the artist at the lower right. Includes a LOA from Robert McKimson Junior. Includes a LOA from Robert McKimson Junior. *From the McKimson Collection.*

30265 Tom McKimson *Mouse Tales* Illustration Original Art (1920s). Original illustration from *Mouse Tales*, illustrated by Robert and Tom McKimson and written by their mother, Mildred Porter McKimson. The drawing by Tom McKimson, featuring three Disney inspired characters, is from the McKimson personal collection. Pen and ink on heavy board, measuring 9" x 10.75". Some paper aging, and soiling; otherwise the work is in Very Good condition. Signed by the artist in the lower portion of the art. Includes a LOA from Robert McKimson Junior. *From the McKimson Collection.*

30266 Pvt. Snafu and Mr. Hook Model Sheet Group (Warner Brothers, c. 1943). During World War II, Warner Brothers produced cartoons for the Army (Pvt. Snafu) and the Navy (Mr. Hook). Here are two rare original studio photostat model sheets for both characters. The Snafu sheet measures 14" x 11", while the Hook sheet is 10" x 8". Both pieces are in Very Good condition. Includes signed LOA from Robert McKimson Jr. for each item. *From the McKimson Collection.*

30270 Robert McKimson Character Size Comparison Production Drawing (Warner Brothers, 1960s). A great character size comparison drawing by Director Robert McKimson Sr., featuring seven of Warner Brothers' most popular characters; Foghorn Leghorn, Tweety Bird, Bugs Bunny, Porky Pig, Speedy Gonzales, Daffy Duck, and Sylvester J. Pussycat. Graphite on 12-field 3-peghole animation paper. Measures 10.5" x 12.5", with character figures from 1.25" (Tweety) up to 5.25" (Bugs). Comes with a C.O.A. from Robert McKimson Jr. There is some light tanning and a little tape residue at the top (outside the image area), otherwise in Fine condition. *From the McKimson Collection.*

30267 *Directed by Robert McKimson* Director Credit Production Drawing (Warner Brothers, late 1950s). Hand-drawn production drawing in graphite and blue pencil for an unnamed cartoon, featuring Robert McKimson's onscreen credit. Image area measures approximately 10.25" x 8", on 2-peghole animation paper. Some tape and very tiny tears along the border edges; otherwise Excellent condition. Includes a signed letter of authentication from Robert McKimson, Jr. *From the McKimson Collection.*

30271 Robert McKimson *Beep Prepared* Wile E. Coyote Model Drawing Original Art (Warner Brothers, 1961). Original production layout drawing of *Hungrii flea-bagius*, Wile E. Coyote by Robert McKimson. Rare drawing by McKimson for this Chuck Jones directed short. Published on page 128 of **I Say, I Say... Son!** Graphite on 10.5" x 12.5" paper. Some light soiling; otherwise the art is in Very Good condition. Includes a LOA from Robert McKimson Junior. *From the McKimson Collection.*

30268 *Ballot Box Bunny* Yosemite Sam Production Drawing (Warner Brothers, 1951). Original production drawing mayor candidate, Yosemite Sam. Graphite on 12" x 9.5" paper. Some paper aging and light edge wear; otherwise the art is in Very Good condition. Includes a LOA from Robert McKimson Junior. *From the McKimson Collection.*

30272 Tom McKimson *Sylvester and Sylvester Jr.* Illustration Original Art (1980s). Original mixed media illustration by Golden Age Warner Bros. animator and layout man, Tom McKimson. The art has an image area of 11" x 8.5" and it is in Excellent condition. Signed by the artist at the upper right. Includes a LOA from Robert McKimson Junior. *From the McKimson Collection.*

30269 Foghorn Leghorn Color Model Production Drawing (Warner Brothers, c. 1960s). An original color model for Foghorn Leghorn, drawn by Director Robert McKimson Sr., the characters' creator. Graphite and colored pencil on 12-field 3-peghole animation paper. In Excellent condition. Includes a C.O.A. from Robert McKimson Jr. *From the McKimson Collection.*

30273 Charles McKimson *I Say, I Say... Son!* **Page 109 Miss Prissy Illustration Original Art (Santa Monica Press, 2012).** Spinster hen, Miss Prissy by Warner Bros. animator and layout man, Charles McKimson. Appeared on page 109 of **I Say, I Say... Son!** Ink and watercolor on textured paper, measuring 5" x 7". In Excellent condition. Signed by the artist at the lower left. Includes a LOA from Robert McKimson Junior. *From the McKimson Collection.*

30275 Tom McKimson *Beep Beep the Road Runner* **#68 "Strictly For the Birds" Preliminary Original Art (Gold Key, 1977).** Original comic book preliminary art for a five-page story featuring Wile E. Coyote and the Road Runner. Drawn on onion skin paper in colored markers, with an average approximate image area of 12.5" x 17.5". In Very Good condition, folded. Includes a signed LOA from Robert McKimson Jr., plus a copy of **Beep Beep the Road Runner** #68. *From the McKimson Collection.*

30274 Tom McKimson *Bugs Bunny* **Illustration Original Art (undated).** Delightful pen and ink drawing of Warner Bros.' greatest cartoon star, Bugs Bunny by veteran animator and layout man, Tom McKimson. The art measures 9" x 11.5" and it is in Excellent condition. Signed by the artist at the lower left. Includes a LOA from Robert McKimson Junior. *From the McKimson Collection.*

30276 Tom McKimson *Beep Beep the Road Runner* **#68 "Early Riser" Preliminary Original Art (Gold Key, 1977).** Original comic book preliminary art for a six-page story featuring Wile E. Coyote and the Road Runner. Drawn on onion skin paper in colored markers, with an average approximate image area of 12.5" x 17.5". In Very Good condition, folded. Includes a signed LOA from Robert McKimson Jr. *From the McKimson Collection.*

30277   Robert McKimson *Sylvester* Coloring Book Preliminary Illustration Sketch (Western Publishing, 1960s). Preliminary illustration sketch for a Looney Tunes coloring book by legendary Warner Bros. cartoon director, Robert McKimson. Published on page 208 of **I Say, I Say... Son!** Graphite on tracing paper, with an image area measuring 7" x 9". Some paper aging and light edge wear; otherwise the art is in Very Good condition. Includes a LOA from Robert McKimson Junior. *From the McKimson Collection.*

30278   Robert McKimson *Looney Tunes* Coloring Book Preliminary Illustration Sketch (Western Publishing, 1960s). Preliminary illustration sketch of Bugs Bunny for a Looney Tunes coloring book by legendary Warner Bros. cartoon director and animator, Robert McKimson. Graphite on tracing paper, with an image area measuring 7" x 9". Some paper aging and light edge wear; otherwise the art is in Very Good condition. Includes a LOA from Robert McKimson Junior. *From the McKimson Collection.*

30279   Robert McKimson *Looney Tunes* Coloring Book Preliminary Illustration Sketch (Western Publishing, 1960s). Preliminary illustration sketch of Bugs Bunny and Porky Pig for a Looney Tunes coloring book by legendary Warner Bros. cartoon director and animator, Robert McKimson. Graphite on tracing paper, with an image area measuring 7" x 9". Some paper aging and light edge wear; otherwise the art is in Very Good condition. Includes a LOA from Robert McKimson Junior. *From the McKimson Collection.*

30280   Robert McKimson Sylvester Jr. Sign Preliminary Original Art (1977). Robert McKimson's last project was drawing this sign, featuring Sylvester Jr., for a 1977 US Marine Corps "Toys For Tots" Christmas campaign. The finished sign is featured on page 229 of Robert McKimson Jr.'s *I Say, I Say...Son!* (Santa Monica Press, 2012). This graphite on animation paper original has an approximate image area of 7.25" x 8", and is in Excellent condition. Includes a signed LOA from Robert McKimson Jr. *From the McKimson Collection.*

30281 Willie Ito *Baton Bunny* Bugs Bunny Lobby Card Rough Pencil Drawing (Warner Brothers, 1959). This cartoon from the Looney Tunes series had Bugs trying to conduct an orchestra despite being plagued by a fly and other annoyances. Art by Chuck Jones unit animator Willie Ito. Signed by the artist and dated 1/59. Excellent condition.

30283 *Gee Whiz-z-z-z-z-z* Wile E. Coyote Production Cel (Warner Brothers, 1956). Hand-inked and hand-painted trimmed production cel of Wile E. Coyote from the Chuck Jones directed short, *Gee Whiz-z-z-z-z-z*. Measures approximately 7" x 4". A Warner Bros. Pictures sticker is applied to the bottom. Paint is cracking, and there is slight old tape on the outer edges; otherwise the art is in Good condition.

30282 Willie Ito *Baton Bunny* Lobby Card Concept Drawing (Warner Brothers, 1959). Chuck Jones unit animator Willie Ito submitted this concept drawing for the lobby card for the Warner Brothers Studio animated short directed by Jones. Signed by Mr. Ito. What a drawing! Graphite with blue highlights on animation paper. Very Good condition.

30284 *Devil May Hare* Tasmanian Devil Production Cel (Warner Brothers, 1954). Taz swallows an inflatable raft which inflates inside him, in this slapstick hand-inked and hand-painted cel featuring the Tasmanian Devil. The cel measures 12.5" x 10.5". Some tape on two four edges; otherwise the work is in Very Good condition.

30285 *Guided Muscle* Wile E. Coyote Production Cel Group (Warner Brothers, 1955). Sequence of four hand-inked and hand-painted trimmed production cels of Wile E. Coyote from the Chuck Jones directed short, *Guided Muscle*. Each trimmed cel measures approximately 4.5" x 8". There is paint cracking and loss, and slight aged tape on the outer edges; otherwise the art averages Good condition.

30286 *Stupor Duck* Production Cel (Warner Brothers, 1956). Three hand-inked and hand-painted trimmed production cels of Daffy Duck as Cluck Trent from the Superman spoof, *Stupor Duck*. Each cel is trimmed to approximately 7" x 4" and each has an applied Warner Bros. Pictures sticker. NOTE: major paint loss and cracking paint, and there is slight old tape on the outer edges; otherwise the art is in Good condition.

30287 *The Bugs Bunny Road Runner Movie* **Bugs Bunny Production Cel (Warner Brothers, 1979).** Hand-painted original production animation cel featuring Bugs Bunny. The work has been matted to an image area of 12" x 9.5" and it is in Excellent condition. Includes a COA, and a Warner Bros. seal at the lower right. Signed by director Chuck Jones at the lower right.

30289 *The Looney Looney Looney Bugs Bunny Movie* **Bugs Bunny Production Cel (Warner Brothers, 1981).** Hand-inked and hand-painted original production animation cel of Bugs Bunny from the Friz Freleng directed animated feature. The work has been matted to an image area of 12" x 9.5" and it is in Excellent condition. Includes a COA, and a Warner Bros. seal at the lower right. Signed by Friz Freleng at the lower left.

30290 *The Looney Looney Looney Bugs Bunny Movie* **Pepe Le Pew Production Cel (Warner Brothers, 1981).** Hand-painted original production animation cel of Pepe Le Pew from this animated feature directed by Friz Freleng. The work has been matted to an image area of 12" x 9.5" and it is in Excellent condition. Includes a COA, and a Warner Bros. seal at the lower right. Signed by Friz Freleng at the lower left.

30288 *The Looney Looney Looney Bugs Bunny Movie* **Yosemite Sam Production Cel (Warner Brothers, 1981).** Hand-inked and hand-painted original production animation cel of Yosemite Sam from this feature directed by Friz Freleng. Matted to an image area of 12" x 9.5" and in Excellent condition. Includes a COA, and a Warner Bros. seal at the lower right. Signed by Friz Freleng at the lower right (faded).

30291 *Bugs Bunny's 3rd Movie: 1001 Rabbit Tales* **Bugs Bunny Production Cel (Warner Brothers, 1982).** Bugs Bunny makes a flying carpet escape from the palace of Sultan Yosemite Sam, in this hand-inked and hand-painted original animation production cel. This art has been matted to an image area of 12" x 9.5" and it is in Excellent condition. Includes a COA, and a Warner Bros. seal at the lower right. Signed by director Friz Freleng at the bottom right.

30292 *Bugs Bunny's 3rd Movie: 1001 Rabbit Tales* **Yosemite Sam Production Cel (Warner Brothers, 1982).** Sultan Yosemite Sam flies high on the carpet, in this hand-inked and hand-painted original animation production cel. This art has been matted to an image area of 12" x 9.5" and it is in Excellent condition. Includes a COA, and a Warner Bros. seal at the lower right. Signed by director Friz Freleng at the bottom right.

30295 *Daffy Duck's Fantastic Island* **Tasmanian Devil Production Cel (Warner Brothers, 1983).** Hand-inked and hand-painted original production animation cel featuring the Tasmanian Devil, a hard character to find in production cels. The work has been matted to an image area of 12" x 9.5" and it is in Excellent condition. Includes a COA, and a Warner Bros. seal at the lower right. Signed by director Friz Freleng at the lower left.

30293 *Bugs Bunny's 3rd Movie: 1001 Rabbit Tales* **Bugs and Daffy Production Cel Set-Up (Warner Brothers, 1982).** Hand-inked and hand-painted original production animation cel set-up featuring Bugs Bunny and Daffy Duck. This art has been matted to an image area of 12" x 9.5" and it is in Excellent condition. Includes a COA, and a Warner Bros. seal at the lower right. Signed by director Friz Freleng at the lower left.

30296 *Bugs Bunny's 3rd Movie: 1001 Rabbit Tales* **Daffy Duck Production Cel Set-Up (Warner Brothers, 1982).** This hand-inked and hand-painted original production animation cel features a close up of Daffy Duck. This art has been matted to an image area of 16" x 12.5" and it is in Excellent condition. Includes a COA, and a Warner Bros. seal at the lower left. Signed by director Friz Freleng at the lower left.

30294 *Daffy Duck's Fantastic Island* **Taz and Yosemite Sam Production Cel (Warner Brothers, 1983).** Hand-inked and hand-painted original animation production cel of pirate Yosemite Sam and his first mate, the Tasmanian Devil. Matted to an image area of 12" x 9.5", the work is in Excellent condition. Includes a COA, and a Warner Bros. seal at the lower right. Signed by director Friz Freleng at the lower left.

30297 *Daffy Duck's Fantastic Island* **Foghorn Production Cel (Warner Brothers, 1983).** Hand-inked and hand-painted original animation production cel featuring Foghorn Leghorn. Matted to an image area of 12" x 9.5", the work is in Excellent condition. Includes a COA, and a Warner Bros. seal at the lower left. Signed by director Friz Freleng at the lower right.

30298 *Adventures of the Road Runner* **Wile E. Coyote Production Cel (Warner Brothers, 1962).** Original hand-painted production cel from the pilot for a TV series, directed by Chuck Jones. The contents were later divided into three theatrical cartoons, the first of which was *To Beep or Not to Beep* (1963). The cel is placed on a hand-painted production background from another Warner's short that appears to be pre-1960s. A great Wile E. Coyote pose, with the image of him in bed measuring 7" x 5". Framed to 18.5" x 15" with an image area of approximately 11.5" x 8.5". The paint is in Fine condition.

30299 *Bugs Bunny's Lunar Tunes* **Marvin Martian and K-9 Production Cel (Warner Brothers, 1991).** An original hand-painted cel featuring Marvin Martian and the ever faithful K-9. "Oh, Mr. DeMille, I'm ready for my close-up!" This one-of-a-kind cel was produced for the home video release of Warner Brothers' *Bugs Bunny's Lunar Tunes* and bears a WB Studio seal on the lower left. The cel has been framed to an overall size of approximately 17" x 19.5", with an image area of 9.25" x 12". In Excellent condition.

30300 *Rabbit Seasoning* **Daffy Duck Production Cel (Warner Brothers, 1952).** Quintessential hand-inked and hand-painted cel of Daffy at his devilish best. Measuring 12" x 10", the work is in Very Good condition.

30301 **Manny Perez** *A Streetcat Named Sylvester* **Production Drawing (Warner Brothers, 1953).** Original production drawing by Manny Perez from the Sylvester and Tweety short. Graphite on 12" x 9.5" paper. Some paper aging, a diagonal crease in the upper left edge, and light soiling; otherwise the art is in Very Good condition.

30302 *Ah Sweet Mouse-story of Life* **Tom and Jerry Production Cel (MGM, 1965).** Original hand-inked and hand-painted production cel of Tom and Jerry together for the MGM theatrical short, directed by Chuck Jones. The cel is placed over a hand-painted MGM production background. Matted and framed to 22" x 18.5", with an image area of 12" x 8.5". The mat is inscribed "All the best to Irvine Barber from Tom and Jerry". An amazing set-up!

30303 *Bugs Bunny's 3rd Movie: 1001 Rabbit Tales* **Bugs and Daffy Production Cel Set-Up with Hand Painted Background (Warner Brothers, 1982).** Hand-inked and hand-painted original production animation cel set-up featuring Bugs Bunny and Daffy Duck with a beautiful hand-painted background. This art has been matted to an image area of 16" x 12.5" and it is in Excellent condition. Includes a COA, and a Warner Bros. seal at the lower right. Signed by director Friz Freleng at the lower right.

The Art of Charlie Brown and Peanuts

"Since 'A Charlie Brown Christmas' first brought the Peanuts comic strip into the hearts of television viewers in 1965, Peanuts animated movies and specials have delighted viewers of all ages," wrote the noted animation writer and historian Charles Solomon in his new book "The Art and Making of Peanuts Animation." Heritage Auctions is proud to offer one of the most impressive collections of Peanuts animation artwork in its inaugural Animation Art auction catalog. Rare title cels, background setups, layout drawings, storyboard drawing segments, and some of the most famous scenes in Peanuts history are represented in this catalog. Included here are Charlie Brown's All Stars, Linus with his famous blanket, Schroeder and Lucy at the Piano, Snoopy and Charlie Brown, and let's not forget The World War One Flying Ace played by Snoopy. A simply amazing selection of one of a kind hand drawn and hand painted artwork is below for your enjoyment.

30304 *Peanuts* "It Was a Short Summer, Charlie Brown" Pan Production Cel Set-Up (Bill Melendez, 1969). Fantastic hand-painted pan production cel set-up featuring 11 *Peanuts* characters, including Charlie Brown, Lucy, Linus, Violet, Schroeder, Pigpen, and Peppermint Patty. Includes hand-painted key master production overlays and a hand-painted key master production background. Framed to 44.25" x 17", with an image area of 35.5" x 8.5"; the characters are all approximately 2.5" tall. The paint is Fine.

30305 *You're a Good Sport Charlie Brown* Tennis-Playing Snoopy Sequence Storyboard Group (Lee Mendelson/Bill Melendez, 1975). Snoopy the Tennis Star struts his stuff (with a little help from Woodstock) in this rare set of original hand-drawn storyboard pages. Peppermint Patty and Sally co-star, but this is really Snoopy's spotlight from the opening sequence of the 14th *Peanuts* television special, which first aired on October 28, 1975. There are forty-eight panel drawings, done in graphite and blue pencil, spread over five pages of 3-peghole animation paper. One page has some additional art taped on and folded. The overall condition is Very Good.

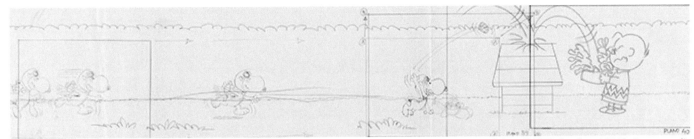

30306 *Charlie Brown and Snoopy Show* **Snoopy and Charlie Brown Production Drawing (Lee Mendelson/Bill Melendez, 1983).** A rare studio layout drawing showing Snoopy as the World War I Flying Ace tossing a hand grenade, which bounces off his doghouse and into the dog tray Charlie is holding. Folded with a few very minor tears and original tape; otherwise in Excellent condition. Included is a copy of the *Peanuts* Sunday strip used during the story development for the cartoon.

30307 *The Charlie Brown and Snoopy Show* **Production Cel Set-Up with Background (Lee Mendelson/CBS, 1983).** Original master pan hand-painted background with two cel set-up of Snoopy as the World War I Flying Ace stuck behind enemy lines. One of the most important pieces of *Peanuts* animation we've seen! Pan hand-painted background is approximately 28" x 10". In Excellent condition.

30308 *The Charlie Brown and Snoopy Show* **Production Cel and Drawing Group (Lee Mendelson/CBS, 1983).** Snoopy, as the World War I Flying Ace, sneaks behind enemy lines in this trio of sequenced hand-painted production cels based on the famous *Peanuts* character. Each cel measures 13.5" x 10" and is placed against a color print background. All three cels include their matching animation drawing. In Excellent condition.

30309 *The Charlie Brown and Snoopy Show* **Production Cel and Drawing Group (Lee Mendelson/CBS, 1983).** Snoopy bails out of his plane as the World War I Flying Ace in this rare sequence of three cels based on the famous *Peanuts* character. Each cel measures 13.5" x 10" and is placed against a color print background. All three cels include their matching animation drawing. In Excellent condition.

BID LIVE

ONLINE AT

HA.COM

30310 *The Charlie Brown and Snoopy Show* **Production Cel Set-Up and Drawing Group (Lee Mendelson/CBS, 1983).** Original hand-painted production cel of Snoopy as the World War I Flying Ace, based on the famous *Peanuts* character. The background is a color photocopy. Includes its matching clean-up and effects drawing. Each cel and drawing measures approximately 13" x 10". In Excellent condition.

30311 *The Charlie Brown and Snoopy Show* **Production Cel (Lee Mendelson Film Productions/CBS, 1983).** Hand-painted production cel of Snoopy as the World War I Flying Ace, preparing to throw a hand grenade (which ultimately lands in his own dog food being carried in by Charlie Brown). The background is a color photocopy. Based on the famous *Peanuts* character, the art measures 13" x 10" and in Excellent condition.

30312 *The Charlie Brown and Snoopy Show* **Production Cel Set-Up and Drawing Group (Lee Mendelson/CBS, 1983).** The Doctor is In. Hand-painted production cel set-up of *Peanuts* characters Charlie Brown, Lucy and Woodstock at Lucy's famed "Psychiatric Help" office. Matching animation drawings of Lucy and Charlie Brown included. Placed on a print background created from the original background. Each cel and drawing measures approximately 13" x 10". In Excellent condition.

30313 *The Charlie Brown and Snoopy Show* **"Snoopy's Trick" Title Cel Set-Up and Drawing Group (Lee Mendelson/CBS, 1983).** Hand-painted title cel set-up, with photocopy background, along with three matching drawings of Schroeder and the title type from the first season episode "Snoopy's Trick." Based on the *Peanuts* comic strip, each cel and drawing measures 13.5" x 10.5". In Very Good condition.

30316 *Charlie Brown and Snoopy Show* **Lucy and Schroeder Production Cel (Lee Mendelson/Bill Melendez, 1983).** Schroeder tells a love-sick Lucy just how it is in this classic "at the piano" pose, based on the famous *Peanuts* characters. This original hand-painted production cel set-up is paired with a color print background, with a combined approximate image area of 13.25" x 9.75". In Excellent condition.

30314 *The Charlie Brown and Snoopy Show* **" Linus and the Blanket" Production Cel (Lee Mendelson/Bill Melendez, 1983).** A rare original hand-painted title cel for the episode "Linus and the Blanket" (later re-titled "Linus's Security Blanket"). This lot includes the matching animation drawings of the *Peanuts* characters, as well as the layout drawing for the title card (four pieces total). Title cards such as these are rarely seen. In Excellent condition.

30317 *Charlie Brown and Snoopy Show* **Baseball Scene Production Cel and Matching Drawings Group (Lee Mendelson/Bill Melendez, 1983).** "All Star" team coach and pitcher Charlie Brown studies the situation with outfielder Snoopy in this original hand-painted animation cel set-up with color print background. The combined image area measures approximately 13.75" x 9.25". Also included are the original matching graphite production drawings for both *Peanuts* characters Charlie Brown and Snoopy, done on 3-peghole animation paper. All three items are in Excellent condition.

30315 *The Charlie Brown and Snoopy Show* **Title Cel (Lee Mendelson/Bill Melendez, 1983).** An original hand-painted title cel for one of the in-show segments, titled simply "Snoopy". This is a rare hand-painted production cel on a key master hand-painted background of *Peanuts* characters Charlie Brown and Snoopy, accompanied by a copy of a Sunday strip with notes used for story development. A director's original one-of-a-kind layout drawing of the scene is also included! In Excellent condition.

30318 *Charlie Brown and Snoopy Show* **Snoopy and Charlie Brown Production Cel and Matching Drawings Group (Lee Mendelson/Bill Melendez, 1983).** Snoopy does his Dinner Time Happy Dance in this cute original production cel set-up with color print background. Also included are the two original production drawings of Snoopy and Charlie Brown on 3-peghole animation paper, stapled together. The cel and background have a combined image area of approximately 14" x 10"; all items are in Excellent condition.

30319 *Charlie Brown and Snoopy Show* **Snoopy and Linus Production Cel (Lee Mendelson/Bill Melendez, 1983).** Linus talks and "guard dog" Snoopy listens (sort of), in this original hand-painted production cel set-up, paired with a color print background. Snoopy on top of the doghouse is always a treat for *Peanuts* animation collectors, and this is a classic pose! The combined image area is approximately 12.75" x 9.75", and the art is in Excellent condition.

30320 *Charlie Brown and Snoopy Show* **Lucy and Linus Production Cel (Lee Mendelson/Bill Melendez, 1983).** Linus hangs onto his blue felt "security blanket" in this charming two-character set-up from the CBS Television series that ran from 1983 until 1986. The 3-peghole cels are combined with a color photocopy background, for an overall size of 13.75" x 10". In Excellent condition.

30321 *Charlie Brown and Snoopy Show* **Snoopy and Charlie Brown Production Cel and Matching Drawing Group (Lee Mendelson/Bill Melendez, 1983).** Snoopy is sitting high on the doghouse in this original hand-painted production cel set-up with color print background. The combined image area measures approximately 13" x 9.75". Also included are the original production drawings for both *Peanuts* characters, each done on 3-peghole animation paper. All items are in Excellent condition.

30322 *The Charlie Brown and Snoopy Show* **Production Cel (Lee Mendelson/CBS, 1983).** Original hand-painted production cel of Snoopy eating and watching TV, with its matching animation drawing placed over a complimentary background created from the original art. Based on the famous *Peanuts* character, the art measures approximately 13" x 10". In Excellent condition.

30323 *The Charlie Brown and Snoopy Show* **Production Cel and Drawing Group (Lee Mendelson/CBS, 1983).** Original hand-painted production cel of Snoopy as the World War I Flying Ace, stuck behind enemy lines, on a print background created from the original art. Includes a matching animation drawing of *Peanuts* star Snoopy. Each cel and drawing measures approximately 13" x 10". In Excellent condition.

30324 *The Charlie Brown and Snoopy Show* **Production Cel Group (Lee Mendelson/CBS, 1983).** Hand-painted production cel of Snoopy with its matching animation drawing placed on a complimentary print background made from the original art. Based on the famous *Peanuts* comic strip, the art measures approximately 13" x 10". In Excellent condition.

30325 *The Charlie Brown and Snoopy Show* **Production Cel Group (Lee Mendelson/CBS, 1983).** Hand-painted production cel set-up of *Peanuts* characters Lucy and Snoopy on a key master hand-painted background. Includes a pair of matching animation drawings of the characters as well! Each cel and drawing measures approximately 13" x 10". In Excellent condition.

30326 *Charlie Brown and Snoopy Show* **Snoopy and Charlie Brown Production Cel and Matching Drawings Group (Lee Mendelson/Bill Melendez, 1983).** Snoopy's hungry, Charlie Brown! Who can resist such a cute pup? Original hand-painted production cel set-up of the famous *Peanuts* characters with color print background, featuring an approximate combined image area of 12.75" x 9.5". Also included are the original production drawings of Snoopy and Charlie Brown, on 3-peghole animation paper. All three items are in Excellent condition.

30327 *The Charlie Brown and Snoopy Show* **Production Cel Set-Up (Lee Mendelson/CBS, 1983).** *Peanuts'* Charlie Brown, The Little Red-Haired Girl and Lucy are here in this hand-painted production cel set-up with a color print background. Each cel measures 13" x 10.5". Some tape along the left and right edges; otherwise the art is in Excellent condition.

30328 *The Charlie Brown and Snoopy Show* **Production Cel Set-Up and Drawing Group (Lee Mendelson/CBS, 1983).** Hand-painted production cel set-up Charlie Brown and Peppermint Patty as part of Charlie Brown's All Stars. The *Peanuts* character set-up is placed on a print background created from the original background. Each cel and drawing measures approximately 13" x 10". In Excellent condition.

30329 *The Charlie Brown and Snoopy Show* **Production Cel Set-Up and Drawing Group (Lee Mendelson/CBS, 1983).** Original hand-painted production cel of Snoopy in his Camp Snoopy outfit, along with Woodstock and a friend, a *Peanuts* bonanza! The background is a color photocopy. Includes two matching clean-up drawings. Each cel and drawing measures approximately 13" x 10". In Excellent condition.

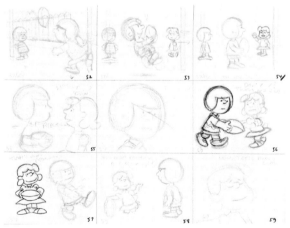

30330 *You're In the Super Bowl, Charlie Brown* **Football Sequence Storyboard Animation Art Group (Lee Mendelson/Bill Melendez, 1994).** Yes, Lucy does it again — pulls away the football as Charlie Brown kicks — in this set of storyboard drawings from the 37th prime-time animated TV special based on Charles Schulz's classic *Peanuts* comic strip. This set of 36 graphite, blue, and green color pencil sketches, co-starring Linus with Lucy and Charlie Brown, are laid out as a nine-panel grid on four sheets of 3-peghole animation paper. There are a few small stains, but otherwise, the pages are in Excellent condition.

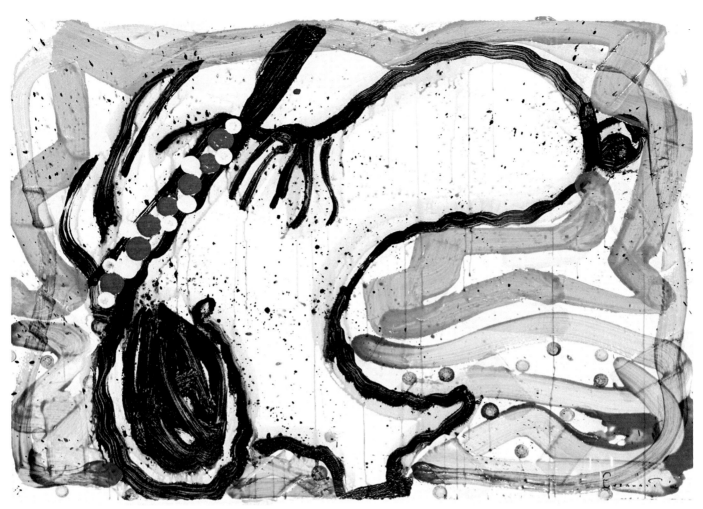

30331   Tom Everhart "Sport Snoopy" Painting Original Art (2006). Tennis star Snoopy cries out over a missed serve in this remarkable fine art painting by Tom Everhart. Mr. Everhart was the only artist authorized by Charles Schulz to use *Peanuts* characters in his work, beginning in 1980. This piece, done in acrylic paints on textured paper, is so vibrant and alive, the colors literally leap off the edges! The art measures approximately 30" x 40", in a floating mat and Plexiglas/wood frame which measures 49.25" x 39.25". In Excellent condition.

YOU'LL FIND CHARLES SCHULZ ORIGINAL ART
FOR THE PEANUTS NEWSPAPER STRIP IN OUR
FEBRUARY 22, 2013 COMIC ART AUCTION!
GO TO HA.COM/7073

THE JACKSON 5IVE

The Art of the Jackson 5ive

After the success of the ABC Saturday morning Beatles animated television series, as well as other networks' success with animated music-themed cartoon shows (" Josie and the Pussycats", "The Archies, and " The Partridge Family," etc.), ABC brought to television the animated series "The Jackson 5ive" It was the weekly adventures of Jackie, Marlon, Tito, Jermaine, and Michael Jackson. The show , like the Beatles cartoon show, featured songs within each episode. It premiered on ABC on September 11, 1971. It was produced by Rankin Bass, and only 22 episodes were produced.

In January of 2013, for the first time, Classic Media released these episodes for the first time on DVD, and the many reviews that have appeared in the press over the last month are testimony to the popularity of this show. Artwork for this series has been rare and hard to find….until now!

30332 *The Jackson 5ive* **Entire Group Production Cel and Drawing (Rankin-Bass, 1971).** Ease on down the road with the Brothers Jackson, in this remarkable oversized 16-field, hand-painted cel set-up. All five are included — Michael, Marlon, Jackie, Tito, and Jermaine. all seen behind the windshield of their vintage jalopy (the front of the car is a color print). This is one of the largest Jackson 5ive cels out there; it has an approximate image area of 10.75" x 10.75". The original production drawing for the scene is also included, and all items are in Excellent condition.

30333 *The Jackson 5ive* **Michael Jackson Production Cel (Rankin-Bass, c. 1972).** The Jackson Five! All five brothers — Michael, Jackie, Tito, Marlon, and Jermaine perform in classic 70's bellbottoms, in this hand-painted production cel. The cel measures 12" x 9.5", and it is in Excellent condition.

30334 *The Jackson 5ive* **Production Cel Set-Up (Rankin-Bass, 1972).** Amazing one-of-a-kind hand-painted pan key master cel set-up of Michael Jackson being mobbed by fair maidens. Measures 34" x 10". In Excellent condition.

30335 *The Jackson 5ive* **Production Cel Set-Up with Key Master Background(Rankin-Bass, 1972).** Hand-painted production cel of Michael Jackson on its key master hand-painted production background from the *Michael in Wonderland* episode (Alice in Wonderland parody) that aired on September 30, 1972. This episode featured the songs "Got to Be There" and "Maria (You Were the Only One)." Measures approximately 13.5" x 10", in Very Good condition.

30336 *The Jackson 5ive* **Production Cel Set-Up (Rankin-Bass, c. 1972).** Hand-painted pan production cel featuring Michael and three of his brothers in mid song. The cel set-up is set against a complimentary color print of the original background art. Measures approximately 27" x 10". In Excellent condition.

30337 *The Jackson 5ive* **Production Cel Set-Up (Rankin-Bass, 1972).** Hand-painted production cel of Michael Jackson at the Mad Hatter's Tea Party from the *Michael in Wonderland* episode that aired on September 30, 1972. The cel is placed on a complimentary printed background created from the original art. Measures approximately 12.5" x 9.5", in Very Good condition.

30340 *The Jackson 5ive* **Production Cel Set-Up (Rankin-Bass, c. 1972).** The Jackson Five sing "I Want You Back!" in this great ¾ close up featuring Michael, Marlon, Tito, Jackie, and Jermaine in full song. Set against a color photocopy of the original background, the two hand-painted cels each measure 12" x 9.5" and are in Very Good condition.

30338 *The Jackson 5ive* **Michael Jackson Production Cel with Matching Drawing (Rankin-Bass, c. 1972).** The young King of Pop is featured in this exquisite hand-painted production cel with photocopy of the original background. Also includes its matching clean-up drawing. The cel and drawing each measure 12.5" x 10.5", and are in Very Good condition.

30339 *The Jackson 5ive* **Production Cel Set-Up (Rankin-Bass, c. 1972).** Jackson brothers Tito, Marlon, Jackie, and Jermaine address Michael at his desk, in this hand-painted production cel set-up with a photocopy of the original background. Each of the four cels measure 13.5" x 10" and the condition of the work is Very Good.

30341 *The Jackson 5ive* **Michael Jackson Production Cel Set-Up with Drawing (Rankin-Bass, c. 1972).** Hand-painted production cel set-up of Michael Jackson, including its matching hand drawn layout drawing. The cel and drawing each measure 12" x 9.5", and they are in Very Good condition.

30342 *The Jackson 5ive* **Production Cel Set-Up (Rankin-Bass, c. 1972).** The Jackson brothers Michael, Jackie, Marlon, Tito, and Jermaine take a drive in this hand-painted production cel set-up with a photocopy of the original background. Each of the six cels measure 13.5" x 10" and the condition of the work is Very Good.

30343 *The Jackson 5ive* **Production Cel Set-Up (Rankin-Bass, 1972).** Hand-painted production cel of Michael Jackson and a witch with an apple from the *Michael White* episode (Snow White parody) that aired on September 16, 1972. Songs in this episode included "Sugar Daddy" and "I Wanna Be Where You Are". The cel is placed on a complimentary printed background created from the original art. Measures approximately 14" x 11", in Very Good condition.

30344 *The Jackson 5ive* **Production Cel Set-Up (Rankin-Bass, 1972).** Jacksons Michael, Marlon, Tito, Jackie and Jermaine appear here in this hand-painted production cel with a photocopy of the original background. The art measures approximately 12" x 10", and it is in Very Good condition. Signed by the show's director Bob Balser at the lower right.

30345 *The Jackson 5ive* **Opening Credits Production Cel Set-Up (Rankin-Bass, 1972).** Rare hand-painted production cel set-up with original background from the opening credits of *The Jackson 5ive* featuring Michael, Marlon, Tito, Jackie, and Jermaine. Each cel measures 12" x 10". There is some paint discoloration in the Michael Jackson figure, and the background art is covered with an acetate sheet, which has been taped along the edges leaving tape staining; otherwise the art is in Very Good condition.

30346 *The Jackson 5ive* **Production Cel Set-Up with Drawing (Rankin-Bass, c. 1972).** Hand-painted pan production cel set-up of all five of the Jackson Five... Michael, Marlon, Tito, Jackie, and Jermaine. Set against a complimentary print background made from the original art, these two pan cels each measure 20" x 10.5". Some edge wear and staples at the lower edge; otherwise the art is in Very Good condition.

TERRYTOONS

The Art of Terrytoons

Terrytoons was an animation studio located in New Rochelle, New York. The studio was founded in 1929 and operated till the late 1960s. This is the studio that brought to life such characters as Mighty Mouse, Gandy Goose, Heckle and Jeckle, and Dinky Duck to name a few. When television came into play, the firm's TV arm developed such new characters as Hector Heathcoat, Deputy Dawg and later on for Captain Kangaroo, the character Tom Terrific.

The founder of Terrytoons was Paul Terry, and the first real star of the studio was Mighty Mouse. Mighty Mouse made his first appearance in 1942. He was originally named Super Mouse. He was in over 80 theatrical animated shorts from 1942 through 1961 and leapt to larger fame when he went to television with the "Mighty Mouse Playhouse" which premiered in 1955.

Terrytoons' other superstar became Tom Terrific, along with his wonder dog, the Mighty Manfred. Directed by Gene Deitch, this animated television series ran for only 26 original episodes in 1957/58. It was part of the Captain Kangaroo children's television show. Tom Terrific was ranked by TV Guide as the 32nd among its 50 Greatest TV Cartoon Characters. Drawn in a simplistic style, it featured a gee-whiz boy hero who lived in a tree house and could transform himself in to anything he wanted, thanks in part to his magical thinking cap. Disappointingly, there has never been an authorized VHS or DVD release of this series!

Heritage is proud to offer an impressive collection of never-before-seen hand painted master backgrounds from Terrytoons Studios. These backgrounds range from 1942 – 1946. They include many Super Mouse/Mighty Mouse cartoons, as well as Gandy Goose theatrical shorts and other theatrical animated shorts form this time period. They have never been seen on the market. The colors on these backgrounds jump! Also included in this auction is one of the largest known examples of original animation drawings from the TV Series Tom Terrific.

30347 *Tom Terrific* **Production Drawings Folder Original Art Group (Terrytoons, 1957).** Vintage drawings from the first year of the short-lived, innovative cartoon featured on *Captain Kangaroo*. This animation folder has 27 drawings of Tom Terrific , one drawing of Fred, and two animator timing sheets, all on 3-peghole, 12-field animation paper. All but one of the drawings are in Excellent condition, the other in Very Good.

30348 *Tom Terrific* **Production Drawings Folder Original Art Group (Terrytoons, 1957).** A production folder full of Terrific-ness! Included in this folder from the cartoon show's first year are 14 Tom Terrific drawings, 12 of Mighty Manfred the Wonder Dog, 15 of the Knight in Armor, and 11 of Fred (all on 3-peghole, 12-field animation paper), two timing sheets, and a mimeograph of the shows logo. Miscellaneous partials and effects drawings are also included. Pages range from Very Good to Excellent condition, most in Excellent.

30349 Terrytoons "Free Lunch" Production Background Painting (Terrytoons, 1940s). Original hand-painted master production background from an unspecified Terrytoons theatrical short. Gouache on board, 13" x 9.5". In Excellent condition.

30352 Terrytoons "Islands" Production Background Paintings (Terrytoons, 1940s). A pair of original hand-painted master production backgrounds from an unspecified Terrytoons theatrical short. Gouache on board, 13" x 9.5". In Excellent condition.

30350 Terrytoons "Train Tracks" Production Background Painting (Terrytoons, 1940s). Original hand-painted master production background from an unspecified Terrytoons theatrical short. Gouache on board, 13" x 9.5". In Excellent condition.

30351 Terrytoons "Ghost Town" Production Background Painting (Terrytoons, 1940s). Original hand-painted master production background from an unspecified Terrytoons theatrical short. Gouache on board, 13" x 9.5". In Excellent condition.

LOOK FOR MORE

ANIMATION ART

IN THE SUNDAY

INTERNET COMICS

AUCTIONS AT

HA.COM

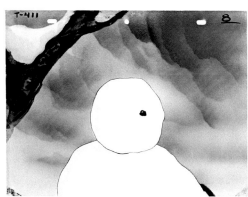

30354 *Shipyard Symphony* **Production Background Painting Group (Terrytoons, 1942).** A set of two original hand-painted master production backgrounds for the wartime theatrical short. Gouache on board, 13" x 9.5". In Very Good condition with staples in the top edges.

30353 *The Snow Man* **Production Background Paintings (Terrytoons, 1940).** A group of three original hand-painted master production backgrounds for the theatrical short, including one featuring a partial image of the titular character. Gouache on board, 13" x 9.5". In Excellent condition.

30355 *Keep 'Em Growing* **Production Background Paintings (Terrytoons, 1943).** A pair of original hand-painted master production backgrounds for the 1943-themed theatrical short. Gouache on board, 13" x 9.5". In Excellent condition.

30356 *Mopping Up* **Gandy Goose Production Background Painting Group (Terrytoons, 1943).** A group of three original hand-painted master production backgrounds for the wartime theatrical short. Gouache on board, 13" x 9.75". In Excellent condition.

30357 *Scrap for Victory* **Gandy Goose Production Background Painting Group (Terrytoons, 1943).** A pair of original hand-painted master production backgrounds for the theatrical short produced to support the war effort. Gouache on board, 13" x 9.75". In Excellent condition.

30358 *The Green Line* **Mighty Mouse Production Background Painting (Terrytoons, 1944).** Original hand-painted master production background for the 1944 Mighty Mouse theatrical short, featuring a conflict between cats and mice. Gouache on board, 13" x 9.5". In Excellent condition.

30359 *The Frog and the Princess* **Gandy Goose Production Background Painting Group (Terrytoons, 1944).** A pair of original hand-painted master production backgrounds for the 1944 theatrical short starring Gandy Goose in a retelling of the classic fairy tale. Gouache on board, 12.5" x 9.5". In Excellent condition.

30360 *Mexican Baseball* **Gandy Goose Production Background Paintings (Terrytoons, 1947).** A set of four original hand-painted master production backgrounds for the 1947 theatrical short in which Gandy Goose and Sourpuss take on the Mexican League Bulls. Gouache on board, 13" x 9.5". In Excellent condition.

30361 *At the Circus* **Mighty Mouse Production Background Painting Group (Terrytoons, 1944).** A pair of original hand-painted master production backgrounds for the Mighty Mouse theatrical short. Gouache on board, 13" x 9.75". In Excellent condition.

30362 *Mighty Mouse Meets Jekyll and Hyde Cat* **Production Background Painting (Terrytoons, 1944).** A very nice original hand-painted master production background for the theatrical short, a twist on Robert Louis Stevenson's classic horror novella. The background features a great image of the cat after he has apparently tussled with our hero. Gouache on board, 13" x 9.75". In Excellent condition.

30363 *Port of Missing Mice* **Mighty Mouse Production Background Painting Group (Terrytoons, 1945).** A trio of original hand-painted master production backgrounds for the 1945 Mighty Mouse theatrical short in which Mighty Mouse rescues sailor mice from a gang of pirate cats. Gouache on board, 12.5" x 9.5". In Excellent condition.

30364 *Mighty Mouse and the Pirates* **Production Background Painting Group (Terrytoons, 1945).** Two original hand-painted master production backgrounds for the theatrical short, the first to feature our hero's arch-nemesis, Oil-Can Harry, as well as the first to have dialogue that was sung rather than spoken. Gouache on board, 13" x 9.75". In Excellent condition.

30366 *The Crackpot King* **Mighty Mouse Background Production Painting Group (Terrytoons, 1946).** A group of three original hand-painted master production backgrounds for the Mighty Mouse theatrical short. Gouache on board, 13" x 9.75". In Excellent condition.

30365 *The Jail Break* **Mighty Mouse Background Production Painting Group (Terrytoons, 1946).** A set of three original hand-painted master production backgrounds for the 1946 Mighty Mouse theatrical short, each featuring images of a cartoon Alcatraz. Gouache on board, 13" x 9.5". In Excellent condition.

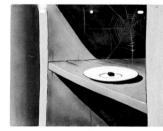

30367 *Beanstalk Jack* **Production Background Painting Group (Terrytoons, 1946).** A set of four original hand-painted master production backgrounds for the theatrical short, a retelling of "Jack and the Beanstalk". Images include the magic bean, the beanstalk, the giant's castle, and some of the golden eggs. Gouache on board, 13" x 9.75". In Excellent condition.

30368 *The Wolf's Pardon* **Production Background Painting Group (Terrytoons, 1947).** A trio of original hand-painted master production backgrounds for the 1947 theatrical short, featuring a typically wacky Terrytoons spin on some classic fairy tale characters. Gouache on board, 13" x 9.5". In Excellent condition.

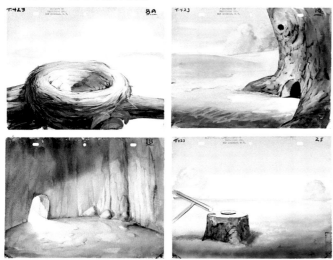

30369 *Cat Trouble* **Heckle and Jeckle Production Background Painting Group (Terrytoons, 1947).** An outstanding group of four original hand-painted master production backgrounds for the 1947 theatrical short, one of the earliest to feature the wisecracking magpies. Gouache on board, 13" x 9.75". In Excellent condition.

30370 *The Intruders* **Heckle and Jeckle Production Background Painting Group (Terrytoons, 1947).** A group of three original hand-painted master production backgrounds for the theatrical short, which pitted the feathered duo against a tenacious bulldog. Gouache on board, 13" x 9.75". In Excellent condition.

30371 *Aladdin's Lamp* **Mighty Mouse Production Background Painting (Terrytoons, 1947).** An original hand-painted master production background for the theatrical short, an operetta parody of the classic tale. Gouache on board, 13" x 9.75". In Excellent condition.

30372 *The Witch's Cat* **Mighty Mouse Production Background Painting (Terrytoons, 1948).** Original hand-painted master production background for the 1948 Mighty Mouse theatrical short, featuring a mouse Halloween party that gets crashed by a witch and her cat. Gouache on board, 12.5" x 9.5". In Excellent condition.

30373 *Camouflage* **Gandy Goose Production Background Painting Group (Terrytoons, 1943).** A group of three original hand-painted master production backgrounds for the war-themed Gandy Goose theatrical short. Gouache on board, 13" x 9.75". In Excellent condition.

30374 *The Flintstones* **"Fred Flintstone in Car" Title Sequence Production Cel (Hanna-Barbera, 1960).** Yabba dabba doo! An original hand-inked and hand-painted production cel of Fred Flintstone from the opening title sequence of the classic 1960-66 TV series — one of the most famous cartoon openings in the history of television. The image of Fred in his car measures 6.5" x 4". The cel is matted to 16" x 12" and placed over a hand-painted non-*Flintstones* production background. The paint is in Fine condition. A wonderful piece of animation history.

30375 *The Flintstones* **Wilma and Betty Model Original Art Drawings (Hanna-Barbera, 1961).** Original concept art/model drawings of Wilma Flintstone and Betty Rubble by Dick Bickenbach for Episode #42 "The Masquerade Ball" that aired on 12/8/61. Signed. The art was done on separate pieces of paper that were glued to a larger sheet. The piece measures approximately 12.5 x 10.5". Good condition.

30376 *The Flintstones* **Pan Production Cel Set-Up (Hanna-Barbera, c. 1960s-70s).** Here is a "rock"-in' 1960's/70's original *Flintstones* hand-painted pan production background (measuring 24" x 10"). A cut cel image of Fred and Wilma, in the Flintstone-mobile has been attached to the background. The cel is from a Flintstone project and the cel was created from Dick Bickenbach drawings. In Excellent condition.

30377 **Joe Barbera** *The Flintstones* **Fred and Dino Illustration (Hanna-Barbera, 1990s).** Original sketch of Fred Flintstone and Dino in a Christmas-themed image by the great Joe Barbera that was later used for a studio holiday card. The rough drawing is accompanied by a color model cel made by Hanna-Barbera's Ink and Paint Department. This gorgeous, one-of-a-kind 12-field cel is also signed by Barbera. The drawing is in graphite on 8.5" x 11" paper, and the cel is stunning. This is something special.

30378 *The Jetsons* **Concept Drawing Original Art (Hanna-Barbera, 1962).** Rare original Hanna-Barbera studio concept/presentation art for *The Jetsons*, featuring entire family (George, Jane, Judy, Elroy and Astro) coming in for a landing to see Rosie the Robot, in an appliance store. Graphite on 16-field animation paper. The entire sheet is filled with magnificent artwork. In Fine condition.

30379 *The Jetsons* Publicity Cel Signed by Entire Voice Cast at Final Taping (Hanna-Barbera, 1985). This hand-painted Hanna-Barbera Studio Publicity cel was done for the final taping of the Jetsons. The show which ran for 19 episodes in 1962 came back with its original cast 23 years later to make more episodes to add to syndication. To mark this historic occasion only a handful of these cels (five) were painted and signed by the voice cast at the final taping. This historic 12-field, hand-painted publicity cel is signed by Don Messick — the voice of Astro, Penny Singleton — Jane, Janet Waldo — Judy, Mel Blanc — Mr. Spacely, George O'Hanlon — George, Frank Welker — Orbity, Jean Vander Pyl — Rosie, Daws Butler — Elroy, and producers Bob Hathcock and Jeff Hall. All of these signatures together on one cel is something we've never seen before. A photo of the group is included on the back of the frame. Framed to an overall size of 14.5" x 19" with an approximate image size of 8.75" x 13.5". In Excellent condition.

30380 *Jetsons: The Movie* Production Cel (Hanna-Barbera, 1990). A huge hand-painted production cel of Judy Jetson and Cosmic Cosmo from the final scene of the movie. The hand-painted background of the Space Age Shopping Mall is truly a spectacular work of art! The movie featured the last performances of George O'Hanlon as George Jetson and Mel Blanc as Mr. Spacely. The cel is an amazing 23" x 24", and in Excellent condition.

30381 *Jetsons: The Movie* Theatrical Banner Painting Original Art (Hanna-Barbera, 1990). Original hand-painted artwork used for the *Jetsons: The Movie* banner-sized theatrical poster, painted on 24" x 17" illustration board. A clear protective cel lies over the artwork. This stunning work showcases the entire Jetson Family in their spaceship! A rare item, this artwork was also used for many of the film's merchandising tie-ins. In Excellent condition.

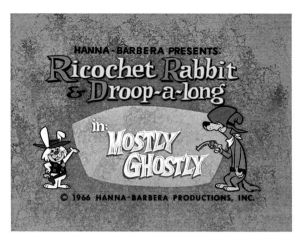

30382   The Magilla Gorilla Show "Mostly Ghostly" Ricochet Rabbit Production Cel (Hanna-Barbera, 1966). Original hand-inked and hand-painted title cel for the "Mostly Ghostly" episode of the 1966 *The Magilla Gorilla Show*, featuring Ricochet Rabbit and Droop-a-long. Three 12-field cels set-up on a hand-painted key master background. An fantastic sample of vintage '60s Hanna-Barbera. In Excellent condition.

30383   Hong Kong Phooey Model Sheet Original Art (Hanna-Barbera, 1974). An outstanding and rare model sheet drawn by famed animator Willie Ito. A note reveals that the original working title for the Number One Superguy was "Kung Phooey." 12-field animation paper marked standard size, Model sheet #3. Signed by the artist. This one should sell "quicker than the human eye!" It's in Excellent condition.

30384   Hong Kong Phooey Penrod Pooch Model Sheet (Hanna-Barbera, 1974). What Clark Kent was to Superman, Penrod Pooch was to Hong Kong Phooey, and you might recall "Penry the janitor" was voiced by the late Scatman Crothers! Marked model sheet #1... "Formerly Kung Phooey". Drawn by famed animator Willie Ito, and signed by him. On 12-field animation paper

30385   The Tom and Jerry/The Grape Ape Show Production Cel (Hanna-Barbera, 1975). One-of-a-kind hand-painted production pan cel set-up of Tom and Jerry from the ABC television show that paired them with the Great Grape Ape. A better Tom and Jerry cel we have not seen. The two-cel set-up measures approximately 20" x 10". In Excellent condition.

30386   The Banana Splits "Hocus Pocus Park" Model Cel (Hanna-Barbera, 1972). An extremely rare Hanna-Barbera Studio 12-field, hand-inked and hand-painted color model cel of Snorky, Drooper, Bingo, and Fleegle. This ABC special was the only time the costume character Banana Splits were animated. In Excellent condition.

30387   Hawley Pratt Wally Gator Little Golden Book Cover Original Art (Western Publishing, 1963). An original gouache on board painting of a lazing Wally Gator and Yogi Bear, created for the cover of the 1963 **Wally Gator** Little Golden book. Hawley Pratt was the long time right hand man of Friz Freleng at Warner Brothers. The reverse of the painting reads "LGB #502 Wally Gator cover art (chartreuse on alligator) 7 ½" x 8 ½"". The colors are amazing. This piece has an image area of 7.5" x 8.5" and is in Fine condition. A copy of the book is included.

30388 *The Simpsons* **Production Cel (Fox, 1990s).** Original hand-painted production cel of Krusty the Clown and Side Show Bob on a print background with a Fox seal on the cel. Outstanding dual full figure poses. Matted with an image area of 11.75" x 9.25". In Excellent condition.

30390 *The Simpsons* **Mr. Burns Production Cel with Background (Fox, 1990s).** Original 12-field hand-painted production cel of Mr. Burns in a "Michael Dukakis" tank reference gag. The cel is with its key master cel painted background. Framed and matted with an image area of 11" x 9". It's in Excellent condition.

30389 *The Simpsons* **Bart and Homer Production Cel with Background From First Episode of First Season (Fox, 1990).** Historic hand-painted 12-field production cel of Bart and Homer from the first episode of the first season, *Bart the Genius*, which originally aired on January 21, 1990. The cel is with its key master painted background. Framed and matted to an image area of 11.5" x 8.75". There are staple damage at the lower left and right corners; otherwise the art is in Very Good condition.

30391 *The Simpsons* **Mr. Burns Production Cel with Background (Fox, 1990).** A perfect pose of Mr. Burns from the very first season of *The Simpsons*. The cel is with its key master hand-painted background. Framed and matted to an image area of 11.5" x 8.5". In Very Good condition.

30392 *The Simpsons* **Homer and Grandpa Production Cel with Background (Fox, 1990s).** This hand-painted 12-field production cel of Bart and Grandpa at the grocery store includes its original hand-painted key master background. Bart with cigar is priceless! Framed and matted to an image area of 11.5″ x 8.5″. In Excellent condition.

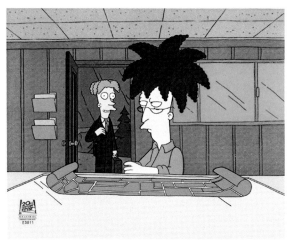

30394 *Simpsons* **"Brother From Another Series" Sideshow Bob and Cecil Terwilliger Production Cel Set-Up (Fox, 1997).** An original hand-painted production cel set-up on a printed background, from Simpsons season eight, episode 16 "Brother From Another Series," that aired on 2/23/97. The set-up features Sideshow Bob (voiced by Kelsey Grammer) and Cecil Terwilliger (voiced by David Hyde Pierce). Includes a certificate of authenticity. The presentation envelope measures 12″ x 15″ with an image area of 8″ x 11″. In Excellent condition.

30393 *The Simpsons* **Krusty the Clown Production Cel with Background (Fox, 1995).** This rare 16-field hand-painted large size production cel of Krusty the Clown includes its original hand-painted key master cel painted background. Framed and matted to an image area of 15″ x 11.5″. In Excellent condition.

HOW BIG IS A 12-FIELD CEL?

PLEASE SEE THE GLOSSARY OF ANIMATION ART TERMS IN THIS CATALOG!

The Art of SpongeBob SquarePants

In its tenth season, SpongeBob SquarePants is the Super Star of Nickelodeon. This series is about a bunch of characters named SpongeBob SquarePants, Patrick, Krabs, Squidward, Sandy and Plankon and their adventures in the underwater city of Bikini Bottom. The Show is Nickelodeon's highest rated show; it has become a media franchise, and is the most distributed property of MTV Networks. It has been nominated for numerous Emmy, Kid Choice, Golden Reel, Annie, and Television Critics Association Awards. It has spawned A feature film, a 2012 Holiday special and again on April 12, 2012, the show celebrated its tenth season. SpongeBob has become a Pop Culture phenomenon.

The series takes place in Bikini Bottom, an underwater city located in the Pacific Ocean beneath the real-life tropical isle of Bikini Atoll . The creator, Stephen Hillenburg, has stated that much of Bikini Bottom was based on his life in the real city of Seattle. The show was originally conceived as far back as 1984 while Mr. Hillenburg was teaching and studying marine biology. It is said that while pitching the show to Nickelodeon executives, Hillenburg donned a Hawaiian shirt, brought along an underwater terrarium with models of the characters and Hawaiian music to set the theme.

Sponge Bob's first season was a modest success during its premier in 1999. It had enough popularity that is was renewed for a second season. It's important to note, that ONLY THE FIRST SEASON USED TRADITIONAL HAND PAINTED CELS. In the second season the show switched over to digital ink and paint. After the success kept rising, and after the third season, a feature film called "The SpongeBob SquarePants Movie was released theatrically.

On July 14, 2009, a Primetime SpongeBob Tenth anniversary documentary titled "Square Roots: The Story of SpongeBob SquarePants" aired on VH1, discussing the history of the show and its impact on popular culture. Then, on July 17th, 2009, Nickelodeon ran a 50½-hour marathon titled, "The Ultimate SpongeBob Sponge Bash". SpongeBob SquarePants surpassed Rugrats as the longest running Nicktoons in number of episodes on April 12, 2012. SpongeBob also has become the first Nicktoon to reach 200 episodes.

Heritage Auctions is proud to have a fine selection of Key Master set ups from the inaugural first season of "SpongeBob SquarePants." The beautiful backgrounds of Bikini Bottom are being sold with their KEY MASTER hand-painted production cels. These one-of-a-kind set-ups represent the beginning of this enormously successful show. This inventory is also rare in that hand-painted cels and hand-painted backgrounds were only used in the first season. All of the characters are well represented in these classic set-ups. Only 41 episodes exist where hand-painted cels and hand-painted backgrounds were used. These rare Key Master and Master set-ups from Season One are one of the first look into what created the SpongeBob phenomenon.

30395 *SpongeBob SquarePants* **First Season "Sandy's Rocket" Production Cel (Nickelodeon, 1999).** This original hand-painted production cel is from the first season of *SpongeBob SquarePants* for the first season "Sandy's Rocket" episode. The 12-field cel is placed over a pan hand-painted key master production background. The background is 19" long and 10" tall! Sponge Bob himself is almost 6" tall. In Excellent condition.

30397 *SpongeBob SquarePants* **"Squidward the Unfriendly Ghost" Production Cel (Nickelodeon, 1999).** An original one-of-a-kind, first season, *SpongeBob SquarePants* hand-painted, 16-field production cel set-up from the "Squidward the Unfriendly Ghost" episode. The large cel is placed on a hand-painted key master production background. Sponge Bob is 2" tall while the impressive background is approximately 13" x 15". In Excellent condition.

30396 *SpongeBob SquarePants* **Production Cel Set-Up (Nickelodeon, 1999).** An original one-of-a-kind hand-painted production cel set-up of Sponge Bob from the first season's "Naughty Nautical Neighbors" episode. The cel has been placed over its original key master hand-painted background. Also a pan overlay cel is over the key master set-up. The pan production background is 17" long and Sponge Bob is 3" tall. A Nickelodeon seal and a Viacom stamp have been added. In Fine Condition.

30398 *SpongeBob SquarePants* **First Season Production Cel Set-Up (Nickelodeon, 1999).** An original first season hand-painted 12-filed production cel set-up of Sponge Bob, placed over a really great original hand-painted production background. Bob is almost 8" tall in all of his over-inflated glory and the background measures 10.5" x 13.5". In Excellent condition.

30399 *SpongeBob SquarePants* **First Season Squidward's House Pan Production Background (Nickelodeon, 1999).** An exquisite original hand-painted *SpongeBob SquarePants* pan production background of the interior of Squidward's Easter Island-head house from the first season episode "I was a Teenage Gary". This huge is background is listed as #164 and is 36" long and 8" high! There have been a few small notches cut from the bottom right edge and there is some tape residue and some slight wear to the the top edge, otherwise in Very Fine condition.

30402 *SpongeBob SquarePants* **"Pickles" Production Cel Set-Up (Nickelodeon, 1999).** This is a pan production cel set-up comprised of 7 different levels! The cel spotlights Sponge Bob, Mr. Krabs, and six friends from the first season episode "Pickles". The pan cels are placed over the key master hand-painted background. A truly great multi-character set-up. The background measures 20" x 10". In Excellent condition.

30400 *SpongeBob SquarePants* **"Sandy's Rocket" Sandy Cheeks First Season Production Cel Set-Up (Nickelodeon, 1999).** This is a hand-painted production cel set-up of Sandy from the "Sandy's Rocket" episode of the first season of *SpongeBob SquarePants*. The cel has been placed on a hand-painted production pan background. The Sandy image is 5" tall, and the great and very detailed background is 25" x 8". A really amazing set-up! In Excellent condition.

30403 *SpongeBob SquarePants* **Sponge Bob and Gary First Season Production Cel Set-Up (Nickelodeon, 1999).** An original first season hand-painted production cel set-up of Sponge Bob and his pet snail Gary, placed over a great first season hand-painted production background. Sponge Bob is about 3" tall and Gary is 1.5" tall. The background measures 10" x 14", and what a background it is! In Excellent condition.

30401 *Ren and Stimpy* **Publicity Cel (Nickelodeon, 1991).** An outstanding 16-field hand-painted cel of Ren, Stimpy, Muddy Mudskipper, Mr. Horse, and Powdered Toast Man on a stylized hand-painted background. Signed near the lower right corner M. Kazagle. Created for use in print advertising. Very Rare, and in Excellent condition.

30404 *SpongeBob SquarePants* **"Jelly Fish Jam" First Season Production Cel Set-Up (Nickelodeon, 1999).** A 12-field hand-painted production cel set-up of SpongeBob SquarePants and the jelly fish from the episode "Jelly Fish Jam." The cel is placed over its original key master hand-painted background. Sponge Bob is approximately 4" long, while the background measures 12" x 10". Some very light ink loss on a few of the black lines on Sponge Bob. In Excellent condition.

30406 *The Gerald McBoing-Boing Show* **Quasi Moto Production Cel (UPA, 1956).** Cels from this show are extremely rare, and this one's on an original UPA matte! From the cartoon "The 51st Dragon" that aired on CBS' Gerald McBoing-Boing Show. Matted to an image area of 10.5" by 7.5". Very Good condition.

30407 *The Gerald McBoing-Boing Show* **Quasi Moto Production Cel (UPA, 1956).** From the cartoon "The 51st Dragon" that aired on CBS' Gerald McBoing-Boing Show. 16-field cel, matted to an image area of 10.25" by 9.5". Excellent condition.

30405 *Gerald McBoing-Boing* **Production Cel Group (UPA, 1950s).** A highly stylized police officer from the 1956 cartoon, *Gerald McBoing-Boing on the Planet Moo*, on a cel with an approximate image area of 2.5" x 4.5"; stapled to a piece of light blue paper bearing the UPA Studio logo in the lower right corner. A synopsis of the original cartoon short is included. Also included is Gerald McBoing-Boing cel from an unidentified cartoon, with an image area of approximately 3.5" x 4.5", attached to a 3-peghole paper, marked "g 011" in the lower corner, and faintly marked with the UPA Studio logo. The paper has been inscribed, "To Mary Lloyd From Gerald Mc Boing-Boing" in graphite. Both pieces in Excellent condition

30408 *Roger Ramjet* **Publicity Cel (Pantomime Pictures/Hero Entertainment, 1965).** Good guys wear white! This cel is signed "Crip" for Fred Crippen, and is consigned to us from the collection of that ace director. Matted to an image area of 9.5" x 7.5". Excellent condition.

30409 Fred Crippen *Roger Ramjet* Scroll Background Production Drawing (Pantomime Pictures/Hero Entertainment, 1965). One of the funniest cartoon series from the 1960s was *Roger Ramjet*, who, with his pint-sized crew, the American Eagles, kept the world safe from bad guys like Noodles Romanoff, Red Dog the Pirate, and Tequila Mockingbird. Each cartoon opened with a theme sung by children that went, "Roger Ramjet, he's our man, hero of our nation; for his adventures just be sure to stay tuned to this station!". This long scroll introduced the crew's intent with an impossibly long list of attributes, drawn on paper affixed to a light blue painted pan background on nine-peghole board, measuring approximately 39" x 4.5". A few elements of the trimmed paper are missing, and some of the lettering (done in colored marker) have faded; the board itself has numerous tack holes, and is in overall Good condition. Consigned to our auction by Fred Crippen, himself. Extremely rare!

30410 *Roger Ramjet* Publicity Cel (Pantomime Pictures/Hero Entertainment, 1965). It would be downright unpatriotic not to love this piece! The show's director Fred Crippen is parting with this one which has been in his personal collection all along. It's nicely framed and matted to an image area of 12" by 9.5". Excellent condition.

30411 *B.C.* "Monroe Safety Tip" Production Cel Progression (1980s). A rare hand-painted progression of four cels on a hand-painted key cel background, featuring Thor from the comic strip by Johnny Hart, used in an animated television ad directed by Fred Crippen for Monroe Shock Absorbers. Signed by Crippen, and consigned to our auction by the director, himself. In Excellent condition.

30412 *Casper the Friendly Ghost* **"Casper and Alice in Wonderland" Unused Production Drawing Group (Famous Studios, 1950s).** A group of 15 pages of original concept art for an unproduced animated short that would have featured Casper encountering Alice in Wonderland. In Fine condition.

30413 *Gulliver's Travels* **Gulliver Production Drawing (Max Fleischer, 1939).** Original one-of-a-kind pan layout drawing of Gulliver walking through Lilliput (sc*/Seq 9), with some amazing detail. In graphite with many color highlights. One of the finest pieces of concept artwork from Paramount Studios' first animated feature film. The drawing, showing two images of Gulliver in the town, is an amazing 30" of artwork, while the pan paper measures 38" long. Mounted on board, which folds in the middle. In Very Good condition.

30414 Winsor McCay *Gertie the Dinosaur* Production Drawing (1914). Drawing #238 from the pioneering animation that is considered the first cartoon to really catch the public's imagination and give birth to the industry. McCay famously drew each scene complete on paper, before the use of acetate cels and separate background art. This is the scene where Gertie picks up a huge bolder in her jaws, which she proceeds to eat. The image area measures approximately 8" x 6", drawn on thin paper affixed to a piece of illustration board. Other than a few tiny stains, the art is in Excellent condition.

30415 Groucho Marx *You Bet Your Life* Title Production Cel Group (c. late 1950s). The secret word is "bid!" Here are six production cels, two featuring Groucho (his car is a pasted-on stat), one depicting his straight man George Fenneman, two have title elements and one depicts an unidentified gal. Very Good condition. Four out of five Dr. Hackenbushes recommend this lot!

30416 *The Yellow Submarine* **Production Cel Set-Up (United Artists/ King Features, 1968).** An original hand-painted three-production cel set-up featuring John Lennon as Frankenstein, Jeremy the Boob (The Nowhere Man), and Fred. The cels are framed with spacing between each cel to create an impressive 3-D effect. Jeremy is 1″, Fred is approximately 3″, and John measures 7″ x 9″! Accompanied by the original Letter of Authenticity with gold seal. One of the best John Lennon-as-Frankenstein images we have seen! In Excellent condition, with an overall size of 21″ x 18″.

30418 *The Yellow Submarine* **Production Cel Set-Up (United Artists/ King Features, 1968).** Original hand-painted three-production-cel set-up featuring John Lennon, Jeremy the Boob (The Nowhere Man), and a large lurking Chief Blue Meanie. The three cels are spaced out in an impressive 21″ x 18″ framed set-up to add a 3-D effect. John is a 6″ full figure, Jeremy is almost 2″, and the Chief Blue Meanie is 9″ x 5″. Accompanied by the original certificate of authenticity with gold foil seal. An impressive piece. In Excellent condition.

30417 *The Yellow Submarine* **Animation Cel Set-Up (United Artists/ King Features, 1968).** One-of-a-kind hand-painted four (4) production cel set-up of Ringo (3) and the Chief Blue Meanie. The four cels are framed with spacing between each to give an impressive 3-D effect. The three Ringos range in size from 2″, 4″, and 5″; and the Blue Meanie is an impressive 7″ x 11″. The original letter of of authenticity with gold seal included. In Excellent condition, with an overall size of 21″ x 18″.

30419 *The Yellow Submarine* **Animation Cel Set-Up (United Artists/ King Features, 1968).** Original hand-painted four (4) production cel set-up of Ringo in his Sergeant Pepper outfit falling, John in his Sergeant Pepper outfit running, long torsos of Apple Bonkers, and a cel of some of the secondary characters. The cels are framed with spacing between each cel to create a 3-D effect. Ringo is 4″, John is 2″, the Apple Bonkers torsos are 8″, and the secondary characters are 5.5″. The original letter of authenticity with a gold foil seal is included. In Excellent condition with an overall frame size of 21″ x 18″.

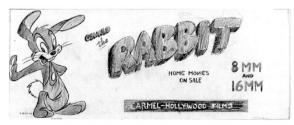

30420 **Oswald Rabbit Production Drawing (Walter Lantz, 1940s).** Rare original artwork for an Oswald the Rabbit promo banner for a series of 8mm and 16mm home movies. Approximately 25″ x 10″ and in Very Good condition.

30421   Dr. Seuss *The Cat in the Hat* Sketch (undated). Original hand-drawn and signed sketch of the Cat in the Hat by Doctor Seuss, with the inscription "Best Wishes! One fish, two fish, three fish. Doctor Seuss". Mixed media on 11" x 11" drawing paper. In Excellent condition.

30422   Lew Keller *Rocky and Bullwinkle* Layout Drawing Group (Jay Ward, 1960s). Rocky and Bullwinkle honor each other in this fun drawing by Lew Keller, renowned artist for the groundbreaking animated television show. The drawing's 13" x 7.5" and in Excellent condition.

30423   *Fractured Fairytales* "Ugly Duckling" Production Cel (Jay Ward, 1960). Extremely rare hand-painted production cel of the Ugly Duckling from the Jay Ward *Fractured Fairytales* series, originally run on December 11, 1960, on *Rocky and His Friends*. The production cel is still in its original Jay Ward Productions mat. Small production background painting beneath the cel set-up. Some discoloration to the mat, but the art itself is in Excellent condition.

30424   Lew Keller *Tom Slick* **Opening Credits Sequence Storyboard Original Art Group (Jay Ward, 1967).** Freckled, All-American racecar driver Tom Slick was a six-minute feature within episodes of the ABC-TV animated series *George of the Jungle*. Tom is seen here revving up his car, the Thunderbolt Grease-Slapper, as girlfriend Marigold and mechanic Gertie Growler look on with pride. A total of six ink and grey wash panels of Lew Keller artwork on two sheets of Jay Ward Storyboard paper measuring 14" x 8.5". Most of the panels are taped on; the bottom row of three panels from the first page are in one taped-on strip. Overall Very Good condition.

30425   *Super Chicken* Publicity Cel and Background (Jay Ward, 1973). An original hand-painted Jay Ward Publicity cel of the wildest superhero ever, Super Chicken, housed in a Jay Ward Studios mat signed by Studio main man Bill Scott. Bill wrote on the cel, "You knew the job was dangerous when you took it, Not! Super Chicken Bill Scott." On the reverse is a letter on Jay Ward stationery, signed by Jay himself, giving permission to hang this piece in a movie project. The image area measures 9" x 7", and the original Jay Ward mat is 13" x 10"; an additional mat brings the overall size to 20" x 16". Both mats display some aging, but the cel and background remain in Excellent condition. Quick Fred, the Super Sauce! *Cluck AWK!!*

END OF SESSION ONE

MORE JAY WARD

TREASURES IN SESSION 2

SESSION TWO

Heritage Live!®, Internet, Fax, and Mail Only Session
Saturday, February 23, 2013 | 3:00PM CT | Dallas, Texas | Lots 31001 - 31278

A 19.5% Buyer's Premium ($14 minimum) Will Be Added To All Lots
To view full descriptions, enlargeable images and bid online, visit HA.com/7052

SPECIAL INTERNET BIDDING FEATURE

Online proxy bidding ends at HA.com two hours prior to the opening of the live auction. Check the Time Remaining on individual lots for details. After Internet proxy bidding closes, live bidding will take place through HERITAGE Live!®, our bidding software that lets you bid live during the actual auction. Your secret maximum will compete against those bids, and win all ties. To maximize your chances of winning, enter realistic secret maximum bids before live bidding begins. (Important note: Due to software and Internet latency, bids placed through Live Internet Bidding may not register in time and those bidders could lose lots they would otherwise have won, so be sure to place your proxy bids in advance.)

WALT DISNEY STUDIOS

31001 Woolie Reitherman Going Away Drawing for Joe Magro (Walt Disney, 1937). Special "going away" drawing for animator Joe Magro by famed Disney animator and Nine Old Man, Wolfgang "Woolie" Reitherman. Magro worked in Reitherman's animation unit at Disney. Graphite and colored pencil on 12-field 5-peghole (10" x 12"). Some paper aging and light soiling; otherwise the art is in Very Good condition. Signed by the artist at the lower right. *From the Joe Magro Collection.*

31002 Bob Wickersham Going Away Drawing for Joe Magro (Walt Disney, 1937). Hilarious and sexy "going away" drawing for animator Joe Magro drawn by Disney animator, Bob Wickersham. Mixed media on 12-field 5-peghole (12" x 10"). Some paper aging and light soiling; otherwise the art is in Very Good condition. Signed and inscribed by the artist at the lower right. *From the Joe Magro Collection.*

31003 Ward Kimball Going Away Drawing for Joe Magro (Walt Disney, 1937). Caption reads: "East Brooklyn on a ramp." This "going away" drawing for animator Joe Magro was drawn by Disney animator, Ward Kimball. Mixed media on 12-field 5-peghole (10" x 12"). Some paper aging and light soiling; otherwise the art is in Very Good condition. Signed and inscribed by the artist at the lower right. *From the Joe Magro Collection.*

31004 Clyde Geronimo Going Away Drawing for Joe Magro (Walt Disney, 1937). Viva Italia! This "going away" drawing for animator Joe Magro was drawn by Disney director/writer, Clyde Geronimo. Mixed media on 12-field 5-peghole (10" x 12"). Some paper aging and light soiling; otherwise the art is in Very Good condition. Signed and inscribed by the artist at the right. *From the Joe Magro Collection.*

31005 Dick Lundy Going Away Drawing for Joe Magro (Walt Disney, 1937). Caption reads: "Now lissen you eastern hombres. I'm Butch Magro of the West!?" This "going away" drawing for animator Joe Magro was drawn by Disney animator/director, Dick Lundy. Mixed media on 12-field 5-peghole (10" x 12"). Some paper aging and light soiling; otherwise the art is in Very Good condition. Signed and inscribed by the artist at the lower right. *From the Joe Magro Collection.*

31006 Mickey Mouse Production Drawing (Walt Disney, 1929/30). An early, 2-peghole Walt Disney Studios drawing of Mickey Mouse. In Very Good, almost Excellent condition.

31007 Mickey Mouse Production Drawing Group (Walt Disney, 1930s). Two lively drawings of the Main Mouse from the 1930s (OPDs #24 and 44A). Each drawing was rendered in graphite and red pencil on a 12" x 10" sheet of animation paper. There is some light paper aging and wear; otherwise, the art averages Very Good condition.

31008 Les Clark (attributed) Mickey Mouse Preliminary Publicity Drawing (Walt Disney, c. 1930). Graphite on 2-peghole animation paper of Mickey Mouse. A similar piece was shown in a Christie's 1997 Animation Art catalog, lot 172, as "two model drawings for publicity" from the private collection of Les Clarke. We believe this is the second piece from that lot. Image area measures approximately 8" x 9". At one time folded, with some penciled writing on the back; Very Good condition.

31009 *The Steeple Chase* Production Drawing (Walt Disney, 1933). Original Walt Disney Studio animation drawing of Mickey Mouse from this short, directed by Burt Gillett. Graphite on 12-field 2-peghole animation paper (12" x 9.5"). Some light paper aging and soiling; otherwise the art is in Very Good condition.

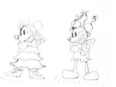

31010 *Birds in the Spring* Production Drawing (Walt Disney, 1933). Production drawing filled with dozens of fine feathered characters, drawn on 2-peghole animation paper. The bottom of the page is numbered "6". The art is in graphite and colored pencil, with an approximate image area of 10.5" x 9". Handling wear and tanning to the paper; overall Very Good condition.

31011 *Mickey's Mellerdrammer* Mickey and Minnie Mouse Production Drawing (Walt Disney, 1933). An original 12-field 2-peghole animation paper drawing of Mickey and Minnie Mouse from the Wilfred Jackson directed 1933 theatrical short *Mickey's Mellerdrammer*. In the story Mickey and Minnie are appearing in a version of "Uncle Tom's Cabin". A great dual image done in graphite. Each figure's image is approximately 3.5" high. Beautifully framed to an overall size of 15.75" x 17.75", with an image area of 6.75" x 9".

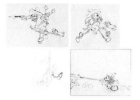

31012 Mickey Mouse *Two-Gun Mickey* Animation Production Drawing Group (Walt Disney, 1934). Mickey, Minnie and Black Pete are featured in this set of four original production drawings from this 1934 Mickey Mouse short. Graphite and red pencil on 2-peghole animation paper, measuring 12" x 9.5". In Very Good condition.

31013 *Peculiar Penguins* Production Drawing Group of Five (Walt Disney, 1934). Set of five rough animation drawings of Polly and Peter from the 1934 Silly Symphony, *Peculiar Penguins*. Graphite on 12" x 10" 5-peghole animation paper. Some paper aging, and light soiling; otherwise the art averages Very Good condition. *From the Joe Magro Collection.*

31014 *The Grasshopper and the Ant* Storyboard Drawing (Walt Disney, 1934). The Queen Ant gives out a proclamation in this Disney Studios storyboard drawing. The art is in graphite and red pencil, with an image area of 5.5" x 4", and is noted as #19. The paper is light brown, and shows considerable tanning; otherwise the art is in Excellent condition.

31015 *The Grasshopper and the Ant* Storyboard (Walt Disney, 1934). The grasshopper feels the cold winter wind blow, in this storyboard drawing for the Disney cartoon classic. The art is in graphite and red pencil on brown paper, noted as #30 in the lower margin. The image area measures approximately 7.25" x 5.5". The paper shows signs of considerable tanning, but the image remains in Excellent condition.

31016 *The Big Bad Wolf* Production Drawing (Walt Disney, 1934). Original layout drawing of the Big Bad Wolf while he is chasing Little Red Riding Hood, on 12-field 2-peghole animation paper. Image is 8" x 6". From the Walt Disney Studio theatrical short directed by Bert Gillett, matted with original Sotheby's sticker.

31017 *Mickey's Service Station* Peg-Leg Pete Production Drawing (Walt Disney, 1935). An outstanding Walt Disney Studios animation drawing (with effects) of Peg-Leg Pete from the theatrical short film. In Excellent condition.

31018 *Mickey's Man Friday* Production Drawing (Walt Disney, 1935). Production drawing featuring Mickey from the 1935 short, *Mickey's Man Friday*. Rendered in graphite and red pencil on a 12" x 10" sheet of animation paper. The paper has some aging; otherwise the art is in Excellent condition.

31019 *Mickey's Circus "Ringmaster"* Production Drawing (Walt Disney, 1936). What a facial expression, as good as they get! It's Mickey Mouse as the Circus Big Top Ringmaster from the 1936 theatrical short that also starred Donald Duck and Pluto. On 12-field 5-peghole animation paper, graphite pencil with red and green highlights. "#71" written in the bottom right corner. Image area measures approximately 4.75" x 3.5". Excellent condition.

31020 Preston Blair *Mickey's Rival* Mortimer Mouse Production Drawing (Walt Disney, 1936). An animation drawing of Mortimer Mouse by Preston Blair, signed by the artist on the acetate. According to Disney Studio legend, Mickey Mouse's original name was Mortimer Mouse but Mrs. Disney talked Walt into using the name "Mickey" instead. A character named Mortimer Mouse made one appearance, in the 1936 cartoon "Mickey's Rival". He humiliated Mickey up to a point and was a star in Minnie's eyes — he was her ex-boyfriend — until Mickey made a comeback and won Minnie back. The drawing and the acetate have been matted to 12" x 16", and background information about the cartoon is attached to the reverse.

31021 *Mickey's Rival* Production Drawing (Walt Disney, 1936). The new rival for Minnie's affections, Mortimer, from the Disney short, *Mickey's Rival*. Rendered in graphite and red pencil on a 12" x 10" sheet of animation paper (OPD #13). The paper has some aging and light surface wear; otherwise the art is in Very Good condition.

31022 *Mickey's Rival* Mickey and Minnie Mouse Production Drawing (Walt Disney, 1936). Mickey and Minnie from the Disney short, *Mickey's Rival*. Rendered in graphite on a 12" x 10" sheet of animation paper. The paper has some aging and light surface wear; otherwise the art is in Very Good condition.

31023 *The Country Cousin* Production Drawing Group (Walt Disney, 1936). Here are five drawings of cousin Abner as he tastes mustard, from the Disney short, *The Country Cousin* (OPDs #7, 23, 27, 43, and 55). Each drawing is rendered in graphite on a 12" x 10" sheet of animation paper. The drawings have a bit of aging and some light edge wear; otherwise they are in Very Good condition. *From the Joe Magro Collection.*

31024 Disney Model Sheet Group (Walt Disney, 1936-37). Set of ten Walt Disney Studio printed animator's model sheets from shorts including *Mickey's Car*, *Three Little Wolves*, *Don Donald*, *Orphan's Picnic*, *Peculiar Penguins*, *Clock Cleaners*, *Two-Gun Mickey*, *Mickey's Rival*, and *Moving Day*. Also includes a model sheet of Donald Duck and one of Pluto. Each sheet measures approximately 12" x 11". Paper aging, edge wear and soiling; otherwise the work averages Good condition. *From the Joe Magro Collection.*

31025 *Snow White and the Seven Dwarfs* Prince Charming Production Drawing (Walt Disney, 1937). Prince Charming leans over to kiss Snow White in this handsome production drawing from Disney's premiere animated feature (OPD #49). Rendered in graphite and red pencil on a 12-field sheet of animation paper (12" x 10", matted to an image area of 11" x 8.5"). Includes color notations for the cel inkers. Aside from some light paper aging, the art is in Very Good condition.

31026 *Don Donald* Donald Duck Production Drawing Group (Walt Disney, 1937). Two animation drawings of Donald Duck from his first starring-role short, *Don Donald*. Graphite on 12" x 10" 5-peghole animation paper. Some paper aging, edge wear, and light soiling; otherwise the art averages Good condition. *From the Joe Magro Collection.*

31027 *Hawaiian Holiday* Goofy Production Drawings (Walt Disney, 1937). An outstanding set of 15 animation "ruffs" of a hot-doggin' Goofy from the 1937 theatrical short, *Hawaiian Holiday*, from which the surf-/skate-/snowboarding term "goofy footed" originated. In Fine condition. *From the Joe Magro Collection.*

31028 *Clock Cleaners* Goofy Production Drawing (Walt Disney, 1937). Original production drawing of Goofy from the short, *Clock Cleaners* (OPD #129). This 12" x 10" drawing was rendered in graphite, and it is in Very Good condition. *From the Joe Magro Collection.*

31029 *The Worm Turns* Pegleg Pete Production Drawing Group (Walt Disney, 1937). Series of three drawings of dogcatcher Pegleg Pete, from the 1937 Disney short, *The Worm Turns*. Graphite and colored pencil on 12" x 10" 5-peghole animation paper. Some paper aging, edge wear, pinholes and creasing; otherwise the art averages Good condition. *From the Joe Magro Collection.*

31030 *The Worm Turns* Production Drawing Group (Walt Disney, 1937). Series of three rough animation drawings of dogcatcher Pegleg Pete, from the 1937 Disney short, *The Worm Turns*. Graphite on 12" x 10" 5-peghole animation paper (#373, 379, and 387). Some paper aging, edge wear, pinholes, creasing, and water damage at the lower right; otherwise the art averages Good condition. *From the Joe Magro Collection.*

31031 *Magician Mickey* Mickey Mouse Production Drawing Group (Walt Disney, 1937). An outstanding group of 33 rough animation drawings of Mickey from the classic short. In Excellent condition.

31032 *Lonesome Ghosts* Goofy Background Layout Production Drawing (Walt Disney, 1937). Background layout drawing featuring Goofy from the classic theatrical short. In Excellent condition.

31033 *Little Hiawatha* Production Drawing (Walt Disney, 1937). Adorable full figure with bow and arrow. From the theatrical short directed by Dave Hand. Graphite pencil with red and green highlights. "#67" in right corner. Image area measures approximately 6" x 7.5". Excellent condition.

31034 *Woodland Cafe* Production Drawing (Walt Disney, 1937). It's a "bump and grind" night on the dance floor for these happy insects! This Disney Studios production drawing is unusually heavy on notes to inkers, but the figures in the drawing are first rate. The image area has an approximate size of 10" x 4.5", not counting the handwritten instructions. On 5-peghole animation paper; in Excellent condition.

31035 *Brave Little Tailor* **Giant Concept Drawing Group (Walt Disney, 1938).** In 1939, the Mickey short *Brave Little Tailor* was nominated for an Academy Award for Best Animated Short Film, but lost to Disney's own *Ferdinand the Bull*. Each of these two concept drawings were rendered in graphite on a 12-field sheet of animation paper. Some paper aging, pin holes, and light soiling; otherwise the art averages Very Good condition.

31036 *Mother Goose Goes Hollywood* **Storyboards (Walt Disney, 1938).** Outstanding pair of Walt Disney Studio hand colored storyboards of Eddie Cantor as Little Jack Horner and Cab Calloway (who breaks into a portion of "Minnie the Moocher" in this scene) from the 1938 short directed by Wilfred Jackson. Possibly the work of Tee Hee. The storyboards measure 5" x 7" and are in Very Good condition with pin holes in the corners.

31037 *Mother Goose Goes Hollywood* **Production Drawing Group (Walt Disney, 1938).** Cab Calloway sings "Hi-de-Ho!" in this set of two original production drawings from the Little Jack Horner sequence of *Mother Goose Goes Hollywood*. Each drawing is rendered in graphite, and red pencil on a 12-field sheet of animation paper (12" x 10"). Some paper aging and light creasing; otherwise, the drawings are in Very Good condition.

31038 *The Practical Pig* **Big Bad Wolf Production Drawing (Walt Disney, 1939).** This theatrical short, directed by Dick Richard, was the sequel to "Three Little Pigs." Outstanding drawing on 12-field 5-peghole animation paper, with "39" written in the right bottom corner. Graphite pencil with red highlights. Image area is approximately 6.5" x 5". Very Good condition.

31039 *Society Dog Show* **Production Drawing (Walt Disney, 1939).** Mickey gets Pluto primed for a ritzy dog show, in this fabulous production drawing. Drawn in graphite and red pencil on a 12" x 10" sheet of animation paper. The art has a bit of aging, and very slight water damage at the left; otherwise the condition is Very Good.

31040 Pluto Production Drawing (Walt Disney, 1940s). Expressive production drawing of Mickey's best friend with animator notes. Measures 15.5" x 12.5". There is paper tanning, a vertical crease in the center, and edge wear; otherwise the work is in Good condition.

31041 *Mr. Mouse Takes a Trip* **Background Production Drawing (Walt Disney, 1940).** Original background layout drawing for the 1940 theatrical short, in Very Good condition.

31042 *Pinocchio* **Production Drawing (Walt Disney, 1940).** A rare Walt Disney Studios rough animation drawing on Pinocchio turning into a real boy, for the classic 1940 animated feature. In Excellent condition.

31043 Shamus Culhane *Pinocchio* **Foulfellow Rough Drawing (Walt Disney, 1940).** A delightful drawing! J. Worthington Foulfellow (Honest John) is shown smoking a cigar. Signed by animator Shamus Culhane. Graphite pencil on 12 filed 5-peghole animation paper. "#100" written in bottom right corner. Image area measures approximately 6.5" x 6.5". Excellent condition.

31044 *The Riveter* **Peg-Leg Pete Production Drawings (Walt Disney, 1940).** Set of three animation drawings (numbered 48, 64, and 73) of Pete from the 1940 animated short. In Excellent condition.

31045 *The Riveter* **Peg-Leg Pete Model Sheet (Walt Disney, 1940).** Original layout drawing of the character for the 1940 theatrical short featuring Donald Duck. In Very Good condition.

31046 *The Nifty Nineties* **Animation Production Drawing Group (Walt Disney, 1941).** This set of two original animation drawings features two song and dance men, "Fred & Ward, Two Clever Boys from Illinois" (caricatures of animators Fred Moore and Ward Kimball who also voiced the characters). Each drawing was rendered in graphite and multi-colored pencil on a 12" x 10" sheet of animation paper. There is some light paper aging and wear; otherwise, the art averages Very Good condition.

31047 Ward Kimball *Dumbo* **Storyboard Art (Walt Disney, 1941).** Original Walt Disney's Studio storyboard drawing of Dumbo for the classic animated feature, signed by Oscar-winning animator Ward Kimball along the top edge. Kimball was one of the studio's legendary "Nine Old Men", and is credited with creating a number of classic characters. Graphite and red pencil on paper, with an image area of approximately 5" x 5". In Excellent condition.

HIGH-RES IMAGES OF EVERY LOT CAN BE VIEWED AT HA.COM/7052

31048 *The Reluctant Dragon* "How to Ride a Horse" Goofy Production Cel (Walt Disney, 1941). Original hand-inked and hand-painted production cel of Goofy and Percy from the "How to Ride a Horse" segment of the 1941 package feature, laminated and placed over a specially prepared background. The cel is in its original mat and 18.5" x 15.5" frame, with the mat featuring a caption that reads "For the Beginner, May we Suggest — 'How to Ride a Horse' Sequence from Walt Disney's 'Reluctant Dragon'". The image of Goofy measures 5" x 4", and Percy is 5" x 4". The paint on Goofy is in Fine condition; there is slight cracking in a few areas of Percy, but no paint loss. the mat is dirty as there is no glass, but everything is original. Originally sold by the Albert Roullier Art Gallery in Chicago, with the original paperwork mounted on the reverse.

31049 *The Village Smithy* Donald Duck Production Drawing (Walt Disney, 1942). Outstanding rough animation drawing of Donald Duck for the 1942 theatrical short. In Excellent condition.

31050 Hank Porter "Big Bad Wolf" WWII Insignia Preliminary Illustration (Walt Disney, c. 1942). This little wolf intends to do some cleaning up! One of Hank Porter's wonderful military insignia designs used as "nose art" on World War II bomber planes. In graphite and blue pencil on tracing paper, with an approximate image area of 5.5" x 8". Other than a small crease touching the top of the Wolf's hat, in Excellent condition.

31051 Hank Porter "Sailor Mickey" WWII Insignia Preliminary Illustration (Walt Disney, c. 1942). Mickey is coming up with a brilliant idea on how to fight the enemy! This is one of Hank Porter's clever military insignia designs used as "nose art" on World War II bomber planes. In graphite and blue pencil on tracing paper, with an approximate image area of 4.5" x 7". Some outer art area was clipped off; otherwise in Excellent condition.

31052 Hank Porter "Beach Head Figaro" WWII Insignia Preliminary Illustration (Walt Disney, c. 1942). This cat isn't afraid of getting wet for the cause! A delightful military insignia design by Hank Porter, used as "nose art" on World War II bomber planes. In graphite and blue pencil on tracing paper, with an approximate image area of 7" X 7". In Excellent condition.

31053 Hank Porter "Bombs Away Thumper" WWII Insignia Preliminary Illustration (Walt Disney, c. 1942). Look out below — Thumper just let loose a blockbuster! A brilliant and wonderful Disney-themed military insignia design from Hank Porter, used as "nose art" on World War II bomber planes. In graphite and colored pencil on tracing paper, with an approximate image area of 7" x 10.75". In Excellent condition.

31054 Hank Porter "Flintlock Donald" WWII Insignia Preliminary Illustration (Walt Disney, c. 1942). Donald pitches in to fight "the good fight" in this inspiring Hank Porter military insignia design, used as "nose art" on World War II bomber planes. In graphite and red pencil on tracing paper, with an approximate image area of 6" x 8.5". In Excellent condition.

31055 Bill Justice *Gremlins* First Edition Book Signed Painted Sketch (Random House, 1943). Painting is across from the half title of the book. Book has significant wear and is in Good condition.

31056 *Victory Through Airpower* Opening Credit Production Drawing (Walt Disney, 1943) The penciled title art that opened one of Disney's patriotic WWII cartoons, this tightly penciled "Walt Disney Presents" art should appeal to any Disney animation fan. The art has a total image area of 10.5" x 8", and is on 5-peghole animation paper, with the number "2" in the far lower right corner. In Excellent condition.

31057 *Hockey Homicide* Animation Production Drawing Group (Walt Disney, 1945). Set of six exuberant rough original animation drawings of Goofy from this hockey satire short, *Hockey Homicide*. Each drawing was rendered in graphite and blue pencil on a 12" x 10" sheet of animation paper. There is some light paper aging and wear; otherwise, the art averages Very Good condition.

31058 *Make Mine Music* Peter and the Wolf Character Model Sheet (Walt Disney, 1946). Outstanding model sheet of the Wolf from the "Peter and the Wolf" segment of *Make Mine Music*. Fine images of the wolf, printed on 13" x 10" photographic paper. In Excellent condition.

31059 *Make Mine Music* Casey at the Bat Production Cel (Walt Disney, 1946). An original hand-painted production cel of the team manager for the "Casey at the Bat" segment of the 1946 package film, with a printed background. In Excellent condition.

31060 *Fun and Fancy Free* **Lulubelle Production Cel (Walt Disney, 1947).** Sweet hand-inked and hand-painted cel featuring Bongo the bear's love interest, Lulubelle. The cel measures 10" x 10". There is some slight ink loss and soiling; otherwise the art is in Very Good condition.

31061 Goofy Production Cel Animation Art (Walt Disney, 1960s). Hand-inked and hand-painted cel matted to an image area of 4.5" x 6.5". In Very Good condition.

31062 *Pluto's Sweater* **Minnie Mouse Production Drawing (Walt Disney, 1949).** Original graphite and red pencil 12-field animation production drawing, with a 5" x 3" image area. Matted and framed with glass to an overall 17.25" x 14.25" size. Excellent condition.

31063 Jiminy Cricket *Mickey Mouse Club* **Production Drawing (Walt Disney, 1950s).** An outstanding 16-field drawing of Jiminy Cricket from the Mickey Mouse Club segment "I'm No Fool", in Excellent condition.

31064 *I'm No Fool* **Mickey Mouse Club Jiminy Cricket Production Drawing and Model Sheet Group (Walt Disney, 1950s).** A series of three animation drawings and two model sheets of Jiminy Cricket from the Mickey Mouse Club short *I'm No Fool*. In Excellent condition.

31065 *Lucky Strike* **Advertising Illustration Original Art (Walt Disney, c. 1950).** Rare example of advertising art by the Disney Studio for Lucky Strike cigarettes. The art is rendered in gouache and collage (the pack of cigarettes is printed, trimmed and collaged with the art), with an image area of 7.5" x 6.5". In Excellent condition.

31066 "Pre-Flight Checklist" Production Background (Disneyland TV Show, 1957). From a "How To Relax" Disneyland television feature aired on November 27, 1957, marked "Prod. 5701 Seq. II B.G. sc 5 2". Measures 14.5" by 13". Very Good condition. The copy says "before takeoff... make out will." Gulp! Remember, you don't have to fly to New York for the auction, you can bid online too!

31067 Fred Moore (attributed) *Peter Pan* **Mermaids Production Drawing Group (Walt Disney, 1953).** Two animator's model sheet drawings of Peter Pan's lovely mermaid friends. Rendered in graphite and red pencil on 16-field animation paper. Some paper aging, edge wear and a vertical fold in the center of the solo mermaid drawing; otherwise the work averages Very Good condition.

31068 *Peter Pan* **Wendy Production Cel (Walt Disney, 1953).** Original 16-field hand-inked and hand-painted production cel of Wendy from the 1953 Disney feature, placed over a complimentary print background. Wendy measures 5", and "c 131" is printed in the corner. Paint is in Fine condition.

31069 *Peter Pan* **Tiger Lily Production Cel (Walt Disney, 1953).** Original 16-field hand-inked and hand-painted production cel of Tiger Lily (#146) placed over a complimentary print background. Tiger Lily is a nice large image of 8". Slight lifting of very small section of black paint in hair; the balance is Fine.

31070 *Grin and Bear It* **Ranger Production Cel (Walt Disney, 1954).** The Ranger's first screen appearance was in this Jack Hannah-directed theatrical short. A 12-field cel with "#19" written in the right corner. Paint is fine. Image is almost 6" tall. Excellent condition.

31071 *Bearly Asleep* **Humphrey the Bear Production Cel Animation Art (Walt Disney, 1955).** Hilarious hand-inked and hand-painted cel featuring Humphrey from the Donald Duck short, *Bearly Asleep*. Measures 16" x 12.5". In Excellent condition.

31072 *Hooked Bear* **Humphrey the Bear Production Cel (Walt Disney, 1956).** This one comes from the Art Corner that operated in the early years of Disneyland, and has the store's seal on the back. The piece is 12" x 9", with an image area of 9.5" x 5.5". There's a wee bit of paint loss at far right, otherwise the art is in Very Good condition.

31073 *Sleeping Beauty* **Production Drawing (Walt Disney, 1959).** Simply beautiful portrait of Princess Aurora as Briar Rose. This Walt Disney Studio animation drawing was rendered in graphite on 16-field animation paper. "#27" written at the bottom and top right corners. Aside from some light paper aging, it is in Very Good condition.

31074 *Sleeping Beauty* **Production Drawing Group (Walt Disney, 1959).** Three lovely full figure drawings of the three fairies — Fauna, Flora and Merryweather. Graphite with red highlights on 16-field animation paper. The numbers #157, 132, and 216 are written in the respective bottom corners. Aside from some light paper aging, the art averages Very Good condition.

31077 *Sleeping Beauty* **Briar Rose Production Drawing (Walt Disney, 1959).** Original one-of-a-kind 16-field Walt Disney Studio animation drawing of Briar Rose. A heartfelt animation drawing, with a great pose. Graphite "#83" written in the corner of the image, which measures 8" x 4". In Excellent condition.

31081 *Sleeping Beauty* **Drunken Lackey Production Drawing Group (Walt Disney, 1959).** Pair of original 16-field animation rough drawings of the drunken Lackey getting drunk! Beautiful pair of drawings in graphite with red highlights (#98/107) with the image measuring 8" tall. A classic Disney secondary character for the 1959 feature film.

31079 *Sleeping Beauty* **Briar Rose and Prince Phillip Production Drawing Group (Walt Disney, 1959).** Unique matched set of Walt Disney Studio 16-field animation drawings of Briar Rose with Prince Phillip. Both drawings are #195. Graphite on paper, with Briar Rose measuring 6" and Prince Phillip measuring 7". Written above Briar Rose is the handwritten dialogue notation "tongue shows THAT". A beautiful pair of Disney animation drawings showcasing the start of their courtship. In Excellent condition.

31075 *Sleeping Beauty* **Production Drawing (Walt Disney, 1959).** A beautiful animation rough of the sinister Maleficent, rendered in graphite on 16-field animation paper. The image area is approximately 9" x 10". "#177" has been written in the bottom right hand corner. Aside from some light paper aging, light soiling, and some edge wear, the art is in Very Good condition.

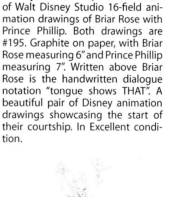

31082 *Sleeping Beauty* **Briar Rose Production Drawing (Walt Disney, 1959).** Rare, original 12-field Walt Disney Studio animation drawing (12" x 10") of Briar Rose, from the classic 1959 feature film. A more beautiful pose we have not seen. Graphite with a slight hint of blue added. The figure is 7" tall. "#19n" written in the corner. In Excellent condition.

31078 *Sleeping Beauty* **Briar Rose and Scarecrow Prince Production Drawings (Walt Disney, 1959).** A pair of 16-field animation drawings featuring Briar Rose on one (E72) and the forest animals' "Scarecrow Prince" on the other (143). Graphite on paper with Briar Rose measuring 6" tall and the Prince measuring 5". A wonderful set of drawings from the same scene. In Excellent condition.

31080 *Sleeping Beauty* **Forest Animals Production Drawing Group (Walt Disney, 1959).** A pair of original 16-field studio animation roughs of the animals creating the Scarecrow Prince. Graphite with brown highlights, #279H and 33. Adorable set of two drawings for a memorable scene. In Excellent condition.

31083 *Sleeping Beauty* **Briar Rose Production Drawing (Walt Disney, 1959).** One-of-a-kind Disney Studios 16-field animation drawing of Briar Rose in the forest. Image area approximately 6". Graphite #241. In Excellent condition.

31076 *Sleeping Beauty* **Production Drawing (Walt Disney, 1959).** Expressive original production drawing of the evil Maleficent, rendered in graphite on 16-field animation paper (OPD #39). The image area is approximately 8.5" x 9". "#111" written in the bottom right hand corner. Aside from some light paper aging and surface wear, the art is in Very Good condition.

LOOK FOR "SLEEPING BEAUTY" CONCEPT ART IN SESSION ONE!

31084 *Sleeping Beauty* **Maleficent Production Drawing (Walt Disney, 1959).** A great original production drawing of the wicked Maleficent, rendered in graphite on 16-field animation paper (OPD #39). Great 9" image. Aside from some light paper aging and surface wear, the art is in Very Good condition.

31085 *Sleeping Beauty* **Maleficent Production Drawing (Walt Disney, 1959).** Original production drawing of Maleficent, rendered in graphite on 16-field animation paper (OPD #169). Great 9" image of a classic Disney villainess! Aside from some light paper aging and light edge wear, the art is in Very Good condition.

31086 *Wonderful World of Disney* **Storyboard Group (Walt Disney, 1960).** Writer Al Bertino's original storyboards from *The Wonderful World of Disney*, including the episode "This Is Your Life, Donald Duck," and various Donald Duck shorts. Twenty two storyboards printed on photographic paper with an average size of approximately 17" x 10" (several boards measure 10" x 29"). In Very Good condition.

31087 *Winnie-the-Pooh* **Animation Production Cel (Walt Disney, 1960s).** Rabbit holds a Hunny jar, in this hand-painted production cel with presentation background. The cel measures 12.5" x 10.5" and is in Very Good condition.

31088 **José Carioca Model Cel (Walt Disney, 1960s).** A large, hand-painted model cel of cigar-smoking parrot Jose Carioca, which was carefully trimmed and laminated between two sheets of acetate, and paired with a non-Disney original art animation background. José has an image area of approximately 4" x 4.25", and the background size is 14.5" x 10.5". An air bubble trails off from Jose's tail feathers; otherwise in Excellent condition.

31089 **No Lot**

31090 *Disney's Wonderful World of Color* **"Mediterranean Cruise" Ludwig Von Drake Production Cel (Walt Disney, 1964).** An original production cel of Ludwig Von Drake in a sea captain's uniform, seen in full-length, hosting the 1964 "Mediterranean Cruise" episode of Disney's *Wonderful World of Color*. Matted to an overall size of 8" x 10", with an image area of approximately 3" x 5.5". In Excellent condition.

31091 *Disney's Wonderful World of Color* **"Mediterranean Cruise" Ludwig Von Drake Production Cel (Walt Disney, 1964).** An original production cel from Disney's *Wonderful World of Color* featuring Ludwig Von Drake in a sea captain's uniform, hosting the 1964 "Mediterranean Cruise" episode. Matted to an overall size of 8" x 10" with an image area of approximately 4.25" x 7". In Excellent condition.

31092 *Winnie-the-Pooh and the Honey Tree* **Storyboard Group (Walt Disney, 1965).** This group includes twelve pages, a complete set of storyboards, from Walt Disney's animated film *Winnie-the-Pooh and the Honey Tree*. The sheets are dated 4/1/65 and are printed on photographic paper measuring approximately 14" x 17". There is a vertical fold line through the center of all of the pages and the top 10 sheets are stapled together. There is some very light soiling and wrinkling; otherwise in Fine condition.

31093 **Alex Ignatiev Dopey Publicity Drawing (Walt Disney, 1960s).** On 16-field animation paper, drawn for publicity purposes. Image area is approximately 4" x 5.5". Very Good condition.

31094 **Alex Ignatiev Dumbo and Timothy Mouse Pencil Drawing (Disney, 1960s).** Done for publicity purposes on 16-field animation paper. Image area measures approximately 13 x 7". Excellent condition.

31095 *Robin Hood* **Little John Production Cel (Walt Disney, 1973).** A 16-field cel with Disney seal from the feature film. Paint is in Fine condition. Matted to an overall size of 16 x 14". Excellent condition.

31096 *The Rescuers* **Penny Animation Production Cel (Walt Disney, 1977).** This hand-painted cel features the young orphan, Penny, from Disney's twenty third feature production, *The Rescuers*. The cel is matted to an image area of 15.5" x 11.5". In Excellent condition. Includes a Disney stamp.

31097 **Winnie-the-Pooh** *Disney Time Annual* **"Pooh and the Honey Pot" Artwork (Walt Disney, 1978).** Original artwork used for the UK publication, a copy of which is included with this lot. Six panels of artwork in mixed media on 11.5" x 16.25" illustration board. In Excellent condition.

31098 **Mickey Mouse as Aladdin Comic Book Preliminary Drawing Group (Walt Disney, undated).** Group of five tightly penciled preliminary comic book pages, featuring Mickey and Goofy in old Arabia. We're not sure what comic this was done for; possibly a foreign edition story. The art is in graphite and colored pencil on tracing paper, with an average image area of 13" x 17.75". The pages have been folded, and have some tears and wrinkles. In Very Good condition.

31099 *Wonderful World of Disney Annual "Alice in Wonderland" Original Art* **(Walt Disney, 1980).** The Mad Hatter, the Cheshire Cat, and friends co-star on this page from a British annual. The art is gouache on board. The two upper panels, the four lower panels, and the lettering (which is original) are on three separate pieces of board, attached to a larger 13" x 18" board. The art is in Very Good condition.

31100 *Winnie-the-Pooh* **Production Cel with Background (Walt Disney, 1980s).** Original hand-painted production cel of Winnie-the-Pooh with effects overlay placed on a hand-painted background. From a 1980's education film. In Excellent condition.

31101 Dumbo Book Project Presentation Cel (Walt Disney, 1980s). A wonderful view of the flying elephant known as Jumbo Jr., or more commonly as Dumbo. This hand-inked and painted 12-field cel and hand-painted background art were prepared for a 1980s Walt Disney Consumer Products children's book. The image area measures 10" x 7", matted and framed with glass for an overall 16" x 13". In Excellent condition.

31102 Gene Ware Pinocchio and Figaro Book Project Presentation Cel (Walt Disney, 1980s). Hand-inked and painted 16-field cel of Pinocchio, placed over a hand-painted background that includes Figaro, done for a Disney children's book project. The background is signed by the artist, the late Gene Ware. The image area measures approximately 15" x 12", and the art as been double matted and framed with glass for an overall size of 21.75" x 25". In Excellent condition.

31103 *The Great Mouse Detective* **Ratigan Production Cel (Walt Disney, 1986).** Deviously delightful production cel of the evil sewer rat, Ratigan. Hand-painted on a 16-field cel (measures 15.5" x 11"), this piece includes the Disney certification stamp, and is in Excellent condition.

31104 *The Great Mouse Detective* **Ratigan Concept Sketch Walt Disney, 1986).** Concept sketch of the Napoleon of Crime, Ratigan, rendered in marker on 16-field animation paper (15" x 12.5"). There is paper tanning, edge wear and some tearing; otherwise the art is in Good condition.

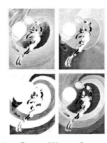

31105 Gene Ware *Sport Goofy* **Illustration Painting Original Art Group (Walt Disney, 1986).** Disney launched a major campaign for Sport Goofy in the late 1980s. The television special *Sport Goofy in Soccermania* was released in 1987, featuring veteran voice actor Russi Taylor's first performance as Huey, Dewey, and Louie, in a story co-written by the late Joe Ranft of Pixar fame. A major poster of Goofy was sold in the mass market world, created from Gene Ware's original artwork. This set of four original mixed-media paintings by the late Ware, is showcasing color models for the proposed poster. Each is signed by him and dated 1986. The paintings are being sold as one lot to keep his color selections together. Framed, they measure a staggering 18" x 14" each. In Excellent condition. *From the Gene Ware Collection.*

31106 *Duck Tales* **Huey, Dewey, Louie, and Webby Production Cel with Background Group (Walt Disney, 1987).** This hand-painted cel features the Duck Nephews and Webby on an original hand-painted background. The art has an approximate image area of 10.5" x 9.5". A Disney seal and certificate are included. In Excellent condition.

31107 *Duck Tales* **Uncle Scrooge, Duck Nephews and Webby Production Cel with Background Group (Walt Disney, 1987).** This hand-painted cel features Uncle Scrooge, Huey, Dewey, Louie, and Webby on an original hand-painted background. A great four character cel set-up! The art has an approximate image area of 10.5" x 9.5" and it includes a Disney seal. In Excellent condition.

31108 *Duck Tales* **Uncle Scrooge and Duck Nephews Production Cel Set-Up with Background Group (Walt Disney, 1987).** This hand-painted cel set-up features Uncle Scrooge, Huey, Dewey, and Louie on an original hand-painted background. The art has an approximate image area of 10.5" x 9.5" and it includes a Disney seal. In Excellent condition.

31109 *Mickey's 60th Birthday* **Production Cel with Drawing Group (Walt Disney, 1988).** From the NBC special that celebrated sixty years of Mickey Mouse, here is a hand-painted original production cel along with its matching clean-up drawing. Each piece has an approximate image area of 11.5" x 9". Framed and matted together, and in Excellent condition.

31110 *The New Adventures of Winnie-the-Pooh* **Production Cel (Walt Disney, 1988).** Large full figure hand-painted production cel of Winnie-the-Pooh from the long running ABC television series. With Disney seal and printed background. In Excellent condition.

31111 Gene Ware *Elves for a Day: Mickey and Friends in Santa's Workshop* **Storybook Illustration (Walt Disney, 1993).** In the early 1990s, Disney stores reigned supreme. This is an original acrylic painting of Mickey Mouse and Donald Duck that was featured on page one of the 1993 Disney Store exclusive children's book. A first edition copy of the book accompanies this beautiful painting. Framed to 20" x 18", with an image area of 10.5" x 8". Signed by the late Gene Ware, and in Excellent condition.

31112 *Aladdin* Genie Color Model Cel (Walt Disney, 1993). Rare hand-painted Walt Disney Studio color model cel of the Genie, used for color reference, publicity, merchandise, and animator reference. There are no painted production cels for this film, making this is a very rare item. Excellent condition.

31113 *Aladdin* Jafar Color Model (Walt Disney, 1993). Rare hand-painted Walt Disney Studio Ink and Paint Department color model cel of Jafar. With no production cels painted for this film, this hand-painted cel of Jafar would have been used for color reference, publicity, animator reference, and merchandise. A very rare item. Excellent condition.

31114 *The Lion King* Hyena Color Model Cel (Walt Disney, 1994). Original Walt Disney Studios 16-field hand-painted color model cel of one of Scar's three hyena henchmen. The image measures 7" x 7". Painted by the Walt Disney Ink and Paint Department for a 1994 Skybox trading card series and other consumer products projects. In Excellent condition.

31115 *The Lion King* Zazu Color Model Cel (Walt Disney, 1994). Original Walt Disney Studios 16-field hand-painted color model cel of Zazu, with an image size of 4" x 7". Painted by the Walt Disney Ink and Paint Department for a 1994 Skybox trading card series and other consumer products projects. In Excellent condition.

31116 *The Lion King* Nala Color Model Cel (Walt Disney, 1994). An original Walt Disney Studios 16-field hand-painted color model cel of Nala, with a 9" x 10" rendition of the lioness. Painted by the Disney Ink and Paint Department, for a 1994 Skybox trading card series, as well as other consumer products. In Excellent condition.

31117 *Gargoyles* Pan Production Cel (Walt Disney, 1994). Original hand-painted pan cel set-up featuring Lexington, Broadway, Brooklyn, Demona, Goliath, and the Captain of the Guard, from the series premiere episode "Awakening (Part I)". One of the finest *Gargoyles* set-ups ever offered for sale, originally sold at Sotheby's June 10, 1995, animation art sale (lot # 557). The image area measures 22" x 9", and the overall set-up measures 31" x 18". The paint is in Fine condition, and the Disney seal is on the lower right corner. A letter of authenticity is mounted on the reverse.

31118 *Snow White and the Seven Dwarfs* "Is Anyone Home" Limited Edition Cel HC 1/25 (Walt Disney, 1995). Limited *hors de commerce* edition xerographic-line, hand-painted character cel set-up recreated from Disney's first animated feature. This two cel set-up recreates Sequence 3C, Scene 2B of the film, as Snow peeks inside the Dwarf's home to see if anyone is home. Framed and matted, with a print background, to an image area of 15.5" x 10", this piece includes a Disney seal and a Certificate of Authenticity. In Excellent condition.

31119 Gene Ware *Peter Pan* Disneyland Storyteller Album Original Preliminary Art and Record Group (Disneyland Records, 1982) Original graphite pencil concept artwork on onion skin paper for a proposed *Peter Pan Storyteller Album*. The pencil drawing is an impressive 14" x 18", and is in Very Good condition. A sealed copy of the album is included in the lot.

31120 *Snow White and the Seven Dwarfs* Promotional Display Group (Walt Disney, undated). An outstanding set of painted foyer displays, probably created for a large theater showing of *Snow White and the Seven Dwarfs*. The displays are all hand-painted on quarter-inch thick sheets of press-board, and cut into the shapes of each character. Included are Snow White, who stands approximately 35.75" tall; and all seven Dwarfs, who average about 25" tall. All have been expertly hand-painted, using ink and gouache. A few stains and scuffs here and there; Doc and Bashful have some minor edge wear, but overall the condition is Very Good, with the Snow White figure in Fine condition. As a special bonus, each figure has been signed on the back, "Voice of Snow White, Adriana Caselotti."

31121 *101 Dalmatians* Coloring Book Concept Art (Walt Disney, 1961). A pair of color roughs dated January 29, 1960, representing original concept art for the cover of the *101 Dalmatians* coloring book, which was published prior to the release of the movie. Gouache on board, 10" x 12.5", and accompanied by a copy of the coloring book. Both are in Excellent condition.

31122 *Mickey Steps Out* **Mickey Mouse Cartoon Script (Walt Disney, 1931).** A ten-page typed duplicate working script for the 1931 Mickey Mouse theatrical short. Forty-two scenes marked in red pencil. In Very Good condition.

31123 *The Delivery Boy* **Mickey Mouse Cartoon Script (Walt Disney Studios, 1931).** A rare original working script (marked "Copy 2") for the 1931 Mickey Mouse theatrical short, bearing its original title *The Expressman*. Thirty-six scenes marked in red pencil. In Very Good condition.

31124 *Mickey's Nightmare* **Mickey Mouse Cartoon Script (Walt Disney, 1932).** A rare four-page typed script for the theatrical short featuring Mickey, Minnie, and Pluto. A rare look into the creative process, in Good condition.

31125 *Touchdown Mickey* **Handwritten Mickey Mouse Cartoon Script (Walt Disney, 1932).** An extremely rare handwritten three-page script for the 1932 theatrical short *Touchdown Mickey*, bearing its original title of *Hold That Line*. Three double-sided pages of 2-peghole animation paper. In Very Good condition.

31126 "Tom Sawyer Island" **Flag and Other Disneyland Memorabilia Group (Walt Disney, 1957-1970s).** The original American flag that flew above Tom Sawyer Island was a gift to our consignor's family. The flag is about 3.5 feet high by 5 feet long and in "distressed" condition. Comes with a vintage Tom Sawyer Island map and a family Press Pass from November 24, 1955 for Disneyland. Lot also includes used and unused Disneyland Tickets (A, B E, C D, are included in five half used ticket booklets), along with 8 1970's park guides/maps.

31127 **Mike Royer** *TV Guide* **"Down and Out" Donald and Daisy Duck Illustration (Walt Disney, 1986).** An original pen-and-ink drawing on 12.5" x 11" illustration board by Disney artist Mike Royer, for an issue of *TV Guide*. In Excellent condition.

31128 **Frank Thomas and Ollie Johnston Seven Dwarfs Ceramic Tile Mural Limited Edition AP 2 (Walt Disney, 2000).** An exclusive item available only at the 2000 "It's a Small World" Disneyana Convention, this framed set of seven ceramic tiles features each of Snow White's little friends, one on each tile in full color. The first tile features the signature of Frank Thomas, while the last features the autograph of Ollie Johnston — two of the original Disney "Nine Old Men," both of whom got their start with this famous animated feature film. This set was limited to only 75 pieces that were all quickly grabbed up at the convention, but this particular item is even more scarce, being one of only a few artist's proofs. Each tile measures a little over 5" square, and the framed size measures approximately 41.75" x 10". Frank and Ollie signed the back of the frame in gold ink, and the mural is in Excellent condition. What a wonderful item for any Disney fan to own!

31129 **Hank Porter** *Snow White and the Seven Dwarfs* **Sunday Strip Preliminary Original Art (Walt Disney, 1938).** Hank Porter's original penciled preliminary art for the first tier of panels of the Sunday strip dated 3-13-39. The chilling moment when the Evil Queen, disguised as an old hag, dips an apple into the vat of poison — "Sleeping Death!" Title panel has been left blank. The image area measures approximately 27" x 5.5", in a mat measuring 35.5" x 14". Very Good condition with a few minor stains and a crease in the third panel.

31130 **Hank Porter** *Snow White and the Seven Dwarfs* **Sunday Strip Preliminary Original Art (Walt Disney, 1938).** Hank Porter's original penciled preliminary art for the first tier of panels of the Sunday strip dated 1-23-38. In this sequence, a frightened Snow White runs deep into the forest after her near-fatal encounter with the huntsman. The title panel has been left blank. The image area measures approximately 27" x 5.5", in a mat measuring 35.5" x 14". Very Good condition with a few tiny stains.

31131 **Hank Porter** *Snow White and the Seven Dwarfs* **Sunday Strip Preliminary Original Art (Walt Disney, 1938).** Hank Porter's original penciled preliminary art for the third tier of panels of the Sunday strip dated 1-23-38. Snow White collapses in the woods after running from the woodsman in this somber sequence. The image area measures approximately 27" x 5.5", in a mat measuring 35.5" x 14". Very Good condition with a few tack holes in the outer borders, and a heavy blue pencil art correction.

31132 **Hank Porter** *Snow White and the Seven Dwarfs* **Sunday Strip Preliminary Original Art (Walt Disney, 1938).** Hank Porter's original penciled preliminary art for the third tier of panels of the Sunday strip dated 3-6-38. Note the different pose for Grumpy in the first panel; the printed version had him looking the other way! The image area measures approximately 27" x 5.5", in a mat measuring 35.5" x 14". Very Good condition with a few minor stains and a crease in panel four.

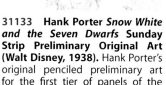

31133 **Hank Porter** *Snow White and the Seven Dwarfs* **Sunday Strip Preliminary Original Art (Walt Disney, 1938).** Hank Porter's original penciled preliminary art for the first tier of panels of the Sunday strip dated 4-10-38. Snow White encounters the old hag, as her woodland friends flee. The first panel is left blank for the title. The image area measures approximately 27" x 5.5", in a mat measuring 35.5" x 14". Very Good condition with a few minor stains.

31134 **Hank Porter** *Snow White and the Seven Dwarfs* **Sunday Strip Preliminary Original Art (Walt Disney, 1938).** Hank Porter's original penciled preliminary art for the third tier of panels of the Sunday strip dated 4-10-38. This is the dramatic scene where Snow White takes a bite of the poisoned apple. The image area measures approximately 27" x 5.5", in a mat measuring 35.5" x 14". Good condition with a few minor stains, some edge wear, and a few small tears.

"ZOOM-ABLE" PICTURES OF EVERY LOT ARE ONLINE AT HA.COM/7052

31135 Gene Ware Hot Wheels Ad Preliminary Original Art (Mattel, 1960s). 1960's "Hot Wheels" Original pencil drawing on onion skin paper, with an approximate image area of 20" x 19". Concept/package design artwork for a proposed Hot Wheels race track toy. One of the children in this drawing is one of Mr. Ware's sons, according to Darlene Ware. Very fragile; otherwise in Very Good condition.

31136 Gene Ware *Bambi* Poster Preliminary Original Art (Walt Disney, 1980s). Original graphite pencil on onion skin paper concept artwork for the mass marketed 1980's *Bambi* Poster, created by the late Gene Ware. This original artwork has an impressive size of 18" x 18", and is in Very Good condition.

31137 Gene Ware *Disney's Adventures of the Gummi Bears* Package Design Preliminary Original Art (Walt Disney, 1985) Original package design artwork by Gene Wear for a proposed Fischer Price Gummi Bear Toy. (A detail of the full image is pictured here.) Graphite pencil on onion skin, with an approximate image area of 18" x 18". Features six Gummi Bears on a log, with beautiful details.

31138 *Feed the Kitty* Mark Antony Model Drawing (Warner Brothers, 1952). From the Chuck Jones-directed and Michael Maltese-written theatrical cartoon. Voted #36 in Jerry Beck's book **The 50 Greatest Cartoons**. 12-field 3-peghole animation paper. "1-M" in bottom right. "Feed the Kitty" in quotes on top of paper. Image area of approximately 6.5" x 5.75". In Very Good condition.

31139 *Lumberjack Bunny* Smidgen Rough Drawing (Warner Brothers, 1954). Rough animation drawing of Smidgen the frisky dog. On 12-field animation paper. Looks like it may have come from the hand of Chuck Jones. Image area of approximately 2" x 4.5". Excellent condition.

31140 Tweety Bird Production Cel Signed by Mel Blanc (Warner Brothers, c. 1950s). A small image of Tweety (about 1.5" tall) on an acetate cel, which has been autographed in green marker by Mel Blanc, who added the inscription, "Oooo — I taut I taw a Puddy Cat!". The matted cel is displayed in a shadowbox frame with a small painted plastic model of Tweety on a perch. The frame includes glass, and measures approximately 12.5" x 15.5", and the cel is in Excellent condition.

31141 Chuck Jones *Rocket Squad* Layout Drawing of Daffy Duck (Warner Brothers, 1956). This Chuck Jones-directed theatrical short was a *Dragnet* parody starring Daffy Duck and Porky Pig. On 12-field animation paper, drawn in graphite. Dialogue of "Right... Truck back" is written on the drawing. "#2" written in the bottom right corner. Image area of approximately 6.5" x 4.5". In Excellent condition.

31142 *Boyhood Daze* Ralph Phillips Layout Drawing (Warner Brothers, 1957). 12-field layout drawing from the theatrical short directed by Chuck Jones. Note ("Willie see Chuck on Clean ups") is a direct message to animator Willie Ito. This drawing looks closely like the work of Chuck Jones himself. Image area is approximately 6.5 x 8". Very Good condition.

31143 Chuck Jones *What's Opera Doc* Elmer Fudd Layout Drawing (Warner Brothers, 1957). This was the feature that the book **The 50 Best Cartoons** by Jerry Beck rated as number one! 12-field animation paper with graphite. "#18" is written on the drawing. Image area approximately 6.5" x 5". In Excellent condition.

31144 *The Bugs Bunny Show* "Tale of Two Kitties" Original Storyboard Group (Warner Brothers, 1962). The ABC-TV's series *The Bugs Bunny Show* was shown during prime time, and featured all-new animated linking segments, as well as classic cartoons from the 1940s-50s. Here is a rare set of hand-drawn storyboards by Dave Detiege for the second season episode entitled "Tale of Two Kitties", which framed the cartoons "Slap Happy Mouse", "Too Hop to Handle" (replaced with another cartoon for the actual broadcast), and "Cat's A-Weigh". The connecting segments star Sylvester and his son Junior, along with Bugs. There are a total of thirteen pages drawn in graphite, plus black and red and grease pencil, and are in Excellent condition. Includes a signed LOA from Robert McKimson Jr. *From the McKimson Collection.*

31145 Bugs Bunny Production Cel (Warner Brothers, 1972). Everyone's favorite "waskally wabbit" is popping out of his rabbit hole, in this cel from an unspecified production. The image area measures approximately 3.5" x 4.75", and is in Excellent condition.

31146 *Carnival of the Animals* **Bugs Bunny and Daffy Duck Production Drawing Group (Warner Brothers, 1976).** Trio of outstanding Bugs drawings as the conductor in sequence (77, 85 and 99), along with a corrected animation drawing of Daffy Duck (#34) from the same Chuck Jones-directed TV special of all-new animation. Excellent condition.

31147 **Charles McKimson** *Daffy Duck* **Illustration Original Art (1980-90s).** Original pen and ink illustration by Golden Age Warner Bros. animator and layout man, Charles McKimson. The art has an image area of 7.5" x 7" and it is in Excellent condition. Signed by the artist at the lower left. Includes a LOA from Robert McKimson Junior. *From the McKimson Collection.*

31148 *Bugs Bunny's Bustin' All Over* **Production Cel (Warner Brothers, 1980).** Original hand-painted production cel of baby Bugs and baby Elmer from the "Portrait of an Artist as a Young Bunny" segment of this 1980 TV special. The art has been matted to an image area of 12" x 9.5" and it is in Excellent condition. Includes a COA, and a Chuck Jones Enterprises seal at the lower left. Signed by writer/director Chuck Jones.

31149 *Bugs Bunny Bustin' Out All Over* **Marvin Martian Rough Drawings Group (Warner Brothers, 1980).** Marvin is a very hard to find character in terms of production artwork! These three drawings were for the "Spaced Out Bunny" segment of this May 21, 1980 Bugs Bunny TV Special which was written, produced and directed by Chuck Jones. Three 12-field animation drawings. Image areas average 2.5 x 4.5" and the art is in Very Good condition.

31150 *Duck Dodgers and the Return of the 24 1/2th Century* **Original Model Sheet of Daffy Duck Plus Printed Model Sheet Group (Warner Brothers, 1980).** Model sheet by Manny Perez from the Chuck Jones-directed cartoon that was the sequel to one of the all-time favorites. 12-field animation paper with 8 poses. Lot also includes four 16.5" x 10.5" printed model sheets (with printed Chuck Jones signatures) for *Bugs Bunny Bustin' Out All Over*, which include images of Marvin Martian, Wile E. Coyote, and Daffy as Duck Dodgers, who ended up not being included in this TV special. Original art is in Very Good condition with a barely noticeable stain at top left, however the prints have noticeable stains at top left and are in Good condition, with two having been folded in half.

31151 *Bugs Bunny Bustin' Out All Over* **Wile E. Coyote Rough Drawing Group (Warner Brothers, 1980).** Outstanding pair of rough animation drawings in sequence (1/16) from the *Soup of Sonic* Road Runner and Wile E. short that was part of this May 21, 1980 Chuck Jones-directed TV special. Excellent condition.

31152 *The Looney Looney Looney Bugs Bunny Movie* **Production Cel (Warner Brothers, 1981).** Hand-painted original production animation cel of Porky Pig from this animated feature directed by Friz Freleng. The work has been matted to an image area of 12" x 9.5" and it is in Excellent condition. Includes a COA, and a Warner Bros. seal at the lower right. Signed by Friz Freleng at the lower left.

31153 *Bugs Bunny's 3rd Movie: 1001 Rabbit Tales* **Production Cel (Warner Brothers, 1982).** Hand-inked and hand-painted original animation production cel featuring Sultan Yosemite Sam. This art has been matted to an image area of 12" x 9.5" and it is in Excellent condition. Includes a COA, and a Warner Bros. seal at the lower right. Signed by director Friz Freleng at the bottom.

31154 *Daffy Duck's Fantastic Island* **Production Cel (Warner Brothers, 1983).** Hand-inked and hand-painted original animation production cel of pirate Yosemite Sam and his first mate, the Tasmanian Devil. Matted to an image area of 12" x 9.5", the work is in Excellent condition. Includes a COA, and a Warner Bros. seal at the lower right. Signed by director Friz Freleng at the lower left.

31155 *Daffy Duck's Fantastic Island* **Production Cel (Warner Brothers, 1983).** Hand-inked and hand-painted original production animation cel featuring Daffy Duck and Speedy Gonzales. The work has been matted to an image area of 12" x 9.5" and it is in Excellent condition. Includes a COA, and a Warner Bros. seal at the lower right. Signed by director Friz Freleng at the lower left.

31156 *Batman the Animated Series* **Gotham City Production Background (Warner Brothers, 1993).** Original one-of-a-kind hand-painted pan production background of Gotham City, from the episode "Mudslide", matted and framed with the original layout drawing that was used to create the painting. The image areas measure 27" x 8"; the overall set-up measures 36.25" x 28.25". Accompanied by a letter of authenticity from Warner Brothers. In Excellent condition.

31157 *The Mouse That Jack Built* **Cartoon Script Group (Warner Brothers, 1959).** One of the funniest cartoons from Warner's late 1950s output was Robert McKimson's *The House That Jack Built*, which actually starred Jack Benny and his cast members Eddie "Rochester" Anderson, Mary Livingston, and Don Wilson. Here is the original script from that cartoon, both in an early version typed on yellow paper (four pages, with a deleted opening scene), and the final version (three pages, typed on white paper). Both sets have numerous notes and revisions penciled in, but are in Excellent condition. Includes a signed LOA from Robert McKimson Jr. *From the McKimson Collection.*

31158 Warner Brothers Studio Animation Master Footage Roster (Warner Brothers, 1959). Extremely uncommon roster, indicating footage for cartoon directors Robert McKimson, Chuck Jones, and Fritz Freleng. Three stapled ledger sheets measuring 11" x 24". Excellent condition. Includes a letter of authentication signed by Robert McKimson, Jr. *From the McKimson Collection.*

31159 *Bugs Bunny-Road Runner Show* **Studio Memo (Warner Brothers, 1968).** An original interoffice memo on yellow Warner Brothers stationery, concerning new bits of animation for the Saturday morning television series, addressed to Joseph Kotler from Bill Hendricks. In Excellent condition. Includes a signed LOA from Robert McKimson Jr. *From the McKimson Collection.*

31160 Terrytoons *Catnip* Production Drawings (Terrytoons, 1940s). Four pages of Storyboard art from the 1940s-era theatrical short. In Excellent condition.

31161 *Mighty Mouse* **Oil Can Harry Production Drawing (Terrytoons, 1940s).** Original animation drawing featuring Oil can Harry and Pearl Pureheart from an unspecified Mighty Mouse theatrical short. In very Good condition.

31162 Mighty Mouse *The Lion and the Mouse* Storyboard (Terrytoons, 1943). A rare storyboard for the theatrical short featuring an early appearance of Mighty Mouse, when the character was (briefly) called Super Mouse. *The Lion and the Mouse* was the last such short to be produced before the name change. In Excellent condition.

31163 *Tom Terrific* **Production Drawings Folder Original Art Group (Terrytoons, 1957).** This animation folder contains 20 drawings of Tom Terrific popping out of the water, 20 of Mighty Manfred the Wonder Dog in the water, one of a sea serpent, and dozens of water effects drawings, all on 3-peghole, 12-field animation paper. This "Terrific" collection showcases the simple yet eloquent animation of the beloved series, here from its first year.

31164 *Tom Terrific* **Production Drawings Folder Original Art Group (Terrytoons, 1957).** Villain Crabby Appleton dominates this group in an animation folder consisting of 18 unique drawings of Crabby, one layout of his diabolical machine, and several effects and mouth drawings on 3-peghole, 12-field animation paper. There are two animator timing sheets included. The pages range from Very Good to Excellent condition, most in Excellent.

31165 *Tom Terrific* **Production Drawings Folder Original Art Group (Terrytoons, 1957).** Five unique drawings of Tom Terrific and Mighty Manfred the Wonder Dog highlight this folder group from the first year of the cartoon's production. Also included are two timing sheets and 20 assorted water effects drawings on 3-peghole, 12-field animation paper. Art ranges Very Good to Excellent condition, most in Excellent.

31166 *Tom Terrific* **Production Drawings Folder Original Art Group (Terrytoons, 1957).** Jam-packed folder of 27 sequential drawings of Tom Terrific turning himself into a chicken — no biggie for our pint-sized hero - plus 17 of Mighty Manfred the Wonder Dog and 12 of Fred, watching the amazing transformation. The folder also includes dozens of miscellaneous effects drawings. The art's on 12-field, 3-peghole animation drawing paper, and in Excellent condition.

31167 Terrytoons Unspecified Production Cel (Terrytoons, 1960s). A rare hand-painted pan production cel, In Very Good condition.

31168 *The Jetsons* Model Sheet Original Photostat Group (Hannah-Barbera, 1962). Two original studio photostatted model sheets, including the entire Jetsons family (image area approximately 14" x 9.5"), and one of Judy Jetson (image area approximately 10" x 8.5"). Both pieces are matted and ready to frame. Excellent condition.

31169 *Hey There It's Yogi Bear* Production Cel (Hanna-Barbera, 1964). Adorable trimmed cel of Yogi and Cindy Bear from the feature film. Approximately 5" x 3.5". Paint is fine. Trimmed and mounted in a cream colored mat. Excellent condition.

31170 Pumpkin Puss, Mush Mouse, and Secret Squirrel Layout Drawings Group (Hanna-Barbera, 1964-65). Pumpkin Puss and Mush Mouse starred in the *Magilla Gorilla Show*, while Secret Squirrel co-starred with Atom Ant. All on 12-field animation paper. Each signed by the original artist, Willie Ito. Excellent examples of vintage Hanna-Barbera Studio artwork. Excellent condition.

31171 Willie Ito *The Flintstones* Fred, Wilma, Barney, and Betty Layout Drawing (Hanna-Barbera, 1964-65). An outstanding layout drawing of America's two favorite couples! Marked sc 151, BG 143. Graphite pencil on 12-field animation paper. Signed by the artist. Excellent condition.

31172 Bob Singer *The Flintstones* The Gruesomes Layout Drawing Group (Hanna-Barbera, 1964). In 1964, the Gruesomes, a cross between the Munsters and the Addams family, appeared in the *Flintstones* series. They reappeared on the *Pebbles and Bam Bam Show* in 1971. This is a set of five detailed layout drawings of Rocksylvania Hotel by noted Hanna-Barbera and animation layout artist Bob Singer. These drawings show the prehistoric hotel entrance, balcony, hotel registration desk, crypt, and train Depot. This concept artwork was for a character named Rockula. This artwork showcases Mr. Singer's genius and the creativity that made *The Flintstones* one of television's most loved animated cartoon series. Image sizes range from 6" x 4.5" to 7.5" by 6". Excellent condition.

31173 *Laurel and Hardy* Ollie and Friend Production Cel (Hanna-Barbera, 1966). From the Hanna-Barbera/Larry Harmon syndicated animated TV series. Trimmed cel placed over a painted background. Image area is approximately 9" x 7". Excellent condition.

31174 *Fantastic Four* Animation Drawing Group (Hanna-Barbera/Marvel Comics, 1967). The *Fantastic Four* animated television show ran from 1967 to 1970, during which time approximately 20 episodes were produced. Offered here are 26 pages of assorted storyboards for the show, including one for the episode "Klaw, The Murderous Master of Sound." The drawings average Very Good condition.

31175 *Fantastic Four* Original Shooting Script Group (Hanna-Barbera/Marvel Comics, 1967). From the animated television show of the late 1960s, over 100 typed pages of voice scripts for four episodes. Two are personal copies used by Jo Ann Pflug who voiced Sue Richards, and one used by veteran voiceover actor Vic Perrin.

31176 *Huckleberry Hound* Production Cel (Hanna-Barbera, 1970s-80s). Hand-painted cel measuring 11.5" x 9.5", matted to an image area of 9.5" x 7.5". Some tape residue at the upper and lower edges; otherwise the work is in Very Good condition.

31177 *The Roman Holidays* Publicity Cel (Hanna-Barbera, 1972). An extremely rare hand-painted 16-field publicity cel used to promote the NBC/Hanna-Barbera Studio animated series. This beautiful cel showcases Gus Holiday, Mr Evictus, and Brutus the Lion. In Excellent condition.

31178 *The Jetsons* Concept Artwork for New Characters Group (Hanna-Barbera, 1973). In 1973 Hanna-Barbera explored the idea of bringing back the Jetsons with the family having grown up since its 1962 premiere. These model sheets by Willie Ito show the development of a grown-up Judy and a grown-up Elroy, as well as a new addition to the family in Astro Pup. Ultimately the series was brought back but without these updates, so this lot may be the only look you'll ever get at these character versions. All on 12-field animation paper. Mr. Ito signed the Astro Pup Model sheet. Excellent condition.

31179 Dick Bichenbach *The New Tom and Jerry/Grape Ape Show* Layout Drawing (Hanna-Barbera, 1975). A beautiful cat and mouse drawing on 12-field animation paper. Very Good condition.

31180 Captain Caveman and Dino Production Cel (Hanna-Barbera). Original Hanna-Barbera Studio hand-painted 12-field cel used for a Hanna-Barbera children's storybook. The cel is placed over a copy of the original background. Captain Caveman originated in 1977 in the series *Captain Caveman and the Teen Angels*, which ran through 1980. A great image! In Excellent condition.

31181 *The Smurfs* Production Backgrounds (Hanna-Barbera, 1980s). Pair of hand-painted 12-field production backgrounds (BG115, and BG194) of the Smurfs' mushroom homes, with one under a full moon. This Emmy Award-winning series ran from 1981-1990 and has since been spun into a series of successful feature films. In Excellent condition.

31182 *The Smurfs* Production Cel Set-Up (Hanna-Barbera, 1981). Outstanding 12-field hand-painted production cel of five Smurfs — including Papa Smurf and Smurfette — placed over a 12-field hand-painted-production background from the same series (BG16). What makes this set-up special is that it is signed by both Bill Hanna and Joe Barbera. You very rarely see production artwork from *The Smurfs* signed by these studio giants. In Excellent condition.

31183 *The Smurfs* Smurfette and Others Production Cel (Hanna-Barbera, 1981). Original 12-field hand-painted production cel of three Smurfs (including Brainy) and Smurfette placed on an outstanding hand-painted production background (BG 61), showcasing the Smurfs' mushroom homes. In Excellent condition.

31184 *The Smurfs* Production Cel and Background (Hanna-Barbera, 1981). Outstanding 12-field hand-painted production cel of Papa Smurf, Smurfette, and one other Smurf on a hand-painted 12-field production background (BG 165) from the animated television series. In Excellent condition.

31185 *The Greatest Adventure: Stories from the Bible* "The Nativity" Production Cel (Hanna-Barbera, 1987). Original 12-field, hand-painted production cel from the episode "The Nativity" of the 1985-1993 series. The scene showcases the three wise men as they arrive at the manger, and this cel was used for the closing credits of the episode. A 17-year pet project for Joe Barbera, very little artwork from this series has been seen. The cel is placed on a hand-painted 12-field production background. In Excellent condition.

31186 *The Greatest Adventure: Stories from the Bible* "The Nativity" Production Cel (Hanna-Barbera, 1987). Original hand-painted 12-field production cel with a hand-painted key master production background. Depicts the three wise men with Mary, Joseph, and baby Jesus. This cel was seen in the closing credits of the episode "The Nativity", and was also used in all creative pitches to sell the series, which was a 17-year pet project for Joe Barbera. In Excellent condition.

31187 *The Greatest Adventure: Stories from the Bible* "Moses" Production Backgrounds (Hanna-Barbera, 1987). Trio of detailed Hanna-Barbera production backgrounds from the episode "Moses". The hand-painted backgrounds are 16" x 12" boards with hand-painted overlays of a cliff, mountain top, and valley. Three beautiful production backgrounds, hard-to-find artwork from Joe Barbera's 17-year pet project. In Excellent condition.

31188 *The Flintstones* Fred Flintstone Presentation Cel (Hanna-Barbera, circa 1980s-1990s). 12-field cel of Fred with his catchphrase "Yabba Dabba Doo!" Used by Hanna-Barbera Studio for publicity and possible merchandising efforts. Placed on a complementary print background. Excellent condition.

31189 Scooby-Doo and Shaggy Publicity Cel (Hanna-Barbera, 1990s). Outstanding Hanna-Barbera Studio 12-field, hand-painted publicity cel of the duo in their classic pose. One of the longest running cartoon characters in the history of television. Hand-painted at the studio for publicity purposes and possible consumer products merchandise use. Placed on a complimentary background. In Excellent condition.

31190 *The Jetsons Movie* Production Drawing (Hanna-Barbera, 1990). Original layout drawing showing George, Elroy, Rosie the Robot, and Astro hidden with friends on a fun 12-field animation drawing. Graphite with blue highlights. Few layouts from this feature have been seen. In Excellent condition.

31191 *The Flintstones* "First Kiss" Limited Edition Cel (Hanna-Barbera, 1990s). During the 1990s heyday of animation art, Hanna-Barbera released many hand-painted limited edition cels highlighting their rich history. One of the fastest to ever sell out, and one of the earliest ever produced by Hanna-Barbera, was the one featuring Pebbles and Bamm-Bamm titled "First Kiss". This hand-painted artist proof (#3 of only 20) features a 12-field cel and print background, and is signed by Bill Hanna and Joe Barbera. In Excellent condition.

31192 *Gravedale* *High* **Character Model Cel (Hanna-Barbera, 1990).** This is a one-of-a-kind hand-painted cast size comparison model cel for the Hanna-Barbera series, which ran for 13 episodes, showcasing the entire cast of 12 characters. A large piece, measuring more than 44" x 10". Very rare, and in Excellent condition.

31193 *Tom & Jerry Kids Show* **"Muscle Beach Droopy" Title Cel Set-Up (Hanna-Barbera, 1991).** A highly desirable original hand-painted title cel set-up for a Droopy cartoon from the 1991 Fox animated television series. An outstanding image on a airbrushed original background. In Excellent condition.

31194 *The Pirates of Dark Water* **Publicity Illustration (Hanna-Barbera, 1991).** Original Hanna-Barbera Studio master painting, used for publicity purposes. This beautiful artwork is on 24" x 20" illustration board and showcases the main characters Ren, Tula (voiced by *The Little Mermaid* star Jodi Benson), Ioz, and villain Bloth. The 1991 series ran on Fox and then over to ABC. A beautiful piece of Hanna-Barbera Studio artwork, in Excellent condition.

31195 *Monster Tails* **Comparison Model Cel (Hanna-Barbera, 1991).** Extremely rare, one-of-a-kind, hand-painted size comparison model cel. This series was part of the *Wake, Rattle, and Roll* show (later retitled to *Jump, Rattle, and Roll*). This amazing character development piece showcases 13 characters from the show, and measures 45" x 10". In Excellent condition.

31196 *Fish Police* **Character Model Cel (Hanna-Barbera, 1992).** Here is one of the rarest pieces of Hanna-Barbera art you will find. In 1992, in attempt to get back into prime-time network animation, Hanna-Barbera debuted *Fish Police* on CBS. Inspired by the comic book of the same name and featuring John Ritter as the lead, it was canceled after only three episodes. This is the one and only hand-painted size comparison model cel featuring all of the characters. The 11 hand-painted figures and the show's logo are enormous, and the cel measures 39" x 13". If you like them rare, this is it!

31197 *SWAT Kats: The Radical Squadron* **Title Cel (Hanna-Barbera, 1993).** A rare title cel for the Robert Alvarez-directed cartoon series that ran on TBS from 1993-95. Hand-painted 12-field cel over a blue complimentary background print. Very little artwork from this series is in circulation. In Excellent condition.

31198 *Once Upon a Forest* **Pan Production Cel (Hanna-Barbera, 1993).** Rare hand-painted pan production cel on a hand-painted key master production background, featuring the characters Cornelius, Abigail, Edgar, and Russell. Production artwork from this feature film is rarely seen. The cel and background are 27" x 10" and in Excellent condition.

31199 *Yogi the Easter Bear* **Yogi, Boo-Boo, and Easter Bunny Production Cel (Hanna-Barbera, 1994).** Original Hanna-Barbera Studio one-of-a-kind hand-painted production cel set-up of Yogi, Boo-Boo, and the Easter Bunny, placed on a complimentary print background from the April 3, 1994 TV special. This was the last appearance of Don Messick as Boo-Boo and Park Ranger Smith. In Excellent condition.

31200 *Daisy-Head Mayzie* **Production Cel (Hanna-Barbera, 1995).** Original 12-field hand-painted production cel of Mayzie McGrew for the Hanna-Barbera television special which aired on TNT on February 5, 1995. The special was adapted from the last book by Doctor Seuss and was narrated by the Cat in the Hat himself. The cel has a Hanna-Barbera Studio seal and is in Fine condition.

31201 *The Real Adventures of Jonny Quest* **Autographed Color Model Cel (Hanna-Barbera, 1996).** Rare 16-field hand-painted color model cel used for reference, showing Jonny, Jessie, Hadji, Doctor Benton Quest, and Race Banyan. The cel is signed by the voices of Hadji (Rob Paulsen), Jonny (Quinton Flynn), and Jessie (Jennifer Hale). The show aired worldwide and ran in the US on TBS (1993-95) and Cartoon Network (1996-97). In Excellent condition.

31202 *Scooby-Doo on Zombie Island* **Scooby and Shaggy Production Cel (Hanna-Barbera, 1998).** Original, one-of-a-kind hand-painted production cel set-up of Scooby-Doo and Shaggy with his snack, from the 1998 Hanna-Barbera direct-to-video feature film. A great pose! This film received positive reviews, was a commercial success, and was dedicated to the memory of Don Messick (the original voice of Scooby-Doo). The matching animation drawing of Scooby is included, as is a DVD copy of the movie. In Excellent condition.

31203 Scooby-Doo Presentation Cel (Hanna-Barbera, date unknown). Funny 12-field publicity cel of Scooby-Doo, one of Hanna-Barbera's most successful characters for over 40 years. Created from original artwork by studio artist Jack Manning. Used for publicity and possible consumer products purposes.

31204 Yogi Bear Presentation Cel (Hanna-Barbera, undated). Yogi Bear, Boo-Boo, and the Ranger are featured in this 12-field cel used for publicity and possible consumer products artwork. Placed on an original hand-painted production background (bg 301). Great image showing entrance to Jellystone Park.

31205 Hanna-Barbera Signed Check and Photo (1964). A canceled 1964 expense check, signed in blue ink by both Joseph Barbera and William Hanna is matted with a black and white photo of the two, receiving an award from the City of Los Angeles. The photo measures approximately 9.5" x 7.5", with an overall mat size of 15" x 17.75". Excellent condition.

31206 Jean Vander Pyl's *The Flintstones* "Curtain Call at Bedrock" Script (Hanna-Barbera, 1966). Original 33-page script for the season 6 episode, from the personal archive of voice actor Vander Pyl, who performed the voices of Wilma and Pebbles Flintstone for the series. In Excellent condition.

31207 Hal Smith's *Fantastic Four* "Klaw" Script (Hanna-Barbera, 1967). Original 21-page script for the fifth episode of the animated series, from the personal collection of voice actor Hal Smith, who voiced the titular villain in the episode. In Excellent condition.

31208 Lew Keller *Cap'n Crunch Cereal* "The Tortoise Race" Storyboard Group (Jay Ward, 1960s). The crew lands on the Galapagos Islands, only to find Cap'n Crunch's nemesis, Jean LaFoote the Barefoot Pirate already there! Fun, nostalgic artwork from one of the Saturday morning commercials of the 1960s, as drawn by artist Lew Keller for Jay Ward. Each of the six pages has art in ink, graphite, colored pencil, and markers on 14" x 8.5" paper. All pages display some degree of minor paper tanning, with some art elements taped on; overall Very Good condition.

31209 Lew Keller *Cap'n Crunch Secret Cereal* "Agent 00" Storyboard Group (Jay Ward, 1960s). Cap'n Crunch introduces a new version of his cereal aboard his Good Ship Guppy, but discovers a spy onboard, as well. This classic vintage storyboard was drawn by long time animator Lew Keller for Jay Ward's original series of commercials for Quaker Oats. Ink, graphite, and marker on forty paper rectangles which were cut and affixed to eight pieces of 14" x 8.5" heavy paper. Some tape discoloration from age, otherwise in Excellent condition.

31210 *George of the Jungle* Tom Slick Concept Drawing (Jay Ward, 1967). Concept sketch of a flying gadget called the Frosto Blast Digaloo for the Tom Slick section of this program. Mixed media on the reverse of an NBC *The Bullwinkle Show* letterhead, measuring 11" x 8.5". Some paper aging, light surface wear and pin holes; otherwise the art is in Very Good condition.

31211 Lew Keller *Cap'n Crunch Peanut Butter Cereal* "Smedley's Track Record" Storyboard Group (Jay Ward, c. 1969). Cap'n Crunch's pet elephant displays is bike riding abilities in this set of storyboard drawings from the Jay Ward Studio, created by artist Lew Keller. Ink, graphite, and red pencil on three sheets of 14" x 8.5" heavy stock paper. Most panels are replacement art taped over earlier drawings, as originally created. Overall condition is Very Good.

31212 *Tom Slick* Production Cel (Jay Ward, 1989). Original hand-inked, hand-painted scene cel of Tom Slick, Marigold, and Gertie with a Jay Ward seal in the lower right corner. The cel is in its original Jay Ward Productions mat. This is the type of cel that was routinely sold at the Dudley Do-Right Emporium on 8200 Sunset Strip, in West Hollywood. In Excellent condition.

31213 *Fairly OddParents* Production Cel Key Master Set-up (Nickelodeon, 2003). Background art with four cel overlays from the first year of the television series. 16.5" x 10" and in Excellent condition.

31214 *Fairly OddParents* Production Cel Key Master Set-up (Nickelodeon, 2003). Godparents Cosmo and Wanda hover over a sickly Timmy in this scene from the popular television series' first year. It's in Excellent condition, with an image area of 15.75" x 11.75".

31215 *SpongeBob SquarePants* Sandy and SpongeBob Production Cel Set-Up Group (Nickelodeon, 1999). A hand-painted production cel set-up of SpongeBob and Sandy. The cel has been placed on a first season hand-painted production background. The set-up has an overall size of 10.5" x 14". The SpongeBob figure is 3" tall and Sandy is 4" tall. The 12-field background has amazing detail. In Fine condition.

31216 *SpongeBob SquarePants* Production Cel (Nickelodeon, 1999). A first season (the only season not done by computer) hand-painted production cel of SpongeBob. The cel has been placed over an original hand-painted production background. The SpongeBob figure measures about 3" x 5". A great 12-field background! In Fine condition.

31217 *SpongeBob SquarePants* **Production Cel (Nickelodeon, 1999).** A hand-painted SpongeBob SquarePants first season production cel set-up. A huge 7" Bob is the focus here! The 12-field cel has been placed over a beautiful hand-painted production background, which measures approximately 10" x 13.25". A Nickelodeon studio seal is on the cel. In Excellent condition.

31218 *SpongeBob SquarePants* **Patrick and SpongeBob Production Cel (Nickelodeon, 1999).** A first season hand-painted production cel set-up of SpongeBob and his best friend Patrick. The cels are placed on a hand-painted original production background. SpongeBob figure is 5" tall and Patrick is 7" tall. Both are wearing rubber gloves on their heads... The set-up has an overall size of 10.5" x 14", and is in Fine condition.

31219 *SpongeBob SquarePants* **Production Cel Set-Up (Nickelodeon, 1999).** An outstanding 16-field first season production cel set-up of SpongeBob. The cel has been placed on its original hand-painted production background. This nice large background makes for a dramatic set-up. The SpongeBob figure is 5" tall and the piece has an overall size of 13.5" x 16.5". In Fine condition.

31220 *Rugrats* **Production Cel and Drawing with Background (Klasky Csupo/Nickelodeon, undated).** Hand-painted cel includes its original matching drawing and key master background. Measures approximately 10.5" x 19". In Very Good condition.

31221 Walter Lantz Production Background (Walter Lantz, 1920s). Blue-and-white painted production background, 10.5" x 8.5". In Excellent condition.

31222 *Cheese-Nappers* **Color Model Cel (Walter Lantz, 1938).** A black-and-white cel of one of the rats from the 1938 short, on a complimentary print background. In Excellent condition.

31223 *Woody Woodpecker* **Opening Credit Sequence Production Cel and Matching Production Drawing (Walter Lantz, 1940s).** Full-figure hand-painted Woody Woodpecker, with green eyes, approximately 4.25" tall, paired with a color copy Title background. Some minor paint loss within the face area; otherwise Fine condition. Matted and framed using Plexiglas, with the original penciled production drawing; overall size 32.75" x 15.5". Includes a FilmArt 1993 Certificate of Authenticity.

31224 Grim Natwick Woody Woodpecker Sketches (Walter Lantz, 1940s). Veteran animator Grim Natwick filled this sheet of animation paper with pencil sketches of Walter Lantz's famous woodpecker, Woody. Graphite and red pencil on animation paper, with an approximate image area of 9.5" x 9.5", triple-matted and framed with glass for an overall size of 22" x 18". Excellent condition. Includes a Vintage Animation Certificate of Authenticity, affixed to the back of the frame.

31225 *Woody Woodpecker* **Production Cel (Walter Lantz, c. 1940s).** A green-eyed Woody fills this 10" x 9.5" image area. Attractively matted and framed with glass to an overall size of 18.5" x 18". Excellent condition.

31226 *Woody Woodpecker* **Opening Sequence Production Cel (Walter Lantz, 1940s).** A green-eyed Woody pecks away in this hand-painted production cel, paired with a color copy of a production title background drawing. Woody has a small crack within his beak, and another within his left foot; Fine condition. The art measures approximately 4" x 3", with a combined image area of 11.75" x 8". Matted and framed with glass for an overall 19" x 15".

31227 *Woody Woodpecker* **Opening Sequence Production Cel (Walter Lantz, 1940s).** Great shot of Woody with motion lines, paired with a color copy background of the cartoon title art. Woody measures approximately 4.75" x 2.5". A small paint crack has developed within the beak; overall Fine condition. Combined image area is 11.5" x 9"; matted and framed with glass to 20" x 16". Includes Vintage Animation Certificate of Authenticity.

31228 Walter Lantz Signed Pan Background Production Drawing (Walter Lantz, 1940s). A triple-sheet detailed drawing of the interior of a pirate ship, drawing in graphite and blue pencil. Approximate image area 28.5" x 8.75". Signed in black ink by Walter Lantz. Excellent condition.

31229 *Woody Woodpecker* **Production Cel (Walter Lantz, 1940s).** Nice action shot of a green-eyed Wood, paired with a color print background. Woody is 7" tall; combined image area measures approximately 11.75" x 8.5", and the cel is triple-matted and framed with Plexiglas to an overall 19.25" x 16". Excellent condition

31230 *Woody Woodpecker* **Production Cel with Background (Walter Lantz, 1950s).** This wild and woolly hand-inked and hand-painted cel includes its original background art. Both items measure approximately 13" x 10". Aside from some light aging; the work is in Excellent condition.

31231 **Woody Woodpecker Production Drawing (Walter Lantz, 1950s).** An outstanding Woody Woodpecker layout drawing featuring a quintessential pose, in Excellent condition.

31232 **Woody Woodpecker Hand-Drawn and Colored Comic Book Page Roughs Group (Walter Lantz, c. 1950).** Twelve pages of hand-drawn and hand-colored roughs starring Woody, Knothead, Splinter, Buzz Buzzard, and villains galore! In average Very Good condition.

31233 *Gulliver's Travels* **Princess Glory Production Drawing (Max Fleischer, 1939).** Pair of animation character drawings/concept artwork of Princess Glory from the 1939 Paramount Studios animated feature film. The artwork is graphite and watercolor, with notations written on both, and the image measures 9". Grim Natwick supervised the animation of this character, and it is quite possibly these two drawings are from his hand. On trimmed animation paper 13" x 8". In Excellent condition.

31234 *Gulliver's Travels* **Princess and Prince, and King Production Drawing Group (Max Fleischer, 1939).** Pair of 12-field animation drawings from Max Fleischer Studios' first animated feature film. One features the Prince and the Princess, and the other is an image of King Little. The Prince and Princess measure approximately 7", while the King is 4". Both pieces are matted and in Excellent condition.

31235 *Gulliver's Travels* **Sneak, Snoop, and Snitch Model Sheets (Max Fleischer, 1939).** Four printed animator's model sheets from of Sneak, Snoop, and Snitch, the three spies from Fleischer's first animated feature. There are three hole punches on each, indicating that they were kept in some type of binder. A fourth model sheet is of a secondary character, Twinkeltoes, from the 1940 Paramount Studio theatrical short "Sneak, Snoop, and Snitch." The drawings are 14" x 11" and are in Excellent condition.

31236 *Gulliver's Travels* **Lilliput Production Drawing Original Art (Max Fleischer, 1939).** Outstanding one-of-a-kind 16-field 3-peghole animation layout drawing for a background for the town of Lilliput. In graphite with red and blue highlights. Along the border is written "Background F.8.1 7-35/Seg 7 Sc 35" A beautiful drawing. In Very Good condition.

31237 *Gulliver's Travels* **Lilliput Production Drawing (Max Fleischer, 1939).** Original 16-field three-peg-hole animation layout drawing for a background from Fleischer's Studios' first animated feature film. A great drawing of the cart the Lilliputians build to bring Gulliver to the town of Lilliput. In graphite with miscellaneous colors on the mountains. A notation along the border reads "Background 7.34". In Very Good condition.

31238 **Dave Tendlar Turtle Model Sheet Original Art (Max Fleischer, 1940s).** Three full body views and two additional head shots of an unnamed turtle cartoon character, done on two separate pieces of paper which have been taped to a sheet of 3-peghole animation paper. The art is in graphite, with a few red pencil highlights, and the combined image area is approximately 8.5" x 6.5". Very Good condition.

31239 **Dave Tendlar "Dog Character" Design Sketch (Max Fleischer, 1940s).** Graphite and colored pencil on 13.5" x 11" animation paper. Some paper aging, a vertical crease in the center, and some light creasing in the right portion; otherwise the art is in Very Good condition.

31240 **Dave Tendlar "Flea" Production Drawing (Max Fleischer, 1940s).** Original character design drawing of a hobo flea, stamped "Return to Dave Tendlar". Trimmed to 8.75" x 7"; otherwise, in Excellent condition.

31241 Dave Tendlar "Spelling Bee" Character Design Sketch (Max Fleischer, 1940s). Graphite and colored pencil on 8.5" x 11" animation paper. Some paper aging, light soiling, and edge wear; otherwise the art is in Very Good condition.

31242 Dave Tendlar *Boos and Arrows* Casper Model Sheets (Famous Studios, 1954). Five original model sheets by Tendlar for the 1954 animated short featuring Casper the Friendly Ghost. In Very Good condition.

31243 *Casper the Friendly Ghost* "Ghost of Honor" Production Drawing Group (Famous Studios, 1957). Three hand-drawn storyboards for the theatrical short. In Excellent condition.

31244 *Rugrats* Production Cel Set-Up with Key Background (Klasky Csupo/Nickelodeon, undated). Hand-painted cel set-up with its key master background. Measures approximately 20.5" x 10". In Very Good condition.

31245 *Rugrats* Production Cel Set-Up with Key Background (Klasky Csupo/Nickelodeon, undated). Hand-painted cel set-up with its key master background. Measures approximately 25" x 10.5". In Very Good condition.

31246 *Rugrats* Production Cel Set-Up with Key Background (Klasky Csupo/Nickelodeon, undated). Hand-painted cel set-up with its key master background. Measures approximately 25" x 10.5". In Very Good condition.

31247 *Mr. Magoo* Studio Model Sheet (UPA, 1960s). On 12-field animation paper. Measures approximately 12.5" x 10.25". Very Good condition.

31248 *Bold King Cole* Felix the Cat Production Drawing (Van Beuren, 1936). Original animation drawing of the title character from the 1936 theatrical short, one of only three produced by the studio. In Excellent condition.

31249 *The Little Lost Sheep* Production Drawing (Columbia, 1939). Original drawing of the Wolf from the 1939 cartoon short, *The Little Lost Sheep*, a Krazy Kat cartoon from Columbia Pictures. Graphite and red pencil on a 12" x 10" sheet of animation paper. Some paper tanning and light edge wear; otherwise the art is in Very Good condition.

31250 MGM Studio Production Drawing Group (MGM, 1940s). Pair of MGM Studio animation drawings from Tex Avery directed cartoons. Droopy is from a 1940's MGM theatrical short, and the policeman is from the 1943 theatrical short, *Who Killed Who?"* Both drawings are rendered in graphite on 12-field 3-peghole paper, measuring 12.5" x 10.5". There is paper tanning and light edge wear; otherwise the art averages Very Good condition.

31251 *The Jerky Turkey* Production Drawing Group (MGM, 1945). Original animation drawing of the Pilgrim and the Jerky Turkey from the 1945 Tex Avery-directed theatrical short, *The Jerky Turkey*. Rare to have both characters in one drawing. Rendered in graphite and red pencil on 12-field 3-peghole paper, measuring 12.5" x 10.5". There is paper tanning and light soiling; otherwise the art is in Very Good condition.

31252 *Yellow Submarine* Captain Fred Production Drawing (United Artists/King Features, 1968). Captain Fred holding onto the submarine's anchor from the classic 1968 feature film. Graphite on 16" x 12.5" animation paper (OPD #F-26). Some surface and edge wear and light soiling; otherwise the art is in Very Good condition.

31253 *Yellow Submarine* Ringo Production Cel (United Artists/King Features, 1968). Everyone's favorite drummer sports his Sergeant Pepper finale outfit. With two other cels in a cel set-up. Placed between clear Lucite for a free-forming display. Ringo is 5" tall and paint is fine. The display measures approximately 18" x 14". Very Good condition.

31254 *Yellow Submarine* Ringo and Yellow Submarine Production Cel Group (United Artists/King Features Syndicate, 1968). Two hand-inked and hand-painted animation production cels from the animated musical fantasy feature film. The Submarine cel measures 16" x 12.5" and the Ringo cel measures 13.75" x 12.5". Some light paint loss; otherwise the art averages Very Good condition.

31255 *The Pogo Special Birthday Special* **Two Hand-Painted Production Cels Plus Matching Drawings (Chuck Jones, 1969).** 12-field production cels with their matching animation drawings of Pogo Possum (pg 9) and Albert Alligator (32) for the Procter and Gamble-sponsored TV special that aired on NBC on May 18, 1969. Directed by Chuck Jones and Ben Ashram and written by Walt Kelly himself. Pogo was voiced by June Foray and Albert was voiced by Walt Kelly. Paint is in Fine condition. The cels and drawings have an approximate image area of 7.5" x 4". In Excellent condition.

31256 *The Pogo Special Birthday Special* **Mam'selle Hepzibah Production Cel with Matching Drawing (Chuck Jones, 1969).** 12-field production cel with its matching animation drawing of Mam'selle Hepzibah (voiced by June Foray). Paint is fine. Image area measures approximately 9.25" x 6.5". Excellent condition.

31257 *The Pogo Special Birthday Special* **Production Cels and Matching Drawing Group (Chuck Jones, 1969).** Three one-of-a-kind hand-painted, 12-field production cels of Pogo running and tipping his hat. (Pg 11, PG 15, PG 17). Each cel comes with its matching animation drawings. Paint is in Fine condition. Each cel and drawing has an approximate image area of 6.5" x 4.5".

31258 **Led Zeppelin Special Project Cel (c. 1970).** An unusual hand-painted Xerox transparency with six versions of the famous early photo of Led Zeppelin — Jimmy Page, Robert Plant, John Paul Jones, and John Bonham. Each version of the black image has been painted from behind like an animation cel, with different colors used for each one. We can't say for sure what this was used for, but it is believed the intention was for backstage passes or as a publicity handbill. The combined image area measures approximately 10.5" x 8.5", in Excellent condition.

31259 **Popeye Television Commercial Production Cel (1970).** Rare one-of-a-kind hand-painted production cel of Popeye hawking for Phoscao Instant coffee. This was a black and white TV commercial that ran in Spain in 1970! Image area measures approximately 9" x 9.5", including the original photostat of the product jar. Excellent condition.

31260 *Horton Hears a Who!* **Dr. H. Hoovey Production Drawing (Chuck Jones, 1970).** Dr. Hoovey hears a "Help!" from a small speck of dust, and says the final line: "Oh, no!," in this drawing from the 1970 television special. Framed and matted with an 11.5" x 9" image area, the art is in Very Good condition. Includes a Certificate of Authenticity, a Linda Jones Enterprises seal, and a Chuck Jones autograph at the lower left.

31261 *The Jackson 5ive* **Michael's Pets Production Cel (Rankin-Bass, 1971).** Original production cel set-up of Michael's pets in the show — his rats Ray and Charles and his snake Rosie. Paired with a color print background made from the original, with a combined image area measuring approximately 12.25" x 9.5". In Excellent condition.

31262 *The Jackson 5ive* **Production Drawing (Rankin-Bass, 1972).** Original layout drawing of the Jackson Five — Michael, Marlon, Tito, Jackie, and Jermaine. Notes read: "At end of scene Mike starts to laugh as in Sc. 78, cut to sc. 181". Very rare glimpse into the making of this series. Graphite and red pencil on 17" x 12.5" paper. Some edge wear, creasing, and a 1.5" vertical tear into the image area at the top; otherwise the condition of the work is Very Good.

31263 **Sheriff Hoot Kloot Production Cel and Matching Drawing (DePatie-Freleng, 1973).** Original hand-painted production cel of Sheriff Hoot Kloot and his horse Fester (both on the same cel) for a 1973 theatrical cartoon short. Paired with a color print background, for a combined image area of 13.5" x 10.25". Excellent condition. Includes the original graphite and red pencil production drawing, which is in Fair condition, with paper loss damage.

31264 *Schoolhouse Rock!* **"Conjunction Junction" Production Cel (David McCall, 1973).** Original 12-field hand-painted two-cel set-up on a complimentary print background from the long-running ABC television series. In Excellent condition.

31265 *New Adventures of Batman and Robin* **Production Cel Set-Up (Filmation, 1977).** Exceptional hand-painted production cel of the Dynamic Duo matted to an image area of 11.5" x 9". In Excellent condition. The background is a color photocopy. Includes a COA, and a Filmation seal at the lower right.

31266 *The Family Circus* **Television Commercial Production Cel Set-Up (1980's).** Notes indicate this hand-painted cel set-up on key master background was created for a Sears television commercial. The art measures approximately 12" x 10" and it is in Very Good condition.

31267 **Don Bluth Signed** *The Secret of NIMH* **Mrs. Brisby Production Cel (Don Bluth, 1982).** Large one-of-a-kind 12-field hand-painted production cel of Mrs. Brisby, hand-signed (with slight fade) by Don Bluth. The movie was Bluth's directorial debut after leaving Walt Disney Studios. The image is a striking 7" tall, with a Linda Jones seal in the corner. In Excellent condition.

31268 Slimer! and the Real Ghostbusters "The Brooklyn Triangle" Production Background Painting (Columbia Television/ DiC Enterprises, 1988). An original hand-painted master production background for a season 4 episode of the popular animated series, featuring an establishing shot of Brooklyn looking into New York City, with the Twin Towers visible in the upper left corner. Gauche on board, 15" x 12.5". In Excellent condition.

31269 Barney the Sheepdog Production Cel (Pegbar, 1988). Hard to find 1988 hand-painted production cel of the popular English animated TV series "Barney" (The Sheepdog, not the American purple dinosaur character), paired with a color print background. Combined image area measures approximately 13" x 10.25". Excellent condition.

31270 Garfield and Friends Production Cel (Paws Inc., 1988). Original hand-painted production cel on a hand-painted production background, signed by Jim Davis with a PAWS seal. Garfield measures 5.5" with his sandwich! Originally sold in Sotheby's animation art sale (Lot #654). Framed to 17" x 15", with an image area of 9.5" x 7.5". The paint is in Fine condition.

31271 The Land Before Time Littlefoot and Mother Production Cel (Sullivan Bluth Studios, 1988). Outstanding hand-painted 16-field production cel set-up of Little Foot and his mother for the feature film directed by Don Bluth. This film sparked a whole series of Land Before Time films. The cel is placed over a print background with studio seal in corner. Perfect pose! The paint is in fine condition.

31272 Superman Publicity Cel (Ruby-Spears, 1988). Original hand-painted publicity cel of the Man of Steel, over a complimentary print background. The image of Superman measures 8.5". Ruby Spears in conjunction with DC Comics brought Superman to Saturday morning TV on CBS. A rare piece from the series.

31273 Shamus Culhane Betty Boop Sketch Original Art (1989). Island girl, Betty Boop by the legendary animator of Pluto, the Seven Dwarfs, Woody Woodpecker, Popeye, the Ajax Elves, and the Muriel Cigar. He was an instrumental animator on the short, Betty Boop's Bamboo Isle (1932). Graphite on paper, framed and matted to an image area of 11" x 9". In Very Good condition. Signed by Shamus Culhane, the work also includes a COA and a Fleisher Studios stamp.

31274 Garfield and Friends Garfield and Jon Production Cels (Paws Inc., 1995). A pair of original hand-painted production cels, one of which is a title cel for a "Garfield Quickie" segment. The two cels are in sequence, placed on a hand-painted production background for the series, and both are signed by Garfield creator Jim Davis. Framed to 31.5" x 16", with image areas of 11.5" x 9" and 10.75" x 7.75". The images of Garfield measure 4" and 3". The paint is in Fine condition. Originally sold at Sotheby's animation art sale (Lot #656), accompanied by a certificate of authenticity.

31275 Toby Bluth The Lord of the Rings Night Rider Concept Drawing (Fantasy Films, 1978). Ink on paper by Bluth, featuring an approximately 7" x 8.5" concept design of a Ringwraith for Ralph Bakshi's animated adaptation of the novel. In Fine condition with some scuffing and a hole near the left edge, none of which affects the artwork.

31276 UPA Studios Holiday Poster (UPA, 1955). Veteran animation artist and director Fred Crippen created this poster-sized (approximately 20" x 30") Christmas card for the studio in 1955. This was Fred's own copy, and he sent it, with an hand-lettered note on the back, to a friend. The poster was mailed folded, and Fred had this one protected with a thin sheet of adhesive plastic on the back. Overall Good condition.

31277 Celebrity-Signed Ceiling Tile from Jim Backus Studio (c. 1960s). A host of important actors, voice artists, directors, and more autographed this unique 23.5" x 23" white ceiling tile that once hung in the sound studio where Jim Backus recorded his Mr. Magoo dialog. Autographs include Jim Backus, Kirk Douglas, Chuck Jones, Paul Frees, George Fenneman, and Herb Ellis, among others. In Good condition. From the Estate of John McLaughlin.

31278 Chitty Chitty Bang Bang Series Proposal Package with Publicity Cel (Rankin-Bass, c. 1970s). Rare folder of pitch material for a proposed animated series based on the Ian Fleming novel and hit movie starring Dick Van Dyke. Includes a full series and character synopsis, a proposed episode script, and ten hand-painted, one-of-a-kind character publicity cels. The outer folder is a bit rough, but the contents are in Excellent condition.

END OF AUCTION

Terms and Conditions of Auction

Auctioneer and Auction:

1. This Auction is presented by Heritage Auctions, a d/b/a/ of Heritage Auctioneers & Galleries, Inc., or Heritage Auctions, Inc., or Heritage Numismatic Auctions, Inc., or Heritage Vintage Sports Auctions, Inc., or Currency Auctions of America, Inc., as identified with the applicable licensing information on the title page of the catalog or on the HA.com Internet site (the "Auctioneer"). The Auction is conducted under these Terms and Conditions of Auction and applicable state and local law. Announcements and corrections from the podium and those made through the Terms and Conditions of Auctions appearing on the Internet at HA.com supersede those in the printed catalog.

Buyer's Premium:

2. All bids are subject to a Buyer's Premium which is in addition to the placed successful bid:
- Seventeen and one-half percent (17.5%) on Currency, US Coin, and World & Ancient Coin Auction lots, except for Gallery Auction lots as noted below;
- Nineteen and one-half percent (19.5%) on Americana & Political, Arms & Armor, Civil War & Militaria, Comic, Manuscript, Movie Poster, Space Exploration, Sports Collectibles, Texana, and Gallery Auction (sealed bid auctions of mostly bulk numismatic material) lots;
- Twenty-two percent (22%) on Wine Auction lots;
- For lots in all other categories not listed above, twenty-five percent (25%) on the first $50,000 (minimum $14), twenty percent (20%) of any amount between $50,000 and $1,000,000, and twelve percent (12%) of any amount over $1,000,000.

Auction Venues:

3. The following Auctions are conducted solely on the Internet: Heritage Weekly Internet Auctions (Coin, Currency, Comics, Rare Books, Jewelry & Watches, Guitars & Musical Instruments, and Vintage Movie Posters); Heritage Monthly Internet Auctions (Sports, World Coins and Rare Wine). Signature* Auctions and Grand Format Auctions accept bids from the Internet, telephone, fax, or mail first, followed by a floor bidding session; HeritageLive! and real- time telephone bidding are available to registered clients during these auctions.

Bidders:

4. Any person participating or registering for the Auction agrees to be bound by and accepts these Terms and Conditions of Auction ("Bidder(s)").

5. All Bidders must meet Auctioneer's qualifications to bid. Any Bidder who is not a client in good standing of the Auctioneer may be disqualified at Auctioneer's sole option and will not be awarded lots. Such determination may be made by Auctioneer in its sole and unlimited discretion, at any time prior to, during, or even after the close of the Auction. Auctioneer reserves the right to exclude any person from the auction.

6. If an entity places a bid, then the person executing the bid on behalf of the entity agrees to personally guarantee payment for any successful bid.

Credit:

7. In order to place bids, Bidders who have not established credit with the Auctioneer must either furnish satisfactory credit information (including two collectibles-related business references) or supply valid credit card information along with a social security number, well in advance of the Auction. Bids placed through our Interactive Internet program will only be accepted from pre-registered Bidders. Bidders who are not members of HA.com or affiliates should preregister at least 48 hours before the start of the first session (exclusive of holidays or weekends) to allow adequate time to contact references. Credit will be granted at the discretion of Auctioneer. Additionally Bidders who have not previously established credit or who wish to bid in excess of their established credit history may be required to provide their social security number or the last four digits thereof so a credit check may be performed prior to Auctioneer's acceptance of a bid. Check writing privileges and immediate delivery of merchandise may also be determined by pre-approval of credit based on a combination of criteria: HA.com history, related industry references, bank verification, a credit bureau report and/or a personal guarantee for a corporate or partnership entity in advance of the auction venue.

Bidding Options:

8. Bids in Signature∗ Auctions or Grand Format Auctions may be placed as set forth in the printed catalog section entitled "Choose your bidding method." For auctions held solely on the Internet, see the alternatives on HA.com. Review at HA.com/common/howtobid.php.

9. Presentment of Bids: Non-Internet bids (including but not limited to podium, fax, phone and mail bids) are treated similar to floor bids in that they must be on-increment or at a half increment (called a cut bid). Any podium, fax, phone, or mail bids that do not conform to a full or half increment will be rounded up or down to the nearest full or half increment and this revised amount will be considered your high bid.

10. Auctioneer's Execution of Certain Bids. Auctioneer cannot be responsible for your errors in bidding, so carefully check that every bid is entered correctly. When identical mail or FAX bids are submitted, preference is given to the first received. To ensure the greatest accuracy, your written bids should be entered on the standard printed bid sheet and be received at Auctioneer's place of business at least two business days before the Auction start. Auctioneer is not responsible for executing mail bids or FAX bids received on or after the day the first lot is sold, nor Internet bids submitted after the published closing time; nor is Auctioneer responsible for proper execution of bids submitted by telephone, mail, FAX, e-mail, Internet, or in person once the Auction begins. Bids placed electronically via the internet may not be withdrawn until your written request is received and acknowledged by Auctioneer (FAX: 214-443-8425); such requests must state the reason, and may constitute grounds for withdrawal of bidding privileges. Lots won by mail Bidders will not be delivered at the Auction unless prearranged.

11. Caveat as to Bid Increments. Bid increments (over the current bid level) determine the lowest amount you may bid on a particular lot. Bids greater than one increment over the current bid can be any whole dollar amount. It is possible under several circumstances for winning bids to be between increments, sometimes only $1 above the previous increment. Please see: "How can I lose by less than an increment?" on our website. Bids will be accepted in whole dollar amounts only. No "buy" or "unlimited" bids will be accepted.

The following chart governs current bidding increments for Signature auctions; Internet-only auction bidding increments are approximately half of these amounts (see HA.com/c/ref/web-tips.zx#guidelines-increments).

Current Bid	Bid Increment	Current Bid	Bid Increment
<$10	$1	$20,000 - $29,999	$2,000
$10 - $29	$2	$30,000 - $49,999	$2,500
$30 - $49	$3	$50,000 - $99,999	$5,000
$50 - $99	$5	$100,000 - $199,999	$10,000
$100 - $199	$10	$200,000 - $299,999	$20,000
$200 - $299	$20	$300,000 - $499,999	$25,000
$300 - $499	$25	$500,000 - $999,999	$50,000
$500 - $999	$50	$1,000,000 - $1,999,999	$100,000
$1,000 - $1,999	$100	$2,000,000 - $2,999,999	$200,000
$2,000 - $2,999	$200	$3,000,000 - $4,999,999	$250,000
$3,000 - $4,999	$250	$5,000,000 - $9,999,999	$500,000
$5,000 - $9,999	$500	>$10,000,000	$1,000,000
$10,000 - $19,999	$1,000		

12. If Auctioneer calls for a full increment, a bidder may request Auctioneer to accept a bid at half of the increment ("Cut Bid") only once per lot. After offering a Cut Bid, bidders may continue to participate only at full increments. Off-increment bids may be accepted by the Auctioneer at Signature* Auctions and Grand Format Auctions. If the Auctioneer solicits bids other than the expected increment, these bids will not be considered Cut Bids.

Conducting the Auction:

13. Notice of the consignor's liberty to place bids on his lots in the Auction is hereby made in accordance with Article 2 of the Texas Business and Commercial Code. A "Minimum Bid" is an amount below which the lot will not sell. THE CONSIGNOR OF PROPERTY MAY PLACE WRITTEN "Minimum Bids" ON HIS LOTS IN ADVANCE OF THE AUCTION; ON SUCH LOTS, IF THE HAMMER PRICE DOES NOT MEET THE "Minimum Bid", THE CONSIGNOR MAY PAY A REDUCED COMMISSION ON THOSE LOTS. "Minimum Bids" are generally posted online several days prior to the Auction closing. For any successful bid placed by a consignor on his Property on the Auction floor, or by any means during the live session, or after the "Minimum Bid" for an Auction have been posted, we will require the consignor to pay full Buyer's Premium and Seller's Commissions on such lot.

14. The highest qualified Bidder recognized by the Auctioneer shall be the Buyer. In the event of a tie bid, the earliest bid received or recognized wins. In the event of any dispute between any Bidders at an Auction, Auctioneer may at his sole discretion reoffer the lot. Auctioneer's decision and declaration of the winning Bidder shall be final and binding upon all Bidders. Bids properly offered, whether by floor Bidder or other means of bidding, may on occasion be missed or go unrecognized; in such cases, the Auctioneer may declare the recognized bid accepted as the winning bid, regardless of whether a competing bid may have been higher.

15. Auctioneer reserves the right to refuse to honor any bid or to limit the amount of any bid, in its sole discretion. A bid is considered not made in "Good Faith" when made by an insolvent or irresponsible person, a person under the age of eighteen, or is not supported by satisfactory credit, collectibles references, or otherwise. Regardless of the disclosure of his identity, any bid by a consignor or his agent on a lot consigned by him is deemed to be made in "Good Faith." Any person apparently appearing on the OFAC list is not eligible to bid.

16. Nominal Bids. The Auctioneer in its sole discretion may reject nominal bids, small opening bids, or very nominal advances. If a lot bearing estimates fails to open for 40–60% of the low estimate, the Auctioneer may pass the item or may place a protective bid on behalf of the consignor.

17. Lots bearing bidding estimates shall open at Auctioneer's discretion (approximately 50%-60% of the low estimate). In the event that no bid meets or exceeds that opening amount, the lot shall pass as unsold.

18. All items are to be purchased per lot as numerically indicated and no lots will be broken. Auctioneer reserves the right to withdraw, prior to the close, any lots from the Auction.

19. Auctioneer reserves the right to rescind the sale in the event of nonpayment, breach of a warranty, disputed ownership, auctioneer's clerical error or omission in exercising bids and reserves, or for any other reason and in Auctioneer's sole discretion. In cases of nonpayment, Auctioneer's election to void a sale does not relieve the Bidder from their obligation to pay Auctioneer its fees (seller's and buyer's premium) and any other damages or expenses pertaining to the lot.

20. Auctioneer occasionally experiences Internet and/or Server service outages, and Auctioneer periodically schedules system downtime for maintenance and other purposes, during which Bidders cannot participate or place bids. If such outages occur, we may at our discretion extend bidding for the Auction. Bidders unable to place their Bids through the Internet are directed to contact Client Services at 1-800-872-6467.

21. The Auctioneer, its affiliates, or their employees consign items to be sold in the Auction, and may bid on those lots or any other lots. Auctioneer or affiliates expressly reserve the right to modify any such bids at any time prior to the hammer based upon data made known to the Auctioneer or its affiliates. The Auctioneer may extend advances, guarantees, or loans to certain consignors.

22. The Auctioneer has the right to sell certain unsold items after the close of the Auction. Such lots shall be considered sold during the Auction and all these Terms and Conditions shall apply to such sales including but not limited to the Buyer's Premium, return rights, and disclaimers.

Payment:

23. All sales are strictly for cash in United States dollars (including U.S. currency, bank wire, cashier checks, travelers checks, eChecks, and bank money orders, and are subject to all reporting requirements). All deliveries are subject to good funds; funds being received in Auctioneer's account before delivery of the Purchases; and all payments are subject to a clearing period. Auctioneer reserves the right to determine if a check constitutes "good funds": checks drawn on a U.S. bank are subject to a ten business day hold, and thirty days when drawn on an international bank. Clients with pre-arranged credit status may receive immediate credit for payments via eCheck, personal or corporate checks. All others will be subject to a hold of 5 days, or more, for the funds to clear prior to releasing merchandise. (ref. T&C item 7 Credit for additional information.) Payments can be made 24-48 hours post auction from the My Orders page of the HA.com website.

24. Payment is due upon closing of the Auction session, or upon presentment of an invoice. Auctioneer reserves the right to void an invoice if payment in full is not received within 7 days after the close of the Auction. In cases of nonpayment, Auctioneer's election to void a sale does not relieve the Bidder from their obligation to pay Auctioneer its fees (seller's and buyer's premium) on the lot and any other damages pertaining to the lot.

25. Lots delivered to you, or your representative in the States of Texas, California, New York, or other states where the Auction may be held, are subject to all applicable state and local taxes, unless appropriate permits are on file with Auctioneer. (Note: Coins are only subject to sales tax in California on invoices under $1500 and in Texas on invoices under $1000. Check the Web site at: http://coins.ha.com/c/ref/sales-tax.zx for more details.) Bidder agrees to pay Auctioneer the actual amount of tax due in the event that sales tax is not properly collected due to: 1) an expired, inaccurate, inappropriate tax certificate or declaration, 2) an incorrect interpretation of the applicable statute, 3) or any other reason. The appropriate form or certificate must be on file at and verified by Auctioneer five days prior to Auction or tax must be paid; only if such form or certificate is received by Auctioneer within 4 days after the Auction can a refund of tax paid be made. Lots from different Auctions may not be aggregated for sales tax purposes.

26. In the event that a Bidder's payment is dishonored upon presentment(s), Bidder shall pay the maximum statutory processing fee set by applicable state law. If you attempt to pay via eCheck and your financial institution denies this transfer from your bank account, or the payment cannot be completed using the selected funding source, you agree to complete payment using your credit card on file.

27. If any Auction invoice submitted by Auctioneer is not paid in full when due, the unpaid balance will bear interest at the highest rate permitted by law from the date of invoice until paid. Any invoice not paid when due will bear a three percent (3%) late fee on the invoice amount or three percent (3%) of any installment that is past due. If the Auctioneer refers any invoice to an attorney for collection, the buyer agrees to pay attorney's fees, court costs, and other collection costs incurred by Auctioneer. If Auctioneer assigns collection to its in-house legal staff, such attorney's time expended on the matter shall be compensated at a rate comparable to the hourly rate of independent attorneys.

28. In the event a successful Bidder fails to pay any amounts due, Auctioneer reserves the right to sell the lot(s) securing the invoice to any underbidders in the Auction that the lot(s) appeared, or at subsequent private or public sale, or relist the lot(s) in a future auction conducted by Auctioneer. A defaulting Bidder agrees to pay for the reasonable costs of resale (including a 10% seller's commission, if consigned to an auction conducted by Auctioneer). The defaulting Bidder is liable to pay any difference between his total original invoice for the lot(s), plus any applicable interest, and the net proceeds for the lot(s) if sold at private sale or the subsequent hammer price of the lot(s) less the 10% seller's commissions, if sold at an Auctioneer's auction.

Terms and Conditions of Auction

29. Auctioneer reserves the right to require payment in full in good funds before delivery of the merchandise.
30. Auctioneer shall have a lien against the merchandise purchased by the buyer to secure payment of the Auction invoice. Auctioneer is further granted a lien and the right to retain possession of any other property of the buyer then held by the Auctioneer or its affiliates to secure payment of any Auction invoice or any other amounts due the Auctioneer or affiliates from the buyer. With respect to these lien rights, Auctioneer shall have all the rights of a secured creditor under Article 9 of the Texas Uniform Commercial Code, including but not limited to the right of sale. In addition, with respect to payment of the Auction invoice(s), the buyer waives any and all rights of offset he might otherwise have against the Auctioneer and the consignor of the merchandise included on the invoice. If a Bidder owes Auctioneer or its affiliates on any account, Auctioneer and its affiliates shall have the right to offset such unpaid account by any credit balance due Bidder, and it may secure by possessory lien any unpaid amount by any of the Bidder's property in their possession.
31. Title shall not pass to the successful Bidder until all invoices are paid in full. It is the responsibility of the buyer to provide adequate insurance coverage for the items once they have been delivered to a common carrier or third-party shipper.

Delivery; Shipping; and Handling Charges:
32. Buyer is liable for shipping and handling. Please refer to Auctioneer's website www.HA.com/common/shipping.php for the latest charges or call Auctioneer. Auctioneer is unable to combine purchases from other auctions or affiliates into one package for shipping purposes. Lots won will be shipped in a commercially reasonable time after payment in good funds for the merchandise and the shipping fees is received or credit extended, except when third-party shipment occurs. Buyer agrees that Service and Handling charges related to shipping items which are not pre-paid may be charged to the credit card on file with Auctioneer.
33. Successful international Bidders shall provide written shipping instructions, including specified customs declarations, to the Auctioneer for any lots to be delivered outside of the United States. NOTE: Declaration value shall be the item'(s) hammer price together with its buyer's premium and Auctioneer shall use the correct harmonized code for the lot. Domestic Buyers on lots designated for third-party shipment must designate the common carrier, accept risk of loss, and prepay shipping costs.
34. All shipping charges will be borne by the successful Bidder. On all domestic shipments, any risk of loss during shipment will be borne by Heritage until the shipping carrier's confirmation of delivery to the address of record in Auctioneer's file (carrier's confirmation is conclusive to prove delivery to Bidder; if the client has a Signature release on file with the carrier, the package is considered delivered without Signature) or delivery by Heritage to Bidder's selected third-party shipper. On all foreign shipments, any risk of loss during shipment will be borne by the Bidder following Auctioneer's delivery to the Bidder's designated common carrier or third-party shipper.
35. Due to the nature of some items sold, it shall be the responsibility for the successful Bidder to arrange pick-up and shipping through third-parties; as to such items Auctioneer shall have no liability. Failure to pick-up or arrange shipping in a timely fashion (within ten days) shall subject Lots to storage and moving charges, including a $100 administration fee plus $10 daily storage for larger items and $5.00 daily for smaller items (storage fee per item) after 35 days. In the event the Lot is not removed within ninety days, the Lot may be offered for sale to recover any past due storage or moving fees, including a 10% Seller's Commission.
36A. The laws of various countries regulate the import or export of certain plant and animal properties, including (but not limited to) items made of (or including) ivory, whalebone, turtle shell, coral, crocodile, or other wildlife. Transport of such lots may require special licenses for export, import, or both. Bidder is responsible for: 1) obtaining all information on such restricted items for both export and import; 2) obtaining all such licenses and/or permits. Delay or failure to obtain any such license or permit does not relieve the buyer of timely compliance with standard payment terms. For further information, please contact Ron Brackemyre at 800- 872-6467 ext. 1312.
36B. Auctioneer shall not be liable for any loss caused by or resulting from:
   a. Seizure or destruction under quarantine or Customs regulation, or confiscation by order of any Government or public authority, or risks of contraband or illegal transportation of trade, or
   b. Breakage of statuary, marble, glassware, bric-a-brac, porcelains, jewelry, and similar fragile articles
37. Any request for shipping verification for undelivered packages must be made within 30 days of shipment by Auctioneer.

Cataloging, Warranties and Disclaimers:
38. NO WARRANTY, WHETHER EXPRESSED OR IMPLIED, IS MADE WITH RESPECT TO ANY DESCRIPTION CONTAINED IN THIS AUCTION OR ANY SECOND OPINE. Any description of the items or second opine contained in this Auction is for the sole purpose of identifying the items for those Bidders who do not have the opportunity to view the lots prior to bidding, and no description of items has been made part of the basis of the bargain or has created any express warranty that the goods would conform to any description made by Auctioneer. Color variations can be expected in any electronic or printed imaging, and are not grounds for the return of any lot. NOTE: Auctioneer, in specified auction venues, for example, Fine Art, may have express written warranties and you are referred to those specific terms and conditions. .
39. Auctioneer is selling only such right or title to the items being sold as Auctioneer may have by virtue of consignment agreements on the date of auction and disclaims any warranty of title to the Property. Auctioneer disclaims any warranty of merchantability or fitness for any particular purposes. All images, descriptions, sales data, and archival records are the exclusive property of Auctioneer, and may be used by Auctioneer for advertising, promotion, archival records, and any other uses deemed appropriate.
40. Translations of foreign language documents may be provided as a convenience to interested parties. Auctioneer makes no representation as to the accuracy of those translations and will not be held responsible for errors in bidding arising from inaccuracies in translation.
41. Auctioneer disclaims all liability for damages, consequential or otherwise, arising out of or in connection with the sale of any Property by Auctioneer to Bidder. No third party may rely on any benefit of these Terms and Conditions and any rights, if any, established hereunder are personal to the Bidder and may not be assigned. Any statement made by the Auctioneer is an opinion and does not constitute a warranty or representation. No employee of Auctioneer may alter these Terms and Conditions, and, unless signed by a principal of Auctioneer, any such alteration is null and void.
42. Auctioneer shall not be liable for breakage of glass or damage to frames (patent or latent); such defects, in any event, shall not be a basis for any claim for return or reduction in purchase price.

Release:
43. In consideration of participation in the Auction and the placing of a bid, Bidder expressly releases Auctioneer, its officers, directors and employees, its affiliates, and its outside experts that provide second opines, from any and all claims, cause of action, chose of action, whether at law or equity or any arbitration or mediation rights existing under the rules of any professional society or affiliation based upon the assigned description, or a derivative theory, breach of warranty express or implied, representation or other matter set forth within these Terms and Conditions of Auction or otherwise. In the event of a claim, Bidder agrees that such rights and privileges conferred therein are strictly construed as specifically declared herein; e.g., authenticity, typographical error, etc. and are the exclusive remedy. Bidder, by non-compliance to these express terms of a granted remedy, shall waive any claim against Auctioneer.
44. Notice: Some Property sold by Auctioneer are inherently dangerous e.g. firearms, cannons, and small items that may be swallowed or ingested or may have latent defects all of which may cause harm to a person. Purchaser accepts all risk of loss or damage from its purchase of these items and Auctioneer disclaims any liability whether under contract or tort for damages and losses, direct or inconsequential, and expressly disclaims any warranty as to safety or usage of any lot sold.

Dispute Resolution and Arbitration Provision:
45. By placing a bid or otherwise participating in the auction, Bidder accepts these Terms and Conditions of Auction, and specifically agrees to the dispute resolution provided herein. Consumer disputes shall be resolved through court litigation which has an exclusive Dallas, Texas venue clause and jury waiver. Non-consumer dispute shall be determined in binding arbitration which arbitration replaces the right to go to court, including the right to a jury trial.
46. Auctioneer in no event shall be responsible for consequential damages, incidental damages, compensatory damages, or any other damages arising or claimed to be arising from the auction of any lot. In the event that Auctioneer cannot deliver the lot or subsequently it is established that the lot lacks title, or other transfer or condition issue is claimed, in such cases the sole remedy shall be limited to rescission of sale and refund of the amount paid by Bidder; in no case shall Auctioneer's maximum liability exceed the high bid on that lot, which bid shall be deemed for all purposes the value of the lot. After one year has elapsed, Auctioneer's maximum liability shall be limited to any commissions and fees Auctioneer earned on that lot.
47. In the event of an attribution error, Auctioneer may at its sole discretion, correct the error on the Internet, or, if discovered at a later date, to refund the buyer's purchase price without further obligation.
48. Dispute Resolution for Consumers and Non-Consumers: Any claim, dispute, or controversy in connection with, relating to and /or arising out of the Auction, participation in the Auction, award of lots, damages of claims to lots, descriptions, condition reports, provenance, estimates, return and warranty rights, any interpretation of these Terms and Conditions, any alleged verbal modification of these Terms and Conditions and/or any purported settlement whether asserted in contract, tort, under Federal or State statute or regulation shall or any other matter: a) if presented by a consumer, be exclusively heard by, and the parties consent to, exclusive in personam jurisdiction in the State District Courts of Dallas County, Texas. THE PARTIES EXPRESSLY WAIVE ANY RIGHT TO TRIAL BY JURY. Any appeals shall be solely pursued in the appellate courts of the State of Texas; or b) for any claimant other than a consumer, the claim shall be presented in confidential binding arbitration before a single arbitrator, that the parties may agree upon, selected from the JAMS list of Texas arbitrators. The case is not to be administrated by JAMS; however, if the parties cannot agree on an arbitrator, then JAMS shall appoint the arbitrator and it shall be conducted under JAMS rules. The locale shall be Dallas Texas. The arbitrator's award may be enforced in any court of competent jurisdiction. Any party on any claim involving the purchase or sale of numismatic or related items may elect arbitration through binding PNG arbitration. Any claim must be brought within one (1) year of the alleged breach, default or misrepresentation or the claim is waived. This agreement and any claims shall be determined and construed under Texas law. The prevailing party (party that is awarded substantial and material relief on its claim or defense) may be awarded its reasonable attorneys' fees and costs.
49. No claims of any kind can be considered after the settlements have been made with the consignors. Any dispute after the settlement date is strictly between the Bidder and consignor without involvement or responsibility of the Auctioneer.
50. In consideration of their participation in or application for the Auction, a person or entity (whether the successful Bidder, a Bidder, a purchaser and/or other Auction participant or registrant) agrees that all disputes in any way relating to, arising under, connected with, or incidental to these Terms and Conditions and purchases, or default in payment thereof, shall be arbitrated pursuant to the arbitration provision. In the event that any matter including actions to compel arbitration, construe the agreement, actions in aid or arbitration or otherwise needs to be litigated, such litigation shall be exclusively in the Courts of the State of Texas, in Dallas County, Texas, and if necessary the corresponding appellate courts. For such actions, the successful Bidder, purchaser, or Auction participant also expressly submits himself to the personal jurisdiction of the State of Texas.
51. These Terms & Conditions provide specific remedies for occurrences in the auction and delivery process. Where such remedies are afforded, they shall be interpreted strictly. Bidder agrees that any claim shall utilize such remedies; Bidder making a claim in excess of those remedies provided in these Terms and Conditions agrees that in no case whatsoever shall Auctioneer's maximum liability exceed the high bid on that lot, which bid shall be deemed for all purposes the value of the lot.

Miscellaneous:
52. Agreements between Bidders and consignors to effectuate a non-sale of an item at Auction, inhibit bidding on a consigned item to enter into a private sale agreement for said item, or to utilize the Auctioneer's Auction to obtain sales for non-selling consigned items subsequent to the Auction, are strictly prohibited. If a subsequent sale of a previously consigned item occurs in violation of this provision, Auctioneer reserves the right to charge Bidder the applicable Buyer's Premium and consignor a Seller's Commission as determined for each auction venue and by the terms of the seller's agreement.
53. Acceptance of these Terms and Conditions qualifies Bidder as a client who has consented to be contacted by Heritage in the future. In conformity with "do-not-call" regulations promulgated by the Federal or State regulatory agencies, participation by the Bidder is affirmative consent to being contacted at the phone number shown in his application and this consent shall remain in effect until it is revoked in writing. Heritage may from time to time contact Bidder concerning sale, purchase, and auction opportunities available through Heritage and its affiliates and subsidiaries.
54. Rules of Construction: Auctioneer presents properties in a number of collectible fields, and as such, specific venues have promulgated supplemental Terms and Conditions. Nothing herein shall be construed to waive the general Terms and Conditions of Auction by these additional rules and shall be construed to give force and effect to the rules in their entirety.

State Notices:
Notice as to an Auction in California. Auctioneer has in compliance with Title 2.95 of the California Civil Code as amended October 11, 1993 Sec. 1812.600, posted with the California Secretary of State its bonds for it and its employees, and the auction is being conducted in compliance with Sec. 2338 of the Commercial Code and Sec. 535 of the Penal Code.

Notice as to an Auction in New York City. These Terms and Conditions of Sale are designed to conform to the applicable sections of the New York City Department of Consumer Affairs Rules and Regulations as Amended. This sale is a Public Auction Sale conducted by Heritage Auctioneers & Galleries, Inc. # 41513036. The New York City licensed auctioneers are: Sam Foose, #095260; Kathleen Guzman, #0762165; Nicholas Dawes, #1304724; Ed Beardsley, #1183220; Scott Peterson, #1306933; Andrea Voss, #1320558, who will conduct the Sale on behalf of itself and Heritage Numismatic Auctions, Inc. (for Coins) and Currency Auctions of America, Inc. (for currency). All lots are subject to: the consignor's rights to bid thereon in accord with these Terms and Conditions of Sale, consignor's option to receive advances on their consignments, and Auctioneer, in its sole discretion, may offer limited extended financing to registered bidders, in accord with Auctioneer's internal credit standards. A registered bidder may inquire whether a lot is subject to an advance or a reserve. Auctioneer has made advances to various consignors in this sale. On lots bearing an estimate, the term refers to a value range placed on an item by the Auctioneer in its sole opinion but the final price is determined by the bidders.

Notice as to an Auction in Texas. In compliance with TDLR rule 67.100(c)(1), notice is hereby provided that this auction is covered by a Recovery Fund administered by the Texas Department of Licensing and Regulation, P.O. Box 12157, Austin, Texas 78711 (512) 463-6599. Any complaints may be directed to the same address.

Notice as to an Auction in Ohio: Auction firm and Auctioneer are licensed by the Dept. of Agriculture, and either the licensee is bonded in favor of the state or an aggrieved person may initiate a claim against the auction recovery fund created in Section 4707.25 of the Revised Code as a result of the licensee's actions, whichever is applicable.

Rev. 12-18-12

Terms and Conditions of Auction

Additional Terms & Conditions:
COMICS & COMIC ART AUCTIONS

COMICS & COMIC ART TERM A: Signature₀ Auctions are not on approval. No certified material may be returned because of possible differences of opinion with respect to the grade offered by any third-party organization, dealer, or service. No guarantee of grade is offered for uncertified Property sold and subsequently submitted to a third-party grading service. There are absolutely no exceptions to this policy. Under extremely limited circumstances, (e.g. gross cataloging error) a purchaser, who did not bid from the floor, may request Auctioneer to evaluate voiding a sale; such request must be made in writing detailing the alleged gross error, and submission of the lot to the Auctioneer must be pre-approved by the Auctioneer. A bidder must notify the appropriate department head (check the inside front cover of the catalog or our website for a listing of department heads) in writing of such request within three (3) days of the non-floor bidder's receipt of the lot. Any lot that is to be evaluated must be in our offices within 30 days after Auction. Grading does not qualify for this evaluation process nor do such complaints constitute a basis to challenge the authenticity of a lot. AFTER THAT 30-DAY PERIOD, NO LOTS MAY BE RETURNED FOR REASONS OTHER THAN AUTHENTICITY. Lots returned must be housed intact in the original holder. No lots purchased by floor Bidders may be returned (including those Bidders acting as agents for others). Late remittance for purchases may be considered just cause to revoke all return privileges.

COMICS & COMIC ART TERM B: Auctions conducted solely on the Internet have a THREE (3) DAY RETURN POLICY: Lots paid for within seven days of the Auction closing are sold with a three (3) day return privilege. You may return lots under the following conditions: Within three days of receipt of the lot, you must first notify Auctioneer by contacting Client Service by phone (1-800-872-6467) or e-mail (Bid@HA.com), and immediately mail the lot(s) fully insured to the attention of Returns, Heritage, 3500 Maple Avenue, 17th Floor, Dallas TX 75219-3941. Lots must be housed intact in their original holder and condition. You are responsible for the insured, safe delivery of any lots. A non-negotiable return fee of 5% of the purchase price ($10 per lot minimum) will be deducted from the refund for each returned lot or billed directly. Postage and handling fees are not refunded. After the three-day period (from receipt), no items may be returned for any reason. Late remittance for purchases revokes all Return-Restock privileges.

COMICS & COMIC ART TERM C: Bidders who have inspected the lots prior to the auction will not be granted any return privileges.

COMICS & COMIC ART TERM D: Comic books sold referencing a third-party grading service are sold "as is" without any express or implied warranty. Certain warranties may be available from the grading services and the Bidder is referred to them for further details: Comics Guaranty Corporation (CGC), P.O. Box 4738, Sarasota, FL 34230.

COMICS & COMIC ART TERM E: Bidders who intend to challenge authenticity or provenance of a lot must notify Auctioneer in writing within thirty (30) days of the Auction's conclusion. In the event Auctioneer cannot deliver the lot or subsequently it is established that the lot lacks title, provenance, authenticity, or other transfer or condition issue is claimed, Auctioneer's liability shall be limited to rescission of sale and refund of purchase price; in no case shall Auctioneer's maximum liability exceed the high bid on that lot, which bid shall be deemed for all purposes the value of the lot. After one year has elapsed, Auctioneer's maximum liability shall be limited to any commissions and fees Auctioneer earned on that lot.

COMICS & COMIC ART TERM F: All comics are guaranteed genuine, but are not guaranteed as to grade, since grading is a matter of opinion, an art and not a science, and therefore the opinion rendered by the Auctioneer or any third party grading service may not agree with the opinion of others (including trained experts), and the same expert may not grade the same item with the same grade at two different times.

COMICS & COMIC ART TERM G: Since we cannot examine encapsulated comics, they are sold "as is" without our grading opinion, and may not be returned for any reason. Auctioneer shall not be liable for any patent or latent defect or controversy pertaining to or arising from any encapsulated collectible. In any such instance, purchaser's remedy, if any, shall be solely against the service certifying the collectible.

COMICS & COMIC ART TERM H: Due to changing grading standards over time, differing interpretations, and to possible mishandling of items by subsequent owners, Auctioneer reserves the right to grade items differently than shown on certificates from any grading service that accompany the items. Auctioneer also reserves the right to grade items differently than the grades shown in the prior catalog should such items be reconsigned to any future auction.

COMICS & COMIC ART TERM I: Although consensus grading is employed by most grading services, it should be noted as aforesaid that grading is not an exact science. In fact, it is entirely possible that if a lot is broken out of a plastic holder and resubmitted to another grading service or even to the same service, the lot could come back with a different grade assigned.

COMICS & COMIC ART TERM J: Certification does not guarantee protection against the normal risks associated with potentially volatile markets. The degree of liquidity for certified collectibles will vary according to general market conditions and the particular lot involved. For some lots there may be no active market at all at certain points in time.

For wiring instructions call the Credit department at 1-800-872-6467 or e-mail: CreditDept@HA.com

Rev. 8-30-10

How to Ship Your Purchases

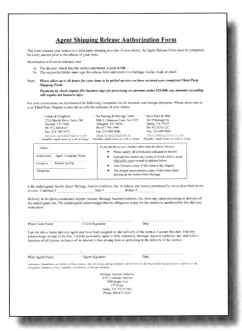

Agent Shipping Release
Authorization form

Heritage Auction Galleries requires "Third Party Shipping" for certain items in this auction not picked up in person by the buyer. It shall be the responsibility of the successful bidder to arrange pick up and shipping through a third party; as to such items auctioneer shall have no liability.

Steps to follow:

1. Select a shipping company from the list below or a company of your choosing.

2. Complete, sign, and return an Agent Shipping Release Authorization form to Heritage (this form will automatically be emailed to you along with your winning bid(s) notice or may be obtained by calling Client Services at 866-835-3243). The completed form may be faxed to 214-409-1425.

3. Heritage Auctions' shipping department will coordinate with the shipping company you have selected to pick up your purchases.

Shippers that Heritage has used are listed below. However, you are not obligated to choose from the following and may provide Heritage with information of your preferred shipper.

Navis Pack & Ship
11009 Shady Trail
Dallas, TX 75229
Ph: 972-870-1212
Fax: 214-409-9001
Navis.Dallas@GoNavis.com

The Packing & Moving Center
2040 E. Arkansas Lane, Ste #222
Arlington, TX 76011
Ph: 817-795-1999
Fax: 214-409-9000
thepackman@sbcglobal.net

Craters & Freighters
2220 Merritt Drive, Suite 200
Garland, TX 75041
Ph: 972-840-8147
Fax: 214-780-5674
dallas@cratersandfreighters.com

- It is the Third Party Shipper's responsibility to pack (or crate) and ship (or freight) your purchase to you. Please make all payment arrangements for shipping with your Shipper of choice.

- Any questions concerning Third Party Shipping can be addressed through our Client Services Department at 1-866-835-3243.

- Successful bidders are advised that pick-up or shipping arrangements should be made within ten (10) days of the auction or they may be subject to storage fees as stated in Heritage's Terms & Conditions of Auction, item 35.

HERITAGE®

ILLUSTRATION ART AUCTION
APRIL 11, 2013 | BEVERLY HILLS | LIVE & ONLINE

Inquiries: 800-872-6467

Ed Jaster, ext. 1288
EdJ@HA.com

Todd Hignite, ext. 1790
ToddH@HA.com

JOSEPH CHRISTIAN LEYENDECKER
Honeymoon
The Saturday Evening Post cover, July 17, 1926
Oil on canvas, 28.25 x 21.25 in.
Estimate: $80,000-$120,000
HA.com/5126-12001

For a free auction catalog in any category, plus a copy of *The Collector's Handbook* (combined value $65), visit HA.com/CATA26012 or call 866-835-3243 and reference code CATA26012.

HERITAGE

THE GENTLEMAN COLLECTOR AUCTION
FEBRUARY 23-24, 2013 | DALLAS | LIVE & ONLINE

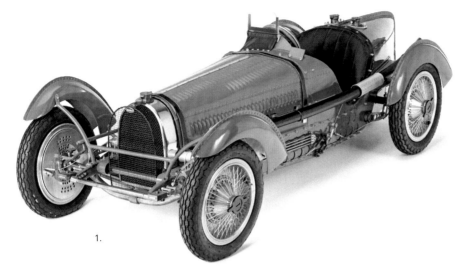

1.

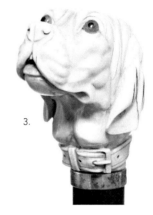

3.

2.

4.

1. MOTORIZED SCALE MODEL OF A
   1924 BUGATTI TYPE 35
   20 high x 32 wide x 75 in.
   From a fine collection of automobilia

2. SYDNEY SPARROW ENGLISH SILVER SHIP
   MODEL: CUTTY SARK
   London, circa 1974
   22 in. high x 54 in. long
   From an extensive collection of marine art
   and ship models

3. CONTINENTAL WOOD AND IVORY
   FIGURAL CANE
   Circa 1900
   38.75 in. long
   Vintage gentleman's walking cane from a
   group of over 80 canes

4. MONTBLANC'S SIR WINSTON
   CHURCHILL LIMITED EDITION 53
   FOUNTAIN PEN
   From an important private collection
   of over thirty rare and extraordinary
   Montblanc and other writing instruments,
   many with first or interesting edition
   numbers.

Visit HA.com/5129 to view
all lots from this eclectic sale.

Inquiries: 800-872-6467
Nick Dawes, Special Collections,
ext. 1605, NickD@HA.com

For a free auction catalog in any category, visit HA.com/CATB26012 or call 866-835-3243 and reference code CATB26012.